The Consultant's Edge

THE CONSULTANT'S EDGE

USING THE COMPUTER AS A MARKETING TOOL

Herman Holtz

JOHN WILEY & SONS
New York   Chichester   Brisbane   Toronto   Singapore

Library of Congress Cataloging in Publication Data

Holtz, Herman.
    The consultant's edge.

    Includes index.
    1. Consultants. 2. Business—Data processing.
3. Management—Data processing. I. Title.
HD69.C6H62 1985   658.4'6'02854   85-5117
ISBN 0-471-81190-4

Printed in the United States of America

10 9 8 7 6 5 4 3 2 1

Preface

The terms *home computer* and *personal computer* are unfortunate choices, implying such things as playing games and doing your personal tax returns. The term *desktop computer* is a far more helpful designator, identifying the microcomputer's role in small business, such as in helping the independent consultant to much earlier and much greater success.

In fact, a desktop computer will help you in a variety of ways, all of which we will explore in some detail in these pages, including these:

☐ It will make great contributions to and hasten your success in marketing your services—in finding clients and winning contracts.

☐ It will relieve you of much of the more tedious administrative chores that must be carried out in even a small enterprise (and/or save you the expense you might otherwise experience in getting help from others to do some of these things for you).

☐ It will take over much of the tedious work that is a part of your consulting service per se, such as making calculations, analyzing data, writing reports, and preparing presentations.

☐ It will increase your profitability as an independent consultant by enabling you to create new profit centers in your practice, such as newsletters and special reports, items which are usually highly salable.

Making this exciting knowledge available to my contemporaries is itself a privilege. However, perhaps the most awesome thing about writing this book is the knowledge that I could not have written it a decade ago—even as few as five or six years ago. Had I attempted this book then, it would have been visionary, an act of speculation. And even if I had that vision I would necessarily have written a book vastly different from this.

It is astounding also to consider that if I or anyone else writes or rewrites this book only a few years hence, it will almost certainly be a book greatly different from today's, if the past is any reliable clue to the future.

A single generation (about 25 years) ago the thousands of glowing tubes in the huge early computers were being rapidly replaced by the tiny transistors that marked a major revolution in electronics. For a while the transistor was the *wunderkind* of electronics engineering, and perhaps the true revolution was in the development of mass-production methods that created intense competition and brought the initially prohibitive prices of transistors down to bargain-counter levels.

Still, the computer remained a large and costly apparatus, owned or leased only by government agencies, major corporations, and other large organizations. No one dreamed that it would ever be different, transistors and tumbling transistor prices notwithstanding. The computer was simply not destined for other applications and environments.

A decade ago a dream of electronics scientists and a new revolution in electronics—the microcircuit—became a practical reality. It was the transistor story again, with marvelous but costly new magic invented by a few geniuses, the ultimate development of the device on a mass-production basis, and the steady improvement and development of entire families of similar and related devices.

With that began the developments that have since reduced the computer in size and price. Today, computers fit easily on any desk or table and some even fit into briefcases and into pockets— and they fit into millions of personal and small-business budgets as well. Also, the word *computer* no longer evokes an image of a room full of metal cabinets and spinning reels of tape in a half-dozen servos, but is often used to refer to something approximately the size of and somewhat similar in appearance to an ordinary table-top TV receiver.

The desktop computer is rapidly becoming as ubiquitous as the telephone and typewriter in even the smallest office. Quite possibly the modern electric—and even the electronic—typewriter will soon be as quaint a relic of the dusty past as the quill pen and inkpot, since computers and their printers can do almost anything the typewriter can do, but more rapidly and more efficiently. However, that is not all that modern computers are likely to make obsolete: Much of what we do today—or, at least, the methods we use today—will become obsolete too.

This is all part of a revolution, perhaps in many ways a new Industrial Revolution, as remarkable in what it is bringing forth as was the original Industrial Revolution of approximately a century ago. Ironically, whereas that original Industrial Revolution all but wiped out the cottage industries of its day, this modern one threatens to bring cottage industries—in the form of electronic cottages, that is—back into existence. Already, many thousands of entrepreneurs have established tiny enterprises in their homes, either based on or made possible by the microcomputer. And others, already established in home-based enterprises, have put microcomputers to work to greatly amplify their efficiency and capabilities.

Some of these enterprises are based on computer technology itself: The entrepreneurs write computer programs and sell computers, computer programs, computer training, and sundry other computer services and supplies. Others are based on selling goods and services made possible by the computer or, at least, made more efficient by the computer—word processing, accounting, newsletters. The entrepreneurs are writers, consultants, accountants, programmers, stenographers, and specialists of many kinds.

On the other hand, a great many people bought personal computers or "home computers" in recent years, and it has been estimated that at least 50 percent of those computers are resting in attics and closets throughout the United States. (I know of a few such cases myself.) They are there because so many people bought computers without knowing what they wanted them for, that is, what the computer could do for them.

This problem not only affects home owners; it has also afflicted many who bought desktop or personal computers for business purposes and then failed to put them to good use. (In some cases known to me, the owner never did *anything* with the new toy, other than plug it in, turn it on, and wonder what to do next.) The reason? They did not know what the computer could do in general, or what it could do for their business ventures, but much worse they did not know where to turn to find out. It is this tragedy—the desire to overcome it, that is—that inspired this book.

For some the computer has been a "natural," as it has been for me: The word-processing capabilities of my computer have amplified my output of books and my proposal-writing services for my consulting clients beyond belief, constituting something of a minor miracle. It has been almost the ideal step forward I could have taken, and I delayed taking it earlier only because of the economic problems: Even the modern desktop computer was too costly for me, for a long time, and only when the prices began to decline did I begin to believe that I could afford to own one. But had I known then what I know now I believe that I would have risked buying one even when the prices were frighteningly high. (Lately, prices have been tumbling faster than ever, as more and more manufacturers begin producing so many models that they compete with themselves, as well as with each other.)

The computer is not quite that perfect a fit or that ideal for everyone. But whether computer support is especially well-suited for your own consulting practice or only ordinarily so, there is little doubt that it can be a boon: It is a rare enterprise or profession that cannot gain great benefits from enlisting computer capabilities in behalf of the venture, when the entrepreneur understands what the computer can, in fact, do.

That is what this book is about—not what a marvel the computer is (although it is, and you will come to appreciate that more and more), not how it works or why it works (although you will inevitably learn some of that), and not how to buy a computer (although this book includes substantial help and guidance in that regard) but how to *use* a computer to help you to greater success in all areas of your practice.

It is not a technical book, and where it is necessary to explain technical concepts all jargon is carefully explained in everyday language. (Moreover, there is a glossary of terms as a final chapter, to which you can refer if necessary, not only while reading this book but also when reading any of the popular literature.) You are not studying computers per se in reading this book but only what you can do to help yourself to greater success by using a computer. In fact, what is addressed in this book is oriented more to the software (programs) and what software can do for you, for the capabilities really reside in the programs; the hardware is only a device for running the software, as a tape player is only a device for converting the magnetic data into words and music. It is necessary to have the right hardware, but you must first analyze your needs in terms of the software programs that are best suited to help you run your practice successfully. And so the major focus is on those software programs.

If you have any doubts about the pervasiveness or importance of microcomputers and the abundance of software for them, reference to a directory, *The Software Catalogue—Microcomputers*, a publication of Elsevier Scientific Publications, will be enlightening. The current edition is 1386 pages long, lists 10,757 programs, and is updated quarterly—updated by adding new crops of programs written by the hundreds of software developers.

HERMAN HOLTZ

Silver Spring, Maryland
June 1985

Contents

PART TWO. THE COMPUTER AS A MARKETING AID

essing is—what it *really* is. A better scenario. Archiving or "backing up."

PART THREE.   THE COMPUTER AS A CONSULTING TOOL

Costs. Custom, in-house seminars. The PR/promotional seminar. Additional income opportunities. A final note.

How newsletter publishing fits the consulting enterprise. A brief look at the newsletter: what is it? Subscription fees. The newsletter as a consulting-services medium. The newsletter as an income source. The newsletter as a PR/marketing/advertising tool. Those other products. The many computer contributions. The editorial "safe." Reviewing material on-screen. Copy fitting. Proofreading. File copies. Mailing.

The two faces of management. What is management? Management versus administration. What do you need to know? How to get the information. Accounting fundamentals. Databases and database management. Miscellaneous other functions.

PART FOUR.   SELECTING THE RIGHT COMPUTER FOR YOUR PRACTICE

The problem of no standards—or is it one of too many standards? Software and hardware are mutually dependent on each other. The "software first" wisdom. Software and market influences. Personal computers and operating systems. The first de facto standard OS. IBM and the PC create a new de facto standard. The conventional wisdom is now a sometime truth only. Some exceptions and clarifications. Facing the future. The software trends. Memory versus storage. The chicken and the egg. Choosing the software. Worksheet 3. Sources of software information. About "user friendliness." The trade-off. Computer languages.

The Consultant's Edge

PART ONE

What You Need To Know About Computers for Professional Applications

A great fuss has been made recently over an alleged need for something called "computer literacy," as though it were some absolute quantity like a cure for a new disease. But whatever computer literacy is, if there really is such a thing, the dosage each of us needs varies widely according to the uses we can and should make of computers in our careers and business enterprises. Certainly the lawyer using a desktop computer to search out precedents in legal databases, the writer preparing a manuscript on a transportable computer, the engineer calculating the volume of concrete needed for a bridge structure, the sixth-grader taking a public school course in general computer skills, and the independent consultant preparing materials for a client have far different reasons to become "literate" about computers.

1

There is no intention here of trying to make you a technical expert in computers, even if I were qualified and able to do so. You do not need to be expert at anything except knowing what a computer can do for you and what you can do with a computer, relevant to your own needs, and how to do it. That, in the form of the most basic, nontechnical orientation, is all that Part One of this book is intended to accomplish.

CHAPTER ONE

The Computer Contribution

The computer represents a far greater revolution than most of us understand or even dream, and it has hardly begun.

IN OUR OWN TIME . . .

The world's first electronic digital computer, ENIAC (electronic numerical integrator and calculator), was designed to calculate artillery firing tables for use in World War II. (The trajectories of missiles, whether ballistic (artillery types) or self-propelled (rocket types), are difficult to calculate, requiring extensive use of mathematics.) Its name, electronic numerical integrator and calculator, and its categorical epithet, computer, both reflected a primary objective and capability for what is today colloquially called "number crunching," namely, mathematical calculations.

It turned out, eventually, that this was a short-sighted idea: the computer, in the hands of the many resourceful geniuses who soon became involved in the infant industry, soon demonstrated that its full potential and capabilities were far beyond the constraints of mere number crunching. In its meteoric rise of only

40-odd years, from that lumberingly clumsy and impossibly expensive behemoth of 18,000 tubes and a roomful of hardware (ENIAC) to today's millions of desktop, briefcase, and pocket computers, the computer has given birth to more than new industry: it has achieved a near dominance of industry generally and has become the foundation for something new, called by many the "Information Industry," that which reportedly is about to replace the traditional "smokestack industries" of the United States and change the very nature of the world's economic and industrial structure. Much of what mankind has accomplished since World War II—satellite communications systems and space sciences generally, for example—would simply not have been possible without the computer. Computers are today under the hoods of modern automobiles, in household appliances, automating entire factories, at the controls of 500-passenger airplanes, in travelers' pockets and briefcases, and on the desktops of professionals, executives, and secretaries in millions of offices.

THE COMPUTER AS GENERALIST

The versatility of the computer is not incidental to its rapid development and proliferation; that versatility is itself the cause of and reason for that rise and proliferation in the myriad of forms in which the computer now appears. The computer is the generalist of the commercial, industrial, and business worlds, and even of other milieus: it can do almost anything we can think up for it to do. (A bit later, when we get into a deeper discussion of computer capabilities and operating principles, you will see why this is true.) Computing—in the literal sense, that is—is only one of the things it does and is certainly not the most important thing nor the thing it is most often assigned to do. In fact, it is reported from a number of sources—and there appears to be general agreement on this—that word processing is by far the most popular use of the desktop computer today. It is even true that word processing is the only use made of the system in a great many offices, and probably a great many users are not even aware that the computer has many other uses and capabilities. Those who have the greatest need for this versatility are the small business entrepreneurs, the self-employed or independent consultants, and other professionals, but unfortunately they are the very ones who tend most often to be unaware of the full potential of computers—of what computers can do to help them to achieve success and how to enlist computers for such help.

THE TWO CLASSES OF APPLICATION

In rather general terms, the independent consultant has two classes of application for a computer: The computer will support (1) the actual processes of consulting—the technical/professional services themselves—and (2) the managerial/administrative functions necessary to the conduct of all enterprises, large and small. In some instances, these services and functions tend to overlap. That is, some functions the computer performs are useful for both applications. That will show up as we review the various functions in general.

MANAGERIAL AND BUSINESS FUNCTIONS

The independent consultant is, at one and the same time, a self-employed professional, an entrepreneur, a small-business chief executive, and a company. But the independent consultant must also be the comptroller/financial manager and chief accountant/bookkeeper, the sales manager, marketing manager, advertising manager, public relations director, troubleshooter, and general factotum, and often the secretary too, if the firm has only one employee.

It's quite a bundle, and many independent consultants have a CPA (certified public accountant) handle their accounting and bookkeeping needs; also, the consultant usually engages a secretary on a full- or part-time basis. But even those measures leave the consultant a large number of managerial/administrative chores to attend to, not the least important of which are all those connected with marketing, directly and indirectly. Marketing is one set of responsibilities the consultant can or should get only partial help with, if at all, but the bulk of the work must be handled personally. Let's have a quick look at what that entails and how the computer can help:

Marketing Functions

The importance of the marketing function is plain enough: without marketing, there are no sales—no clients, that is. And the consequences of having no clients needs no extended discussion: without clients the practice soon passes into oblivion, joining all those other ventures that suffered the inevitable consequences of unsuccessful marketing—or the lack of marketing effort. (Perhaps business failures are more often the result of a complete lack of true marketing effort—so often, entrepreneurs delude themselves into thinking that what they are doing is marketing, when it is not marketing at all—than of ineffective marketing.)

Despite the analyses and reports of the Small Business Administration and others who profess expertise in such matters, no other fault or deficiency in the conduct of a small business (or even a large business, for that matter) is as often responsible for the demise of a business as is the failure to market well. Somehow, most ventures can survive all other weaknesses and disasters when they have adequate sales volume, but no amount of expert management of inventory, accounting, finances, and other such matters can overcome the fatal thrust of insufficient sales volume. For that reason I deem marketing to be by far the most important managerial/administrative function of any venture, and the one an entrepreneur can least afford to delegate or be the least bit careless about.

The functions within marketing include advertising, sales promotion, such as PR (public relations), and sales ("sales" is not identical with marketing, but is one of the marketing functions). Those functions demand the performance of many chores, including writing, mailing, and personal calls. It is necessary to prepare, write, and deliver speeches and to write and mail brochures, letters, and other literature. Some consultants develop little newsletters as sales promotional tools and often find that these are effective in winning clients.

Perhaps the most important writing the consultant must do in marketing is the writing of proposals, that increasingly more important and more widely used tool of marketing and sales. It has become a cliché—but nonetheless a recognized truth—that contract awards go to those who write the most effective proposals, whether or not they happen also to be the most qualified or most competent contestants for the contract. And if proposal-writing skills are among the most important marketing skills, help in writing effective proposals is among the most effective and important contributions a computer can make to your success. But it is not only as a word processor that the computer is an important contributor to your success in writing proposals that win assignments; there are other functions and capabilities of the computer that make substantial contributions too. (Later, we will devote an entire, separate chapter to this subject.)

Accounting Functions

A great many people appear to be laboring under the mistaken notion that accounting systems are conducted for the benefit of the Internal Revenue Service and its counterparts in state and local jurisdictions. And admittedly these organizations often do appear to be the chief beneficiaries—and perhaps, in some cases, the only beneficiaries—of the accounting functions. That is not as it should be, for accounting does not have records for tax purposes as its chief objective or reason for being. In fact, that is, or certainly should be, an entirely subordinate consideration in the design of an accounting system, and an accounting-system design should never be skewed to that consideration, particularly at the expense of the true purpose of any accounting system, namely to provide sensible and necessary management information to the decision makers. The accounting system must serve the proprietor, not the tax collector. The purpose of accounting is to provide managers the information they need to make intelligent and useful decisions about the enterprise. Information for other purposes, such as taxes, are byproducts that fall out of the system without making special efforts to achieve them.

One problem with turning over your accounting chores to a contractor, such as a CPA, is that the CPA generally knows nothing about your needs as a manager and entrepreneur, much less about the field of consulting as a professional enterprise. And, all too often, the CPA doesn't even care and pays little more than lip service in acknowledging that you need information for management. (Many CPAs appear to believe that management information is an annual profit and loss statement, an annual balance sheet, a net-worth statement, and monthly bank statement reconciliations.)

Personal experience has convinced me that delegating accounting to another firm is almost as much a mistake as delegating your marketing to a stranger, and can be almost as deadly in its effects. Again, the computer can be a great help. However, there is this difference: whereas it was understandable that the average consultant did not feel able to manage functions as specialized and tedious as accounting, today the computer makes it possible to do exactly that without knowing the first thing about accounting! In later chapters, we'll discuss this in greater depth and demonstrate its validity.

Miscellaneous Administrative Chores

There are a great many miscellaneous chores that you may elect to delegate and contract out, such as making large mailings. However, the computer makes it possible for you to do these things yourself, in your own office, without extravagant effort, and almost surely at far lesser cost than it would entail to contract it out. In fact, you can use your desktop computer to do the following things:

1. Maintain your mailing lists, keep them up to date, organize and reorganize them in various orders, and/or select out any given name or sets of names you wish.

2. Maintain as many form letters as you wish in files, drawing

on any you want, whenever you want, as they are or with changes to adapt them to the needs of the moment or to individual applications.

3. Type out form letters individually, for mass mailings, addressing each individually to the recipient, in such a way that the recipient cannot tell that the letters are form letters, were mass produced, and were not composed individually.

4. Address all the envelopes automatically.

Your computer is also a communications device, and you can use it to communicate with others, via their own computers, and to draw upon information stored in other computers.

There are many other uses that we will discuss later in more detail.

TECHNICAL/PROFESSIONAL CONSULTING FUNCTIONS

There are at least two classes of technical/professional consulting functions your computer can be called on to perform, depending primarily on what your own consulting field is: (1) the inherent capabilities of the computer may themselves be some of the services you provide or contribute directly to providing those services, such as statistical analyses and inventory planning; (2) even if you are not in some field where the computer is directly involved in the services you offer, you must still do many things, as part of your professional services, that the computer can help you with, such as render reports, make presentations, and do research.

Direct Contributions

If you happen to be a consulting engineer, the computer can be called upon directly to help with CAD (computer assisted design) functions and/or with engineering calculations. Or you may use your computer to dial up relevant databases of engineering data somewhere, as an efficient method of research.

Your computer can help you immeasurably in making statistical analyses, managing inventory, making projections, modeling, searching out information available elsewhere, and otherwise making direct contributions to your professional services, even constituting some of the services.

The available databases—banks of information made available to anyone who wishes to subscribe, and many free databases as well—are themselves the basis for many services you can provide. There are: financial databases, reporting up-to-the-minute news from the stock markets and other financial centers; services offering information on bid opportunities; electronic newsletters and magazines; and databases offering information on drugs and medicines, taxes, legislation in progess, and sundry other subjects. And the availability of online information you can access swiftly via computer is growing steadily.

Indirect, General Contributions

As a consultant, regardless of what your technical/professional field happens to be, you will have to prepare and submit reports, make presentations, do research, communicate with others, read relevant literature, and otherwise perform a large number of chores that are more or less standard for any consulting practice. Here, again, the computer can help you—as a word processor, as a communications device, and as a time-saving helper.

Later, when we examine the software programs available, you will find that they also fall into the two classes of general programs: (1) those that are generally adaptable to and useful for most business enterprises; and (2) those that are specialized and industry-specific, written to suit the special needs of various industries and professions. There are, for example, many accounting programs, some for large organizations, some for small organizations, but generally suited to any and all kinds of businesses and industries. On the other hand, there are special accounting programs suited especially to the accounting needs of specific industries, such as retail sales and architectural services.

MORE ABOUT ONLINE SERVICES

Through the use of many online services, some of which are yet to be described, you may be able to do more than expand your services and deliver them with greater efficiency: you may, in fact, be able to offer new and different services relevant to your field— actually *add* services, that is. You may, for example, add an information service to whatever else you do. (One local specialist, Matthew Lesko, operates a new company he calls "Information USA," after the title of a successful book he wrote; among other services, he offers to search out appropriate online databases for clients in any field for a suitable fee.) You may be able to help investors who do not know the field learn about and understand stock reports, or you can furnish demographic data to marketers. But these are only the barest samples of ways to spin off new products and services out of access to online databases; these convey only the bare idea, where there are almost countless possibilities. The main point is that information is itself a product today, and you can gather and refine the raw materials—raw data—into processed outputs as new products, or provide related services as new services. At present, the door to this field has barely opened.

Other Online Services

Originally, the online databases were conceived as rich stores of readily accessible information, and computer owners began to sign up for the information itself. Today a great many people still conceive of the online system exclusively as information stores. But information per se is only one product; things have begun to change or, perhaps more accurately, to expand and evolve into other services than pure information. Here are a few of the other services, many of which can contribute directly or indirectly to your consulting practice and your income base:

☐ Use of other, larger computers and the relevant software via modem-link to your own computer. This will enable you to provide services your own personal computer would not be big enough to handle. Or it can enable you to provide services that require software other than the programs you have available.

☐ Some online services provide access to other online databases, making it unnecessary for you and your clients to maintain a large number of subscriptions, especially when you want access to some of these databases only once in a while. This can save both you and your clients money, while expanding your spectrum of available information.

☐ Most systems have some kind of bulletin board service, where you can post notices; sometimes, this can even be used as a kind of public relations or advertising service.

☐ Many systems offer an electronic mail facility, in which you can send "letters" to other subscribers. (Privacy and data security are maintained through the use of identification and log-on codes.)

☐ Some systems offer storage facilities, where you can place important data for safekeeping or as a kind of insurance against loss through any cause.

☐ In some systems you can participate in discussions of technical and other subjects, often getting the equivalent of free consultation from other consultants and specialists, in a kind of exchange among peers.

HYBRIDS AND BILATERAL FUNCTIONS

Some of the functions can serve both kinds of applications. Newsletter preparation is one such example. Many consultants develop newsletters as part of their income-producing activities, and charge for subscriptions, whereas others develop newsletters to use for sales promotion.

The online communications and research functions are often useful for both technical/professional and management/ administrative purposes too, inasmuch as they can be helpful in market research, in purchasing functions, in publicity and advertising, in communications, and in sundry other ways, as should be apparent by now. (Today a personal computer and modem can be used quite efficiently as a telex system and can communicate anywhere in the world via telegram and cable traffic. This is useful in marketing, especially for those consultants who take assignments in foreign countries and wish to respond to what many other governments call "tenders," which are equivalent to our own government's solicitations for bids and proposals.)

Obviously, the word processing capabilities of your computer also work in your behalf in preparing reports and presentations, as they do in correspondence, proposal writing, and the development of other marketing and sales literature. Of course, word processing is also a boon to the development and operating of some of those other profit centers, such as newsletters, reports, and manuals.

Overall, then, we see that the personal computer can make important contributions to, and work great improvements in, just about every facet of your practice.

CHAPTER TWO

What Is a Computer?
What Can It Do?

Although the computer is an idea almost everyone in the civilized world knows about, in many ways it remains a complete mystery to most people. It would be useful to dispel at least some of that mystery and place this revolutionary invention in its proper perspective.

THE IDEA OF COMPUTER LITERACY

It is, of course, not necessary to know computer technology to own and operate a personal computer effectively and efficiently. The majority of personal-computer owners, even those who have learned to use the jargon knowingly (or, at least, glibly), have only rather superficial technical knowledge of their computers (although there are notable exceptions because enthusiasm for some is so high that they absorb the information thirstily, almost through their pores, and often become more expert than the professionals in the field).

There is, however, this quality called "computer literacy," about which we hear so much today. But even if we acknowledge that there is such a characteristic and that everyone ought to become "literate" about computers, just what does that mean? And if the need exists, is it the same for everyone? Does the sixth-grader need the same degree of computer literacy as the small-business executive or the engineer? Does the user doing corporate accounting have the same "need to know" as the writer developing a technical manual or the mathematician making probability projections?

Obviously, even conceding the need for computer literacy (and assuming that we know what that means), the need does vary, and in this chapter I am going to subject you to what I believe you ought to know about computers. Of course, I can't prevent you from skimming this chapter rapidly or even from skipping it entirely. And I am not at all certain that you will lose anything important by so doing. (In fact, you may already be more computer literate than I suspect!)

On the other hand, I am going to try my best to make the material easy to understand, interesting to read, and useful to know. And in any case it will not be an especially long chapter to struggle through, if indeed you find yourself struggling to keep your eyes open.

WHAT A COMPUTER IS—AND IS NOT

The choice of the epithet "computer" was an unfortunate one. It led everyone to believe that the computer is some kind of supercalculator. And perhaps that is understandable, since the original mission of the world's first electronic digital computer, ENIAC (electronic numerical integrator and calculator) was to calculate artillery trajectories and firing tables for use in World War II.

So the computer is, in many of its applications, a kind of calculator, used for what is colloquially referred to today as "number crunching," or calculations of various kinds. And there are many kinds of calculations, from simple accounting work to the complex calculations required in celestial mechanics for such things as satellite launching and control.

But number crunching is only one kind of work the computer does, and not necessarily its most important work, either. The general-purpose computer that rests easily on your desktop can do lots of other kinds of work, such as the following examples:

Control inventory
Present training material
Communicate with other computers
Do word processing
Indexing
Serve as telex
Prepare tax returns
Print payroll checks
Keep golf scores
Forecast results (weather, stock market prices, other)
Prepare invoices
Maintain mailing lists
Address letters and envelopes

In short, the computer is a versatile tool, adaptable to a great variety of functions as a result of its inherent capabilities and fundamental concepts upon which the computer is based. In fact, there are two major kinds of computer elements that determine its total capabilities: hardware and software. Many computer enthusiasts are vehement in their belief that the software—programs—are the more important elements, and they have some basis for this: software *is* quite important, and much of computer sophistication is the result of the ingenuity exercised by software developers. However, hardware developers—engineers—have also been ingenious in their inventions and designs, and the truth is that neither hardware nor software is of value without the other. Together, they offer this enormous range of capabilities.

A BRIEF HISTORY

A brief review of modern (recent) computer history will help explain why hardware and software are so interdependent, and perhaps also why many assign even more importance to software than to hardware: in the beginning, only a few decades ago (circa 1950), there was only computer hardware. The digital computer had the potential for flexibility and diversity in application, but it had to be laboriously rewired for each application. That is, each wiring or rewiring represented a new program. A step forward was a plugboard, resembling an oversized cribbage board. By rewiring the computer, via this plugboard, the program—what the computer could *do* —was changed. And every program change might thus take several days to plan and carry out.

The punch card, also referred to popularly as the "IBM card," was an improvement on this, but it required that the computer have an internal memory, in which the data represented by the holes and spaces on the punch card might be represented and stored temporarily. In early computers, a major engineering developmental objective was to improve and increase the size of computer memories.

Memory is a transient quality in a computer, useful usually for only a given program and sometimes only for a given portion of the operation. Computers also need storage, a kind of long-term or permanent memory, and a great deal of effort went into developing ever-improving storage systems also. (Punch cards were, in fact, one form of storage, but a rather inconvenient form for many applications.)

It was because of these demands that early computers were rather large, ponderous, cumbersome, and costly. Early systems tended to be "brute force" systems, accomplishing their goals by sheer massiveness in expenditures of materials, time, and money. They also required special installations and environments—rooms with false floors, so that the mare's nest of cables and wires could be accommodated under the false floor, and heavy air-conditioning to help disperse the thousands of calories of heat generated by these monstrous machines, with their thousands of tubes and, even later, with their vast arrays of transistors.

In the past decade or slightly longer, computers have reached a stage of relative sophistication, where achieving adequate storage, memory, and software are no longer serious problems. Today, computers are compact, quiet, efficient, and inexpensive, and they can function in ordinary office environments, even without air-conditioning. Today, computers are more or less standardized, as hardware, and have quite enormous versatility, as a result of a quite enormous array of available software.

The modern computer is therefore probably more a product of its software than of its hardware, and it is probably fair to say that the software industry is even more dynamic—changing, evolving, and producing new products—than the hardware industry. Software developers have proved to be remarkably resourceful and inventive in exploiting the hardware potentials and in solving problems—at least as resourceful as the engineering geniuses who have climbed many technological Mount Everests in developing the modern desktop computer. Many problems have, in fact, been solved by both hardware and software measures. For example, because the computer operates at speeds far higher than those of even the fastest printers, printing slows the computer down: it has to wait for the lumbering printer to accept the information, which means the computer is unavailable to the user while the printer is running. To enable the computer to go on and do other work while the printer is doing its job, a hardware device known as a "buffer" can be used. It will intercede, accepting the data to be printed, storing it temporarily, and taking over control of the printing, so that the computer can turn to other tasks. But there is a kind of software program, called a "spooler," which can accomplish that same result, and at lesser cost.

IS THE COMPUTER A GREAT BRAIN?

It is a tribute to the versatility of computer capabilities that many think of it as a virtual brain, and a great many science fiction stories have been based on that idea. And there is, in fact, an entire segment of the computer industry devoting itself to the development of "supercomputers" and investigating "artificial intelligence," to the extent that the latter is virtually a science in itself. So the modern scientific community accepts that the computer probably has the potential for eventually becoming an artificial brain in some distant future. Or perhaps not so distant, given the unbelievable speed at which the computer sciences and engineering professions have been setting and reaching ever more ambitious goals.

Whatever the case, the computer is today still only a machine, albeit a "talented" one. And those "talents" lie in the software—programs—at least as much as they do in the hardware. Today's computers can do what their programs order, but the programs were written by humans, and the capabilities of the machines and their programs are the capabilities of the humans who designed the machines and wrote the programs. Make no mistake about that. As a brain, the computer is only as "smart" as its human engineers and programmers were: it is a reflection of human intelligence.

THE COMPUTER'S MAIN TALENT: SPEED

To a computer, data is a series of electrical pulses, arranged in a great assortment of patterns, each pattern representing something. There are enough different patterns of eight pulses each to represent all the alphanumeric characters and symbols, in both upper- and lowercase letters, plus a number of other symbols. These pulses can also be assembled into combinations that can represent words, sentences, numbers, and various graphics—charts, plots, and even line drawings. In short, the computer, under the instruction of the programs, can develop, represent, and print out just about any and every idea that humans can conceive, discuss, record, and/or present on paper.

To accomplish this, the computer has the capability for manipulating data—those sets of pulses—thereby adding, subtracting, comparing, selecting, moving, saving, discarding, accumulating, or otherwise operating on the data as humans would (and thereby giving birth to that notion that the computer is a giant calculator, as well as a giant brain). And it does these things mechanically, according to the instructions it gets from the software. But in fact the computer is something of a moron, as

Peter Drucker has accused it of being, for it carries out all these things in rather laborious and dull-witted fashion, multiplying and dividing, for example, by repetitive addition and subtraction. (Even a grade-school youngster is smarter and better educated than the greatest of computers in that regard!)

Electrons move along conductors at nearly the speed of light, which is approximately 186,000 miles per second—virtually instantaneous, in terms of everyday experience here on Earth. And even though not all electrical events in the computer take place at quite that high speed, they do take place at almost literally lightning speeds. And therein lies the computer's great "brain power": its power is *speed*, nothing else. Even the slowest computer can add 7243 to itself 4324 times and get the result of 31,318,732 far faster than the fastest human can multiply those two numbers together. It is because of this speed that a computer can do in minutes what would take teams of mathematicians days to calculate, and this speed permits the computer to carry out tasks that humans would simply never find practical to tackle by older methods.

THE MAIN ELEMENTS OF THE COMPUTER

While it is neither necessary nor desirable to probe into the technical details of how the computer is built and how it works, getting a general idea about the main elements of the computer and how they work helps to dispel much of the mystery, thereby helping many people to overcome much of the fear they have of this frighteningly complex device.

Figure 1 shows the basic components of a typical computer at the most elementary level. That which we refer to as a "computer" is actually a system of several components, only one of which is the computer or "central computer," as it is sometimes referred to in mainframe (big computer) installations.

In the typical personal computer, there are two methods for entering information and instructions, the keyboard (usually a typewriterlike arrangement of keys) and the disk drives, most of

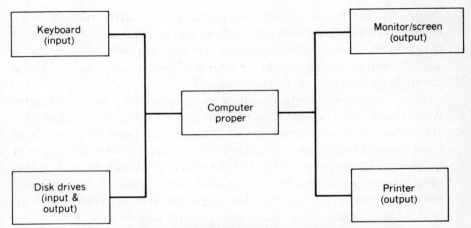

Figure 1. The basic components of a typical computer.

which are built to accommodate floppy disks or diskettes. Similarly, most personal computer systems have two output devices, a TV-like monitor screen, which displays data ("soft" copy or soft display), and a printer of some sort, to make "hard" copies of the information you wish to save on paper.

WHAT'S IN THE COMPUTER?

Within the computer itself there are a number of electrical circuits and elements. The most significant, as far as you are concerned, is the memory, which is kind of a short-term storage: it is used for handling data, and is wiped clean when you turn the machine off, although you can erase what is in it at any time. (Whatever you wish to save you must transfer to one of the disks, which represent long-term or permanent storage.)

Internal memory is in the form of a miniature device, a microchip called RAM (random access memory), which is jargon meaning that you can readily enter, gain access to any area of it, and erase or change data in the device.

The other major element of interest is the CPU (central processing unit), also called the *microprocessor*. This is the heart of the computer's capabilities for handling data. Until fairly recently, most personal computers had CPUs that handled data in groups of eight bits at a time. More recently, a 16-bit CPU has become popular and is appearing in most personal computers of more recent origin. And some machines have appeared with 32-bit CPUs, and these are likely to become more and more common.

The final device of interest—one which you really do not need to know anything about at this early time, but which is mentioned here because you will see its jargon name mentioned frequently and might wonder what it is—is the ROM (read only memory). This device contains certain computer instructions permanently inscribed in it. The CPU reads it, but cannot erase or change what is in it, nor enter anything else into it.

There are other devices, but none that we need to discuss now.

THE BASICS OF OPERATION

In the typical personal computer, you begin operations by inserting a floppy disk in the drive (Drive A, normally, if your system has more than one drive) and pressing the ENTER or RETURN key. That sends the data (or part of the data) on the disk to the computer's memory, and asks you to load the program you wish to run. (You can arrange also to have an "auto load" instruction that will automatically load the program when you press ENTER.) "Loading" the program means, simply, transferring it from the disk to the computer's internal memory. And "transferring" it does not mean literally taking it from the disk—it is not erased—but means *copying* it from the disk and sending the copy to the memory device. (It does this in a few seconds.)

From that point on, you are in control via your keyboard. You can now enter new data by typing it out on the keyboard or from the disk (or from another disk), and issue instructions to manipulate data, transfer it back to disk, or otherwise do whatever the program permits and whatever you wish to do. And, finally, when you are finished, you either save the final results by storing it on a disk, printing it out, or both.

HOW TO BUY A COMPUTER

Later chapters will explore the subject of choosing a computer in some depth. This task presents a serious problem for most newcomers to computers. It's a problem for many reasons, and it is in preparation for helping you solve this problem—as a first step, in fact—that this introductory material is offered. Here are a few of the reasons that most newcomers to computers shy almost instinctively at the task of choosing a computer:

The fear many have of this strange kind of office equipment

The enormous diversity of makes and models

The equally enormous diversity of peripheral devices and accessories

The avalanche of conflicting claims and promises

The outpouring of books purporting to teach the subject to the lay person

The strange and indecipherable language—jargon—spoken in this field

THE CONVENTIONAL WISDOM

The conventional wisdom offered so often by so many is that the software must come first—that you must choose the programs you want, first, and then choose the computer best suited to run those programs. In many ways, that was sound advice a few years ago, but the advice is somewhat dated and certainly not immutable truth today. At the least, there are many exceptions to that wisdom in today's computer environment, and there are certainly some other considerations than those of favored software to be taken into account in choosing a system. In those later chapters on the subject of choosing the right computer, we'll take a closer look at these other considerations.

CHAPTER THREE

What Can a Computer Do for You?

What a computer can do generally and what a computer can do for you are usually two entirely distinct and separate questions, with quite distinct and separate answers.

THE GENERAL COMPUTER CONTRIBUTION

The introductory chapters discussed the application of computers to consulting ventures in the most general terms, pointing out that the computer can be most useful in supporting both the technical/professional functions and the managerial/administrative functions of an independent practice. Those are the two most general categories of computer applications for the independent consultant, but each of these has far more significant ramifications, especially as they apply to individual cases. For on the one hand, there is no question but that no matter what your consulting specialty is, a computer can assist you and contribute to your success generally in a variety of ways, probably all of these:

1. By expanding and adding to your consulting capabilities.

25

2. By increasing your efficiency.

3. By increasing your income through supporting the diversification of your practice and the development of additional income-producing centers in your practice.

4. By making substantial contributions to the marketing of your services and/or products.

THE SPECIAL, INDIVIDUAL COMPUTER CONTRIBUTIONS

On the other hand, everyone has individual and sometimes unique needs and problems, so inevitably you will use a computer somewhat differently than others do, and you will therefore have your own, perhaps different, software needs than others, and perhaps even different hardware needs.

In my own case, for example, my original and sole purpose in buying a computer was to use it as a word processor, for my work is primarily writing. (Most of the time, when I am not writing books I am writing proposals for clients; that's the major element in my consulting work.) At the time, I had no thought of other uses, and for many months the only software I used was the word processor and the spelling program, despite the several other valuable programs that were "bundled" with the machine. They remained undisturbed on my shelves in their original polyfilm envelopes.

It was not then my expectation that the computer/word processor (the word processor is the software, of course, not the hardware) would appreciably boost my output. At most I expected the electronic cut-and-paste and other features of the system to reduce considerably my use of whiteout fluids, correction tapes, and mucilage, save me a little time, and give me, at most, a modest boost in my daily output.

I was both right and wrong. I was right in that it did not give me much of an overall boost in output, as far as I could determine. But I was right for the wrong reason: the limited increase in my daily productivity was not because the system was not considerably more efficient than my older methods—it was and still is. The reason was far more complex: in fact while using the system I began to write a great deal more every day, but produce about the same amount of final product. That was because I began to do a great deal more rewriting, revision, and polishing of copy. If I did not produce significantly more final pages every day, I produced final pages of far greater quality than ever before. Revision and rewriting had become so easy that it was almost fun to revise and rewrite. And every time I read my copy on-screen, whether proofing for typos or refreshing my own memory on what I had written, I yielded to the temptation to do still one more round of improvement. And where before I always pondered whether to cut and paste pages to make an insertion, to rewrite the entire section, or whether the improvement was worth the trouble of rewriting and revision at all, now I make the insertion without pondering it for a moment. It has become that easy.

Despite my technical knowledge of computers, stretching back some years, all of this was a revelation since I had never personally used a computer in my work. My entire view changed considerably after a short time of such personal use. Originally a rather reluctant tyro at the keyboard, determined to try to be objective about word processing, despite my snobbish disdain for the new "in" methodology, I soon became a highly enthusiastic aficionado, only slightly below the status of "hacker," which is the modern—computer—equivalent of the radio "ham" of early radio days.

It was only a few months later that I sought out a spooler program to increase my efficiency. (I hadn't even known what a spooler was!) Spooler software buffers the computer–printer interface, taking over the job of feeding data to the printer, so that the computer can then go on accepting new work and working at new tasks while the printer is running. This meant that I did not have to sit idle, waiting for the printer to finish its chattering before I could do more writing with my word processor, or wait until the end of the day to print out my hard copy. That meant a major boost in my efficiency overall—in the amount of copy I turned out every day—by reducing my idle time.

Still later, I decided that it was necessary for me to be able to go online and communicate with other computers and information sources. I therefore bought a modem and communication software and now enjoy the added benefits of my online communications capabilities, with the expanded information access the online capability adds.

I have also now "installed" the rest of the software that was bundled with my system—there were actually seven different packages of software included—in preparation for using it in marketing my services. One of the programs is a database manager, suitable for managing mailing lists, and I plan to start building a new mailing list, which I shall computerize. Some of the other software I have made ready to use with my system will permit me to do some programming, and I plan to use those to create several new useful products for others to use in their own computers. And no doubt I shall find many other new things I want to do, as time goes on. Experience has already taught me that while I may not be able to anticipate precisely what the desirable new uses will be, I can be sure that there will be many I will want to take advantage of. Some will result from new developments in this ultradynamic industry, while others will result simply from my own growing knowledge and discovery of potentials I did not know about a short time ago.

That is the lesson of computers generally. A great many new computer owners find that they have grossly underestimated what their computers can do for them and for their enterprises, and how their own interest in "computerology" will grow. Once they have become comfortable and efficient in using their systems, their horizons as computer users will begin to expand steadily, and they will begin to develop computer-related interests they did not have originally. This is a factor to be taken into account when buying a system: unless you happen to be a most unusual human being, you are quite likely to experience this same evolution of interest and felt need. That is, you are likely to buy far less initially in both hardware and software than you ultimately discover you need, if you are to get all the benefits possible from your system. But there are ways to cope with this problem, and they will be presented later, in discussing the specifics of software and hardware and their selection for your initial system.

TYPICAL USES AND USERS

The range of things a computer can do is extremely broad. Many of the popular computer applications cut across the lines of all professions and industries by being useful to virtually everyone. On the other hand, many of the more popular applications are more useful for some specific classes or categories of enterprise than for others—needs vary from one profession to another and from one industry to another. A physician, for example, normally sees many patients and, like many other enterprises, bills a large number of people regularly. The physician and others with that kind of need therefore would probably have use for special programs to send out bills, statements, and reminders. The typical independent consultant, on the other hand, generally works with a small number of clients and does not have a need to do a great deal of billing and reminder follow-up, and so would not normally need a special program for that use.

There is also the case of many computer applications that are specialized in the sense of being specific to a given profession, discipline, or industry. The consulting engineer, for example, will be interested in many programs that pertain especially to some specific field of engineering—electronics, stress analysis, aerodynamics, or earth-moving, for example—whereas the training consultant would be interested in programs pertaining to training or presenting actual courses. But both might be interested in some mathematics programs, since both use mathematics in their work.

We'll consider here those uses and applications most likely to be useful to the independent consultant, while recognizing that there may be (and probably are) some exceptions to what is presented as the general rule here.

Word Processing

Among the general uses for which almost all consultants are likely to find the computer valuable is word processing, reported generally as by far the most widespread general application of computers. This is obviously because everyone in even the smallest of professional or business enterprises has occasion to do some writing—at least normal business correspondence, files, memoranda, reports, and all the other typical paperwork of the modern venture.

A second reason for the popularity of word processing applications of computers is the sheer versatility of word processing: with a little imagination, a good word processor can be used to do many other things—make up forms, sketch simple graphs and charts, do some automatic tabulation, and otherwise make itself extremely useful. (There are many special programs that do these things more easily and swiftly than you can do them with a word processor, but these programs are usually quite expensive and not at all necessary or justified if you have only occasional need for these other applications.) In short, most small offices can handle probably 75 percent of their computer needs with a good word processor. But there are many types of word processors offered today, which vary widely in their levels of sophistication and the things they can do, so the adjective *good* is used here advisedly to mean sophisticated, versatile, and convenient word processors.

Word processing can support you well in both marketing and in technical or professional applications—in winning clients and in the services you provide, and in the efficiency with which you operate. In the coming chapters we'll discuss many specific applications.

Accounting

Every business venture, even the simplest sole proprietorship, has a need for accounting. Not only do all governments now demand a virtual share of your venture, but they also claim the right to look at your books, and even require that you keep books. So although the prime purpose of keeping books is to help you manage your enterprise effectively and not to make life easier for the tax collector, it is necessary to have records that will satisfy the demands of the aforementioned authority too.

There is a great number of word processing programs, but there is an even greater number of accounting programs, a far greater number, in fact. And they vary in many ways: there are general accounting programs for small businesses, with all elements included in a single program. But there are many special accounting programs for larger enterprises, which need separate programs for such functions as payroll preparation, listing payables, listing receivables, invoicing, journalizing, preparing financial reports, and sundry other accounting and bookkeeping necessities. Of course, most businesses—even nonprofit corporations, associations, and institutions—must maintain journals and ledgers and do all of these things, but the small organization, and especially the self-employed independent practitioner, can make do quite well with a small, single program that provides all the functions in one.

Number Crunchers

There are many programs designed for mathematics applications. In a sense, accounting programs are number crunchers too, because they do work with numbers primarily, but the term is generally reserved for those applications that are primarily mathematical in nature or that rely heavily on capabilities for manipulating quantitative data.

This would be an application for some independent consultants, but not for all. The consulting engineer, demographer, psychologist, statistician, or other technological specialist working as an independent consultant is likely to have use for such programs to handle fairly complex calculations and statistical determinations, while other consultants may not have such needs.

Database Management

A database is any body of related information. Any set of files, or even a mailing list, may be considered to be a database. A database must be managed, and can be managed far more effectively and efficiently with the help of a computer program than by any of the earlier systems. A database manager (program) can be used, for example, to sort mailing lists, organize and reorganize them in almost any order, print out portions selectively, and otherwise do in minutes what would take you hours, perhaps days, to do by any other method. It can also be used to design forms, generate reports, and perform many other tasks to handle your data. In fact, it can be the mechanism for building the database, to begin with! It would be a rare consultant who could not find useful things to do with a database manager.

Spreadsheets

Spreadsheet programs are quite special and have become extremely popular, having "caught on" immediately after their introduction to the market. In one way, it is somewhat difficult to define spreadsheet software because so many definitions fit it, which is a tribute to its versatility and at least one outstanding reason for its early success.

The spreadsheet program is a means for realization of "what if?" speculation: the user can set up a model and "plug in" different variables to see what the effect of each would be. That makes it a modeling program, which can be used for a wide variety of applications: statistically, to determine the parameters of greatest sensitivity, for example—in engineering, to "build" prototypes or models theoretically, instead of actually; in business management, to calculate the effects of various decisions; and in military applications, to play war games on the computer, instead of in the field—to name just a few of the myriad of possible applications. So it is a kind of gaming device, too, although gaming for serious purposes, and not for amusement.

Communications

Communications software and a modem are a must for the consultant, later if not sooner. There is already an enormous amount of available information resources—online databases, most of which can be tapped for relatively modest fees, and some of which are entirely free. Nor is this the only beneficial use of online communciations that the consultant can make, but it is of itself ample justification for going online. (For one thing, as more and more offices install personal computers, and as more and more progress is made to enable different computers to "talk" to each other despite technological differences, it will become as necessary to have a desktop computer as it is today to have a telephone.)

Inventory, Purchasing, and Miscellaneous

Ordinarily, inventory control and management, purchasing, retail sales, wholesale distribution, and other such highly specialized programs are of interest to the independent consultant only if the consultant's services to clients are in connection with that specialized field, since rarely does the independent consulting practice have need itself for such programs.

SOME TYPICAL PROGRAM CATEGORIES

To give you a somewhat better idea of the wide variety of choices already available—and the list is growing rapidly—here are some classes and kinds of software programs:

General Business Software

Accounting	Marketing/sales
Business graphics	Office administration
Communications	Purchasing
Decision support	Project management

File/mailing list management
Financial management
Inventory
Shipping
Small business management
Telemarketing

Industry Specific

Accounting (for specific
   industries)
Advertising
Agriculture, farm management
Architecture
Automotive
Banking
Broadcasting
Chiropractic
Construction
Consulting
Contracting
Dentistry
Distribution
Electronics
Energy
Engineering
Government services
Hospitality
Import/export
Insurance
Leasing & rental
Legal services
Mail-order services
Manufacturing & processing
Medicine, health care
Personnel agencies
Printing services
Publishing
Real estate, property
   management
Retail sales
Transportation & travel
Utilities
Veterinary medicine
Wholesale sales

Special Disciplines

Amateur radio
Auctioneering
Authors, professional writers
Astrology
Design
Membership management
Music
Science & research
Social sciences
Sports & leisure

Geography

Mathematics

Market research

Statistics

Visual arts, photography

Education

Computer-aided instruction

Computer literacy aids

Educational administration

Special education

Teacher aids, courseware

Systems Software

Communications

Compilers

Database management

Hardware management

Languages

Operating systems

Program development aids

Utilities

PRELIMINARY ANALYSIS OF YOUR NEEDS

The very word *consultant* is difficult to define, as everyone who has tried to create a definition for it has found out. Definitions tend to range from one extreme to the other, depending on the individual's personal bias. One extreme has it that a consultant must be someone with at least one graduate degree, unusually qualifying experience, some remarkable achievements, or some combination of these and that the resulting outstanding expert renders counsel—advice (or is it *opinion?*)—as the sole service, namely, "consulting." At the other extreme, a consultant is defined as just about anyone who provides a service that requires any degree of special qualification.

Obviously, the reasonable answer lies somewhere between the extremes. The one definition would restrict consulting to a triflingly small number of qualified practitioners, and the other would mean that virtually every tradesperson would qualify as a consultant. Probably there can never be a precise definition, nor is it necessary that one be devised. It is enough that an individual claims the title consultant and clients are willing to pay for the

GENERAL BUSINESS APPLICATIONS

[ ]	Word processing*	[ ]	Telemarketing
[ ]	Accounting*	[ ]	Financial management
[ ]	File/list management*	[ ]	Office administration
[ ]	Marketing/sales*	[ ]	Inventory
[ ]	Advertising	[ ]	Management information
[ ]	Contracting	[ ]	Database management
[ ]	Market research	[ ]	Government services
[ ]	Management information system	[ ]	Purchasing
[ ]	_____	[ ]	_____
[ ]	_____	[ ]	_____

TECHNICAL/PROFESSIONAL APPLICATIONS

[ ]	Word processing*	[ ]	Publishing*
[ ]	Project management*	[ ]	Database management*
[ ]	Contracting*	[ ]	Electronics
[ ]	Communications*	[ ]	Statistics
[ ]	Management information systems	[ ]	_____
[ ]	_____	[ ]	_____
[ ]	_____	[ ]	_____

NOTES: _____

_____

*Indicates recommended type of software or application.

Worksheet 1. Preliminary applications recommendations and estimates.

services of bearers of the title. (It's a different matter with lawyers, physicians, and other specialists who must be licensed by law and who must pass certain examinations to be licensed; in those cases, the definition is a legal one and is legitimatized by the licensing authority.)

In any case, the point is that only you, the practitioner, decides finally whether or not you are a consultant and what kinds of services you offer. And it will be only you, finally, who decides what your business and professional needs are and what you need in hardware and software to best satisfy your needs.

A series of worksheets will be offered to help you identify your needs, immediate and potential, and reach the right decisions. The first one, presented here, is a general one, based on suggested applications that appear to be appropriate for all consultants and on other uses or applications that are probably appropriate for some, but not all, consultants. Blank spaces are provided so that categories not offered in the printed lists can be added. Refer to the general list provided earlier for ideas, and check off all items you consider to be probable applications in your own practice or intended practice.

Note that some categories appear in both lists—business and technical/professional applications. That is because many kinds of software fit both kinds of applications, and only you can judge whether a given application is suitable for one or the other—or both.

This is entirely preliminary, a rough estimate of your probable needs, and is by no means binding. You will have ample opportunity to review these listings and refine them, as we proceed, but it is useful to begin now to think about your needs and applications.

PART TWO

The Computer as a Marketing Aid

Marketing is probably the most essential function of most enterprises. In fact, most enterprises cannot exist without marketing. Even nonprofit organizations find it necessary to market: associations market to recruit new members and persuade members to attend conventions and seminars. The U.S. Postal Service has a marketing division to attract business and to try to regain some of the business they have lost to better services provided by the private sector. Even the Federal Supply Service has a marketing department now, to persuade other government agencies to buy from them rather than from the open market.

The computer is a valuable aid to marketing in a variety of ways, with word processing probably being the leading contributor to marketing applications, although not the only one. Marketing your services as a consultant often requires that you create written material for the purpose—newsletters, proposals, articles, brochures, and sundry other such material for both general marketing promotion and for specific sales presentations.

The word processor is a powerful tool in this, when used properly, and pays off in this use alone—it is, in fact, a completely worthwhile investment if used for nothing else but word processing in your marketing operations.

CHAPTER FOUR

Proposal Writing
With a Computer

To be a good proposal writer it is far more necessary to be a good marketer than to be a good writer. But to be both a good marketer and a good writer is to be a great and gifted proposal writer.

A SHORT HISTORY OF PROPOSAL WRITING

Proposal writing has become an increasingly important marketing activity. A few years ago a proposal was little more than an item description or set of specifications, a bid price, and a set of contract terms. The proposer might throw in a brochure or two, but that was gratuitous and not deemed necessary. Even the government did not require a great deal more, in earlier days. However, government procurement exploded after World War II and the requirements were for increasingly complex, sophisticated, and costly procurements. Competition became intense, and bidders went to ever greater pains to present their cases in their submittals. And government agencies demanded more and more detailed information to satisfy increasingly sophisticated evaluation schemes by which to select the winner of each contract competition.

The federal government, especially the Department of Defense, which then and since has led all government agencies in scope, size, and diversity of procurement, blazed the trails. Under the influence of their multimillion-dollar procurements and proposal requirements, proposal writing has grown and matured into methodologies and models that have been emulated widely by other governments—state, local, and foreign—and even by private sector organizations. All of today's proposals, from the simple letter proposals of two or three pages to the mammoth multivolume proposals of thousands of pages, owe their forms, formats, and concepts to those antecedents.

Today, most contracts for services of any size above that of casual small purchases are allowed only after a proposal competition, and even when a contract is to be allowed without competition, clients are nevertheless likely to insist on a proposal.

WHY DO CLIENTS WANT PROPOSALS?

The "why" of proposals has two sides to it: the client's side and your side. Each party has a purpose embodied in the proposal, but the two purposes are somewhat at odds with each other. The client is trying to decide who is the best consultant, and you are trying to demonstrate that you are the best consultant, the one who ought to be favored with the contract.

It has become conventional wisdom among those whose enterprises consist primarily of contracting with government agencies that government contracts are won by those who write the best proposals and not necessarily by those who are the best contractors. In fact, it is possible that the proposal approach to selecting consultants may sometimes be self-defeating in this regard. Some individuals become more expert at writing proposals than at whatever skills and methodologies their work entails. But that is not peculiar to proposal writers: many products and services are successful more because of effective marketing than because of the merits of their product or service. A mediocre service with capable marketing is far more likely to succeed than is an excellent service with mediocre marketing. The mission of marketing is not merely to create sales or to get orders; the true mission of marketing is also to create customer satisfaction, just as a good proposal creates an impression of quality.

The tendency for awards to be made to the best proposal writers is not hard to understand. It is because it is on the basis of what the proposal says that the client makes a judgment as to who is the best consultant. Of course, the client does make other efforts to verify the original judgment, but the bulk of the judgment is based on the impact the proposal makes because there is little else the client can judge by. Hence we see the importance of the proposal.

WHAT THE CLIENT WISHES TO SEE IN THE PROPOSAL

Typically, a proposal must include as detailed a description of the proposed project or service as possible; this description must be very specific in terms of your interpretation of the client's needs. A general description of your services will not usually prove very persuasive, for most clients have a highly specific need or problem when they call on you for aid, and they want a highly specific remedy proposed.

The client wants also to see explanations of why your services will do the job—he or she wants to be educated, in a sense. It dosen't help you very much to offer the finest consulting skills and the most useful project plan if the client does not understand them. It is the client's perception that counts, not yours and not anyone else's. Never ask the client to simply take your word for it that you are the best and that your plan is the best: you have to prove your case. In fact, the client wants to see three things, even if they are not specifically articulated:

1. A proposed plan that appears to be one that will do the job effectively, efficiently, and dependably.

2. A capability for doing the job proposed—human skills and experience, resources, facilities—whatever is needed.

3. Dependability of the consultant as a contractor.

In short, every client, whether an individual or a huge organization, wants to believe in you, your abilities, and your plans—all the way. The job of creating that confidence is yours, and you have to do it primarily via what you present in your proposal.

Try to bear this simple message in mind, for it explains, in a nutshell, what sales and marketing are all about, and these concepts will come up again and again.

WHY YOU SHOULD BE DELIGHTED TO WRITE A PROPOSAL

Many consultants groan when they are asked to write a proposal. For one thing, they don't like to write. For another thing, they know that writing a proposal—at least, a good proposal—is hard work. And for still another thing, they have the notion that they can sell far more effectively in person than they can in writing.

Word processing ought to be especially attractive to any consultant who feels this way. Word processing takes much of the pain out of writing for those who find writing difficult, it improves the quality of most people's writing, and there is no question but that when it is used properly it can add a great boost to the persuasiveness of one's written presentations—make for more powerful sales copy, that is.

The fact is that every proposal opportunity is a great sales opportunity: the request for a proposal is a client inviting you, even begging you, to tell your story and do some selling. The proposal request is a message that says, "Help me. I have need of you. Tell me how you can help me and why I need you. *Sell* me."

DON'T WAIT TO BE ASKED

The opportunity represented by a request for a proposal is so great that the wise consultant *seeks* opportunities to write proposals, that is, always volunteers the proposal and never waits for a client to ask for one. Whenever a prospective client shows serious interest in my services, I say some such thing as, "I'll prepare a simple proposal for you and lay out everything we've talked about in greater detail, so you can review it at your leisure and go over it with others in your organization." Or if a prospect queries me by mail and I believe that there is serious interest, I will respond with a letter proposal, rather than a simple letter alone. What's the difference? The difference is that I will do far more than furnish a bare quotation or answer a question or two, and I will not merely react in what is essentially a passive response, but will proact in what is essentially an aggressive and positive response. I will *propose* some plan of action, making it as specific as I can, given the information available to me at the time. (And I make efforts to gather some advance information.)

This does one or more of several things for the prospective client, depending on his or her situation:

☐ Organizes the information into a coherent plan of action.

☐ Gives him or her time to study it and think about it, perhaps to respond after some thought.

☐ Enables him or her to present it internally to superiors, committees, staff people, or others for study, discussion, concurrence, and/or approval—or even to present it as a basis for general discussion without revealing the source. (Suppose your prospect takes credit in his or her own organization for what are really your ideas and your plan. Do you care, as long as you wind up with a contract?)

It also does things for you, of course. It gives you time to think things out and present the strongest possible plan. It gives you time to polish your language and present your plan in the strongest possible selling words. It gives you a basis for specific follow-up. Perhaps you are more effective at selling in person than in selling via written instruments, but for a great many people, if not most people, the proposal is among the most powerful of selling tools. And word processing makes it even more powerful.

For example, one client recently wrote and asked if I would care to undertake one of three one-day seminar training sessions they planned to conduct for their staff. They enclosed outlines and asked me which I would prefer to teach, if any, and if so, for how much?

My response was a letter in which I selected one of the days, expanded the outline the client had provided to one that was more than three times longer (and, hence, far more detailed), and quoted a price. The result? More correspondence, a telephone conversation, a meeting, a negotiation, and an award of an assignment to do all three days, plus the probability of a return engagement!

This kind of thing *is* work, especially if you have to do it by the already "old fashioned" ways of the typewriter and paste pot. But word processing makes this work so much easier that it is almost fun. (Not quite, but almost.) If you were to prepare an outline, cut it up into individual lines, and lay all the lines out on a table, where you could easily move them around and rearrange them into various orders and sequences, it would be far easier to develop an outline. The problem is that this is an awkward thing to handle, and still gives you a great deal of work to do to fasten it all down and then retype the entire mess. But in effect, that's what you can do easily and swiftly with a word processor, and you never "type" (print out) the final result until you are satisfied with all your changes. Moreover, you can make as many changes of wording as you like, while you are finding the best sequences and patterns, do any footnoting you think necessary, change spacing, vertically and horizontally, and generally experiment to your heart's content before you print the copy. And even then, if you have other changes of mind, it's quite easy to go back for still further alterations and get a revised printout.

THE ESSENCE OF MARKETING

The essence of marketing involves understanding what and why people buy, first of all. Truly knowledgeable marketing professionals have learned that people do not buy things; they buy what things do. Note the tiresome "ring around the collar" commercial on TV: it doesn't try to sell the detergent; it doesn't even sell clean laundry or clean collars; it sells freedom from embarrassment. (Or does it?) It's effective, far more effective than those other commercials that sell "bright colors" and "soft fabrics." That's why those others constantly try new messages and new scenes and keep changing them, always seeking more success. But this commercial remains on the air and goes on, year after year, with many changes of scenes and characters but never a change in the message. Why? Because it sells. And we'll analyze why it sells in a moment, and even *what* it sells. (You really think that it sells freedom from embarrassment? You may get a surprise shortly.)

Note how beer is sold. That is, *what* the beer commercials sell: fun—good times at the neighborhood tavern and at the beach or on the macho fishing trip or mountain climb. The beer itself? That's an afterthought, far less important than being macho and having fun.

How is insurance sold? Note again that no one sells insurance. They sell security and—even more important—freedom from the fear of disaster and financial ruin and freedom from the guilt of not providing for one's loved ones.

But in the end, what do all of these (and other) commercials sell? Do they really sell freedom from embarrassment? Fun? Security? (When was the last time somebody turned your collar or your husband's collar up and sneered, "Ring around the collar!"?) So what are they selling? They are all selling the same thing: a PROMISE. You get the *promise* of freedom from embarrassment, the *promise* of fun and feeling mucho macho, the *promise* of feeling secure and proud that you took care of your family.

In all these cases and in many, if not most, others, customers buy promises. They buy promises because that is all that is offered. No one can deliver security, fun, or most of the other things that enlightened and effective marketers offer. Study effective commercials—and you can tell which are the effective ones; they are the ones that go on forever, seemingly, without change, because they *work*. The magazine advertisement that had the headline "DO YOU MAKE THESE MISTAKES IN ENGLISH?" ran for 40 years without change because it worked. (It was also based on the "avoid embarrassment" theme.) "THEY LAUGHED WHEN I SAT DOWN" also ran for many years, for the same reason, as did a great many other now-famous advertising headlines. In retrospect it is easy to see why: the reader *wanted* to believe the promise. And that is the "secret" of it: give them a promise they *want* to believe, and then give them some grounds for believing it ("proof"). For we cannot assume that the prospect will accept even the most alluring promises without some kind of evidence. Perhaps they do want to believe the promise, want it with all their hearts. Yet, we live in a world where people have become fairly sophisticated, and they will not accept wild promises without some kind of proof.

"Proof," or even "evidence," is not something that can be measured on some absolute scale. Quite the contrary, it is whatever the prospect will *accept* as evidence. (Remember the earlier admonition about a prospect's perception?) If the prospect will accept that "person in the street" dramatization as convincing evidence, so be it. The legal "rules of evidence" do not apply here. Whatever the prospect accepts will suffice. (Obviously a great many people do accept that dramatization as sufficient evidence.) But don't underestimate the intelligence of the prospect. People may try a detergent, even without very good evidence, because the risk is small—a few dollars, at most. But when the risk is hundreds or even thousands of dollars, it's a different story. The evidence has to be much stronger to persuade prospects to accept the risk.

All of this is perfectly relevant to proposal writing. Like the TV commercial, the proposal must make tempting promises of much-to-be-desired results and then provide some kind of evidence or proof to aid the prospect in accepting and believing in those promises. But let's look first at the nature of the promise.

WHAT TO PROMISE

If you promise a prospective client some substantial increase in efficiency as a result of whatever service you provide, it is likely that the prospect will be interested enough to listen to whatever evidence you offer that you can and will deliver that result. However, that promised benefit of increased efficiency is equivalent to promising a prospective buyer of detergent that the product will produce cleaner laundry. It offers a benefit, certainly, but a rather general benefit, one that is almost an abstraction. It lacks the appeal of the more concrete promise—freedom from embarrassment, in the case of that detergent. Greater efficiency is a benefit, but not a *direct* benefit. Clients operate their businesses for various reasons—or so they will say—but the underlying reason is profit. Greater efficiency produces greater profit. The promise of more profit is, therefore, a much more attractive promise to the average prospect. If you make your promise one of producing more profit, you increase the appeal of your promise, and that increases the prospect's *desire to believe the promise.*

That is extremely important. The more the prospect wishes to believe your promise, the better your chance of convincing the prospect that you can and will make good on the promise. You are, in fact, trading off two factors, in framing the promise, that affect the proof desired in opposite directions:

1. The more extravagant the promise, the greater—stronger—the proof required to validate the promise.
2. The more the prospect wishes to believe the promise, the greater the effect of the proof in persuading the prospect to believe in the promise.

In short, then, if you are going to make an extravagant promise of some sort, be sure that it is a promise the average prospect will want very much to believe. For example, if you believe that you can double the prospect's efficiency, you can make that promise easier to validate—more believable, that is—by expressing it in terms of increasing profitability by some appropriate percentage. But even that is not the only nor necessarily the most powerful way of expressing the promise.

MOTIVATIONS: FEAR AND GREED

You may have noted by now that two motivations are used generally in selling. That is, there are two kinds of benefits: gaining something desirable and avoiding or preventing something undesirable. Having fun at the beach, being the life of the party, making money, becoming more secure, and winning the admiration of others are all gain benefits. Avoiding embarrassment, preventing financial disaster, and achieving freedom from guilt are all examples of fear benefits.

Note something else highly significant about motivation: invariably, successful sales and advertising material are based on *emotional* appeals. Much as we humans wish to believe that we are entirely rational creatures who act out of logic, we are far more emotion-driven and act out of emotional drives. Fear of consequences and desire for gain are basically emotional drives, as are all effective motivators.

The promise must be emotional. The "proof" must be basically logical (although pseudo-logic is often used), but emotional appeals may also play a part here. However, because we are reasoning humans we tend to mistrust our emotional impulses enough to want some proof that our impulses are justified. Hence we need some kind of evidence that we can accept as proof behind the promise.

This explains, of course, why fear and gain are such powerful motivators. In fact, they are probably the most powerful motivators underlying all or nearly all human decisions and actions and are sometimes expressed colloquially as fear and greed.

It is almost certain that fear is by far the more powerful of the two motivators for the majority of us. Many humans face life and all its problems courageously, but a great many people, even the most successful among us, go through life with an almost constant dread of terrible things that could happen. So conscious are they of ever-present dangers that fear—the need to avoid or prevent those disasters from happening—is by far their major motivator.

The enormous success of most insurance companies—of insurance as an industry—is one indication of how powerful a motivator fear is. Insurance is almost invariably sold principally via fear motivations. Burglar alarms, fire alarms, locks, and other security devices are sold the same way. Security is itself a powerful motivator, but the threat (fear) of insecurity is even more powerful. And, interestingly enough, either orientation is possible: motivation by promising greater security—gain motivation—or motivation by pointing out or reminding the prospect of the risks (the lack or implied lack of security)—fear motivation.

Note that when the choice is possible—when, that is, the advertiser can express the promise in either gain or fear motivational terms—fear is almost invariably chosen. And if the thing to be feared is not clearly evident, the prospect must first be "educated" and made well aware of the hazard to be avoided: the prospect must be given a "worry item," for it is on the basis of those worry items that most advertising, sales, and proposals succeed or fail. Experienced proposal writers deliberately seek out worry items, especially those which, there is reason to believe, the client is already aware of and concerned about. But if none of those kinds of worry items can be found, the successful proposal writer seeks items the client ought to be concerned about and creates worry items, about which to build the promises and motivators. (Never forget, either, that in the final analysis it is the promise itself that you are selling.)

The choice of motivators is readily available to the proposal writer quite often. Many propositions and promises lend themselves to being expressed in either gain or fear motivational terms. To return to the earlier example of more profit arising out of greater efficiency, it is possible to express this in the fear motivation by promising the reduction of the risk factor in business. Instead of promising greater profits as the main motivator, the appeal would focus primarily on reducing the possibility of losses. The backup promise would be greater profitability as the mechanism for reducing the hazard of losses, and the promise of increase in efficiency would become part of the evidence—the chain of logic—used to validate the main promise.

WHAT KIND OF PROOF?

Proof—even proof of the kind required in a proposal—is elusive. Rarely is even that proof which is required in a court of law absolute in any respect. Most of the time, proof is whatever others will accept as proof—that is, whatever it is that makes the promise believable. So while we use such terms as *proof* and *evidence*, what we are really talking about is credibility.

In general, there are these kinds of evidence that are accepted as evidence, if not absolute proof, and that help the prospect find the promise credible:

- [ ] Chains of logic or what appears to be logical reasoning and/or appeals to "common sense," supported by "the facts." This takes the literary form known as "technical argument" and builds a case for the proposition.

- [ ] Graphic support for the foregoing presentations, such as charts, plots, photos, and line drawings.

- [ ] Testimonials, preferably by well-known public figures, especially any who have been clients at some time. (Second choice: individuals whose names and faces are not well known, but who have credentials of some sort, making them highly credible. Third choice: "person in the street" kinds of witnesses and, especially, those who are past clients.) Brief quotes help, but letters of commendation or testimonial letters are much better and should be reproduced in the proposal, if practicable, or cited as available for inspection, if it is not practicable to reproduce them in the proposal.

- [ ] Certifications (where appropriate).

THE MORE YOU TELL

Some people in mail order have an expression, "The more you tell, the more you sell," by which they mean that the effectiveness of the copy is proportionate to the amount of detail and explanation—sales argument—presented. I can testify from personal experience that this is a general truth. Obviously, the more information you present, the more overpowering your arguments appear to be. And, especially, the more detail you provide, the more convincing your arguments become. The simple fact is this: anyone can generalize, so generalization is not very convincing nor persuasive. An abundance of detail *is* convincing and is generally accepted as proof that you know what you are talking about.

The basic proof, then, is logical argument, supported by as many relevant graphics—illustrations of the key points in your arguments—as you can produce and reinforced with testimonials and whatever else of similar nature you can develop to add strength. But what has all of this to do with the use of a computer in proposal writing? Let's address that now.

SOME BASICS OF WORD PROCESSING

To get a full understanding of what a computer can do to help strengthen your proposal writing, it is necessary to gain at least a working understanding of computers and, especially, of word processors. The word processor is the chief tool you will use in getting the computer to help you in preparing proposals and other marketing documents. Later, we will probe computers in greater depth, but we need to get at least a basic grasp now.

There is such a thing as a "dedicated" word processor. That is a computer designed especially for word processing and for nothing else. It has a few special features because it is so designed. For example, it may have the monitor screen—a cathode ray tube (CRT) of the type used in TV and now used almost universally to display computer data—turned in opposite orientation to the way most of the computer and TV screens are oriented, so that the screen corresponds to a sheet of paper and displays a full page of text. (Most computer screens display only about one-half page of text.) It may be a little easier to use as a word processor, also, because it is built to do that and nothing else. But dedicated word processors are the exception to the rule. Most word processors in use today are employed in general-purpose desktop computers. The word processor is not the machine; it is the software program that is installed in the machine. You can install and run any of thousands of other programs in most of these computers because they are general-purpose computers. (The dedicated word processor is a special-purpose computer.) The information written in these pages refers to a general-purpose desktop or personal computer, for that is what you are most likely to already own or go out to buy. (Actually, few dedicated word processors are even offered today.)

Even among those word processors most commonly used, namely the software program installed in a general-purpose personal computer, there are variations in what they offer. For example, while some word processing programs include graphics capabilities—the ability of the program to convert sets of figures into graphic representations and otherwise generate line drawings—most do not. Most word processors are designed strictly to generate text, and special programs are required to generate graphics. There are other special programs that relate closely to word processing, but are rarely found to be part of the word processors per se. Spellers are one example of this. They are dictionaries on tape or disk (usually on floppy disk or "diskette," for desktop computers), and the program checks all the words in the file by comparing them with the dictionary entries for spelling accuracy.

THE MAIN FUNCTIONS OF WORD PROCESSING

The two basic functions in word processing are editing and formatting, although sophisticated word processors can do a great many other things with the copy. In my own system, a Morrow Designs Micro Decision MD3 desktop computer, I run the acknowledged best-seller granddaddy of all the word processors, WordStar®. There are, of course, numerous other word processors on the market today, many resembling WordStar in some respects and many claiming to be better or more sophisticated than WordStar. However, WordStar is representative of the larger and more complete word processors and is useful as an example of what is to be found in word processors.

WordStar offers these sets of commands and functions. First the two main sets of functions, editing and formatting:

Editing.   The editing functions include entering and correcting text, forming sentences and paragraphs, searching for and finding specific words in the text, replacing items found with corrections, moving text about, inserting and deleting items, and a number of commands connected with these functions and making them easier to perform or automatic.

Formatting.   Formatting includes setting margins and tab stops, centering items horizontally on the page, setting line spacing, identifying and displaying beginnings and ends of pages, displaying the print-control command characters ("embedded commands," which are not printed), automatic hyphening, right justification, and word wrap. (Word wrap is equal to automatic carriage return, with the cursor going automatically to the beginning of the next line when the line is full.) Most of these are "toggle" commands, which means that they can be turned on or off.

The use of the terms *editing* and *formatting* to describe these commands and functions is somewhat arbitrary, as you will see, because other commands also affect the functions described. In fact, there are almost always several ways to accomplish any given function, and you can opt for whichever way you find most convenient or efficient.

Deleting.   Commands and functions listed under this heading enable you to delete single characters, whole lines, and/or whole blocks of copy—paragraphs, pages, or sets of pages, and even entire files. (But there is a better way to delete files.)

Cursor Moving and Scrolling.   The cursor is a dot of light on the screen, which tells you where whatever you command next will occur or where the next character you type will appear. Cursors are of different shapes and sizes in different systems. The cursor can be a solid small block of light, a short line, an arrow, or some other shape, and it can be of steady intensity or blinking. The cursor moves automatically, as you "type" or "keyboard" (enter text), but you can move it about by various commands. You can move it horizontally and vertically, jump it to the beginning or end of a line, page, or entire file. In any movement that would take it off-screen, the copy will move, too, so that the cursor never moves off-screen. This becomes the basis for "scrolling," which is how you flip rapidly through the "pages" of the file, forward or backward, and at a choice of speeds.

Blocks.   This set of commands deals with blocks of copy (and a block is anything you want it to be), enabling you to move blocks about, erase them, transfer them to another file, or otherwise manipulate them. It also enables you to use another mode of text entry and formatting: column mode, wherein your copy appears in two or more columns on the page.

Files.   These commands deal with copy as entire files, rather than as smaller segments, and enable you to "save" the copy (transfer it from the temporary storage of memory to the permanent storage of disk filing), to save entire files, abandon files, copy files, rename files, and erase files.

Help.   These are commands dealing with menus and other tutorial material available to help you remember the right commands and functions. They are useful when you are still new to the system, but ultimately you will have little or no use for them as you become experienced in the system and can remember all the commands and the functions they perform.

Dot Commands.   These are special commands, concerned primarily with formatting and controlling page numbers (as they will be printed), spacing, page length, and sundry other special commands, such as one that enables you to add text as commentary but instruct the program not to print it.

Printing.   There are a number of commands for the printer. They appear on the screen, but are suppressed—do not appear—on the printed page. (They are sometimes called "embedded commands" for this reason.) They include commands to underscore, print as superscripts or subscripts, change pitch, and print in boldface, among others.

In WordStar and other true word processors all of these things can be done on-screen, and in most cases, "what you see is what you get." That is, the copy is displayed on the screen exactly as it will be printed, except for the embedded commands or control characters. There are other programs, some which are called word processors too, although many would argue that these programs do not merit the term. That's because these are "editors" and "formatters." One can be to edit the program—create and organize the text—and the other to format it or prepare it for printing. But they are separate programs or subprograms and cannot be active at the same time: you must switch from one to the other to complete all the work. And what will be printed out may not be exactly what you see displayed.

HOW WORD PROCESSING CONTRIBUTES TO EFFICIENCY

Word processing contributes to proposal writing in two ways. On the one hand, it makes the work easier and faster—much faster. You must "type" at the computer keyboard as you would at a typewriter keyboard, but you get many time- and labor-saving benefits:

☐ "Carriage return" (called "word wrap") is automatic. You need never check to see whether you have come to the end of a line; the computer does it for you and goes on to the next line, if there is insufficient room on the current line for the next word.

☐ You do all "cut and paste" electronically, swiftly, easily, and as much of it as you want, even experimental shifting of copy to evaluate the effect and make comparisons—and as many trial-and-error moves as you want—before you print a single word.

☐ Centering copy—headlines, for example—is automatic, as is page numbering, printing running heads and feet, and many other functions.

☐ If you need to use something more than once in a proposal—perhaps a reference, a table, a chart, or a quotation, for example—you can make additional copies of anything in a file by simply pressing a key or two.

☐ If you need to make minor changes to something, while saving the original—for example, modifying something you have in a permanent file or using something more than once, slightly modified in each use, such as showing several versions of a given table or progressions of some sort—you can make additional copies, make the changes for each copy, and then enter the modified copy into whatever files you wish.

☐ Collecting tables of contents and indexing are greatly simplified, and there are also special programs to help you do these things.

HOW WORD PROCESSING CONTRIBUTES TO QUALITY

One of the great misunderstandings of word processing is the notion that it is useful only for making the writer's work easier—that it is primarily a labor-saving and efficiency-raising system. The fact is that word processing can and should make major contributions to the *quality* of the writer's work. Some of those features already listed as labor-saving and time-saving also add quality to the work—or can be made to do so.

Among the many clichés of writing is one that says that all good writing is rewriting. It is accepted generally that virtually no one, not even the seasoned professional, writes really good first drafts or, at least, does not do his or her best writing in the first draft, but can almost surely make great improvements by preparing a second draft, and probably even greater improvements doing additional drafts.

There are several problems with this, where proposals are concerned, at least two of which are of direct concern here:

☐ Proposals generally have "short fuses"—tight schedules, with never enough time for a careful job and with severe difficulties in even getting a first draft out in time, let alone rewriting and producing a second draft.

☐ Proposals are generally written by individuals who are technical/professional experts, are well educated, and are highly intelligent, but who are not writers—not professional writers, in any case—and who therefore often fail to recognize that truth about first drafts and rewriting. In short, they are likely to believe that their first and original draft is as good as they can do and is, in fact, a fine piece of writing.

Word processing is a help immediately in that it is a time saver: it eliminates a great deal of time spent in minor editorial chores and enables you to concentrate on the content. Here is how it can save you time, in addition to eliminating all the laborious literal cut and paste with paste pot and scissors, by establishing "swipe files," for use in proposal writing:

☐ You can establish a standard format for proposals (one suggested format will be supplied in these pages) and standardize many other features: chapter titles, generic headlines, and forms of many kinds. Set these up in appropriate reference files and make copies of them. This saves all the time you might otherwise spend designing them and constructing them laboriously by hand for each proposal. Figures 2 and 3 are examples of forms that could be kept in files, copied, and filled out for each proposal. But the same idea could be applied to résumé formats and other materials.

☐ Analogous to this is the establishment of boilerplate files. These are files of material, usually text, that will be used with little or no change in proposal after proposal. One type of ma-

Labor-Loading Estimates

Task/subtask	Staffing & Hours			
	Proj. Mgr.			Totals
1. Meeting w/client				
2.				
3.				
Totals:				

Figure 2.   Task/labor estimating form.

Milestone Chart

Tasks	Working Days After Start of Project											
	5	10	15	20	25	30	35	40	45	50	55	60
1. Phase I:												
2.												
3.												

Figure 3. Form for milestone chart.

terial so used would be your own résumé, or several forms of your résumé, if your work is such that you need more than one version. (Or this might be in the previous kind of file, a basic text that you expect to modify in each use.) You should have "canned" descriptions of your general qualifications as a consulting entity (not qualifications as an individual; those are covered in the résumé)—experience, past projects, resources, and facilities—as standard boilerplate material that requires little or no change, to be used over and over.

A letter format might be standarized, too, after you have developed one that pleases you and seems to work well.

☐ These swipe files are not or should not be static and unchanging. As you go on writing proposals, you will make many improvements in your methods, in your copy, and in your swipe files. Over time, your files should improve steadily in their quality, if you keep updating and polishing them, as you discover what works well and what doesn't. Pay careful attention to clients' reactions to your proposals, and use that source of information as valuable feedback to incorporate constant improvement into your files. But be influenced primarily by results—by what works well for you—and make changes carefully and gradually, so that you do not inadvertently destroy something useful.

☐ Build and maintain extensive reference files. Many winning proposals are developed by extensive use of reference materials. When you acquire or discover useful reference material, material that you can use in many of your proposals, convert that material from ink on paper to magnetic spots on disks so that you can add it to your swipe files or general reference files. One reason for this is that the computer can look something up on a disk far more rapidly than you can look it up in a book or filing cabinet. Another reason is that you can store the material easily. One 5¼-inch diskette can hold nearly 200 pages of double-spaced copy. Another is that you can usually find the diskette containing the material far more easily than you can find the book on a shelf. (I have about 40 such diskettes on two "diskette trees" on my desk, within arm's reach.)

☐ Keep a good speller program available and use it, not only to check spellings and make such corrections as necessary, but also to help in proofreading your copy. In fact, spelling programs are probably more often used as proofreaders than as spelling checkers, and are probably more useful as proofreaders, although both are useful functions.

Beware of expecting spelling programs to do all your proofreading, however; they are severely limited because they cannot make judgments. If you absentmindedly wrote "bear" when you meant "bare," the speller will not catch the error, of course; it will only verify that "bear" is spelled correctly. If you leave a verb or noun, or some other part of speech, out of a sentence, or use the wrong tense, the speller will go blithely on, merely verifying your spelling.

Spellers do not relieve you of the necessity to do ocular proofreading. In fact, not only do I do at least two ocular proofreadings of my own copy before I turn it over to the speller (which invariably catches some things I missed), but ocular proofreading also gives me the opportunity to do final editing, rewriting, and polishing of my copy. I make many changes I would not make if I were using a typewriter because with a typewriter I would have to weigh whether the improvement is worth all the time and effort to make the change, whereas with a word processor the change takes virtually no time at all and is easy to make. Hence, I do far more rewriting and polishing now.

Take Figures 2 and 3, as one example. What you see here is the final product, after five revisions. Each time I printed out copies of these I decided they needed improvement to clarify what they were intended to be. And even after I had done the fourth revision and had models I thought were reasonably satisfactory, I was still not entirely satisfied. At the same time, I did not want to tamper further with the originals in my files, for fear that I would do more harm than good. (Although it did not take long to create the originals, it was tedious, and I didn't want to have to redo them from scratch.) So I copied that file into a new working file, which I called "X" because it was for experimental purposes. There I could safely cut and try changes to the originals. When I had finally found what I thought the presentations ought to be, I copied these back in the original file and replaced the original contents of that file. File X having served its purpose and needed no longer, I erased. This final effort required only about 20 minutes to carry out! Even such relatively slow computers as these microcomputers with their slow floppy-disk drives are lightning fast, compared with any of the older methods.

Even without special graphics programs you can construct many graphic representations, such as these, which were done with WordStar and without special graphics software. Nor are you confined to tabular formats, either. You can construct bar charts, organization charts, and plots easily, as Figures 4, 5, and 6 reveal.

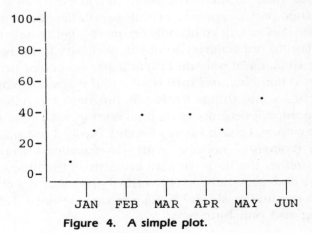

Figure 4.   A simple plot.

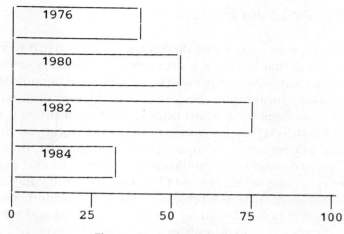

Figure 5.   A bar chart.

The plot of Figure 4 should be finished manually—the curve connecting the dots drawn by hand, that is—if you are using a letter-quality (daisy wheel) printer. It is possible to do it on-screen and by printer, but is rather awkward and tedious to do so. (A dot-matrix printer offers advantages when it comes to printing graphics.) Doing graphics generally without graphics software and a plotter, or at least without a dot-matrix printer, requires some compromise, although it still offers great advantages over the older and more conventional methods.

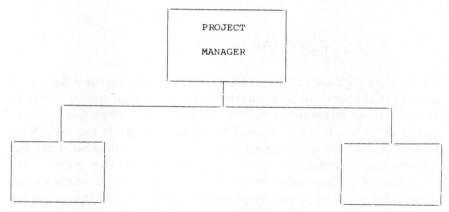

Figure 6.   Basic organization chart.

BUILDING SWIPE FILES

One thing a word processor does for you, if you use it to your best advantage, is that it makes it unnecessary to keep reinventing the wheel. The experience and materials you have accumulated and have stored in references files or project-history files (which you should have established and built during each project) are a resource for this. Whenever you find that something you did earlier is useful in preparing a proposal for a new project, that material should be considered a candidate for transfer to and permanent residency in one of your swipe files. The first time you have to design something, such as a progress report, final report, audiovisual program, oral presentation, or any of those forms and graphics already discussed, you search out models wherever you can find them and modify them to suit your own need. Or you build them from scratch in some cases. And when you next need to explain what will be in your final report or presentation, as you prepare a proposal, you can dig out the old model or the version you last used and build on that. You can bring the old material up on-screen and make any necessary changes swiftly, or make no changes at all if they are not needed. In short, some of the most valuable swipe files are your own copies of earlier proposals and records of past projects. That's as true for text as it is for forms, tables, and charts, and *everything* you have stored in files anywhere should be considered for recycling.

A TYPICAL PROPOSAL FORMAT

The basic proposal rationale follows the same essential logic and approximate order of presentation whether the proposal is a two-to three-page letter proposal or a multivolume proposal of thousands of pages. If you respond to a formal request for proposals issued by a government agency or by some large organization, the request may suggest, specify, or mandate a format and sequence of coverage. Obviously, it is wise to obey the mandate in such a case. Otherwise, you must use your own judgment. The following sequence of address is recommended and, in fact, will probably be quite close to whatever a requestor requires when issuing a formal request for proposals.

1. Introduction to the proposer.
2. Understanding of the client's problem/requirement.
3. Discussion of the problem/requirement.
4. Approach to the solution of the problem/satisfaction of the requirement.
5. Specific program/services proposed.
6. Qualifications of the proposer, assurances.
7. Cost.

Item 1 should be brief, with the details appearing in item 6, to which the first item is merely introductory. Item 2 should be brief, as well, and serves as an introduction to the third item, where the requirement is discussed, analyzed, and argued at far greater length. Item 4 is the logical culmination of that discussion, recommending a course of action and explaining the logic of that recommendation. In fact, it is in these two items, and especially in the second of the two (item 4), that the principal sales arguments are made. Item 5 is extremely important, for that is what you will commit yourself to do and deliver in specific and quantitative terms—what you pledge. Finally, in item 6, you present your credentials, to demonstrate that you have the necessary experience, resources, and record of accomplishment to ensure the results you promised in the previous items. And if the proposal is one submitted to a government agency or other large organization, in response to a formal request, you will almost surely be asked to submit your cost statement in a separate envelope, to ensure that those evaluating the technical merits of your proposal are not influenced by costs.

Depending on the nature of your consulting practice—what kinds of services you offer and what kinds of clients you serve— you may be writing formal proposals often, occasionally, or not at all. In either case, the general format recommended here should appear in your proposal via the following generic sections. (These will be sideheads or captions in simple letter proposals, and section or chapter titles in formal proposals.)

Introduction

Who the offeror is. An understanding of the problem or requirement (Items 1 and 2).

Discussion

Analyses, technical arguments, alternatives possible, approach selected (Items 3 and 4).

Proposed Program

Specifics, including project organization, management, procedures, end products, schedules (Item 5).

Qualifications

Résumé(s), experience, past projects and achievements, facilities and resources, testimonials, references (Item 6).

THINKING ON PAPER: GENERATING A LEAD

Many writers (perhaps even most writers) and experienced professionals, as well as those for whom writing is not a vocation nor a favored activity, find it necessary to develop a "lead" before they can make any real progress with their writing. I confess to being one of those. Even after developing a reasonably detailed and complete outline in advance, I usually require time to work out my lead before I can get down to serious writing. And that applies to every unit—the book, the chapters, and even the paragraphs, although the latter are admittedly not much of a problem.

Such writers, working at typewriters, tend to fill a wastebasket with aborted efforts to develop or find a lead, during the beginning phases of a new writing project. If you are one of those afflicted with this kind of need you are simply unable to proceed until you have a lead that satisfies you. And even after finally getting the lead on paper, you sometimes find, many pages later, that the lead is simply "not working." You must then go back and rewrite it, possibly with paste pot and scissors, possibly with a total discard and fresh effort. (On occasion, I have personally discarded as much as the first 50 pages of the draft for a new book.)

In this process of developing a lead, you are "thinking on paper." You are actually reasoning out the best way to approach this subject, how to organize the material, what to say about it, how to introduce it, and how to lay the groundwork for what you will be saying later. (The writer ought to prepare the reader with a preview of what is to come, to maximize the probability of clear understanding and minimize the possibility of misunderstanding.) Even though you have already done much of this planning on paper, in the form of an outline, the translation of that outline into text is far from automatic or even mechanical: it is very much an art, and the outline is only about one percent of the product it is supposed to specify and describe.

Somehow, seeing the words appear helps you think out all these things. And yet, it is not entirely a rational process, but an art, for somehow you can *feel* it when your lead is "right."

In this area alone the word processor is invaluable in its ability to present, modify, erase, and transpose words instantaneously. If it did nothing else for you but help you develop your leads, it would still be worth far more than its cost in money and the time required to learn how to use it well.

All writers evidently "block" at the typewriter, at least on occasion. Having inserted a clean sheet of paper, they sit and stare at it, searching for the words. They resort to all sorts of favorite devices to try to unblock their minds and get the flow of thought—and words—started. Some simply type anything that comes to mind, knowing that they will discard what they have written, later, when they have gotten the word pumps in their minds properly primed. Others are reluctant to do that. For many, if not all, the word processor is a solution. You can sit and write as much nonsense or random thought as you wish, until ideas begin to fall into place. You can then go back and make any changes you wish, discarding it all as nonsense or saving any portions you believe to be worth saving. You then proceed, but you can return to the lead and revise or at least polish it again and again, and you may very well do just that. (I find myself doing this, usually several times, and at least once again, as I proof my copy by eye before turning it over to my speller.)

A FEW APPROPRIATE WRITING TIPS

If you observe the way dramatic shows are introduced on TV and in the movies today, you'll notice that most use a "hook" at the beginning, something to capture attention and arouse interest or curiosity immediately. This is intended to persuade you to sit through what might be fairly boring material that is necessary to the story.

Writers can and should use the same idea in proposals by using some attention-capturing, interest-arousing idea in the opening lead. Of course, the proper time to write an introduction is last—after you have written whatever it is that you must introduce. The word processor makes it easy to do this, of course, but it also helps you find and use that attention getter in the opening. After you have completed the proposal, you select whatever you believe to be the most striking idea or bit of information in your proposal, and you present it in your introduction.

Credibility is always a problem in proposals, as it is in sales and advertising generally. The public has become so used to extravagant claims and pure hyperbole that it is futile to make unsupported claims. That is, to claim that you are "best," "oldest," "most dependable," or otherwise use such superlatives is wasting time. No one will pay very much attention to such claims because that is what they are—merely claims.

To overcome this problem you must write in such a manner that you appear to be—*are*, in fact—reporting objectively, rather than claiming passionately. And there are three rules that enable you to achieve this:

1. Minimize as much as possible your use of adjectives and adverbs, and shun hyperbole entirely.

2. Quantify as much as possible, even if you must furnish estimates.

3. Never round off numbers. Report them as accurately as pos-

sible, and favor numbers that are not obviously rounded off (e.g., 950,000 versus 1,000,000 or one million).

Here again the word processor can help. In the heat of writing, you usually do not want to stop to search out the numbers. With word processing you do not need to. You can just go on—leave a blank or marker of some sort, if you wish, although it is not necessary—and fill in the numbers later, after you have had time to look them up or estimate them. Or, if you have them in one of your files, simply have the program copy the file or that portion of the file you want to use.

Use graphics as much as possible. The use of graphics has more than one direct benefit:

1. It makes life easier for you, if the graphics are well conceived, because a good illustration takes the place of more than its "weight" of text. (That, in fact, is the test of an illustration: the less explanation it requires, the better it is.) It therefore eases your job as a writer.

2. It helps the client understand what you present.

3. It saves both your time and the client's time, which the client always approves.

4. It has far greater impact, normally, than do words.

Although I mentioned it earlier, it is useful to mention this again: provide as much detail as possible—detail about every aspect of what you are discussing. Detail = knowledge = credibility. Again, this becomes increasingly easier as you accumulate details in your files and are able to summon them up at the press of a key or two. But provide details about other things, too. If, for example, your work will result in a report and/or presentation of some kind, explain in detail what will be included in that report/presentation, about how big/long it will be, and whatever else you can project.

Be sure to identify the end product, which is often a report or presentation, such as that just referred to. But if that is the only tangible result or product the client will have after spending the money to fund the project, it assumes great importance, and you must recognize that in your proposal and give it adequate coverage. Describe the end product(s) in as much detail, qualitative and quantitative, as possible.

But apply that philosophy to the schedule also. Be as specific as possible. If you foresee contingencies, spell them out as precisely as you can, but do introduce them.

Be completely open and honest. Try to project any problems you anticipate and explain how you propose to handle them. (Some clients will rate you on this specific point, as well as on general honesty.)

Explain everything you expect to do in as much detail as possible, for that matter. Aside from the fact that it lends credibility and helps establish your credentials generally, it explains to the client what your estimated costs are going to cover and justifies those costs. That's one reason you want that labor estimating form of Figure 2, so that the client can actually see how many hours of professional endeavor you anticipate as necessary to achieve the result desired. The form demonstrates to the client your capability for analyzing the requirement and planning the project in great detail, but it also permits the client to evaluate your proposed effort in terms of at least these specific factors:

- The effort and cost for each task or subtask.
- The effort and cost for each principal.

In connection with that figure and the effort and cost for each prinicpal, it is possible that you work alone, except possibly for office help. However, you may enlist the aid of colleagues or associates for specific projects that require more than one consultant specialist, or you may wear more than one hat on a given project and want to demonstrate that. In any case, you can adapt that form to whatever situation that exists.

AVAILABLE WORD PROCESSOR SOFTWARE

It would be futile to attempt a complete listing of word processor software here; there are simply too many programs to list, and new ones are being marketed frequently. But a few general notes on word processors may be helpful in your search for a suitable one:

First of all, be sure that the word processor you select is a true word processor—that it has all the general capabilities listed earlier and can do both editing and formatting on-screen, present copy as you will see it when printed (other than control signals), and that it matches your hardware.

The most popular operating systems today are PC-DOS (for the IBM PC), MS-DOS (for those computers claimed to be compatible with the IBM-PC, where capability means "able to run the same programs"), and CP/M, which was the de facto standard operating system for personal computers until IBM introduced their PC and PC-DOS. Until recently, the popular Tandy Corporation/Radio Shack TRS-80 computers used their own operating system, TRS-DOS. Apple computers also have their own operating system. A few other, less popular computers have their own operating systems too.

You must be sure that the word processor you buy matches the operating system of the machine you have. The vendor of the program can advise you on that, as long as you are sure that you know what machine and what model you have. (Different models manufactured by the same manufacturer may use different operating systems.)

You should have a speller program to help you proof your copy and turn it out letter perfect. These are relatively inexpensive and abundant also. Many of those who have developed word processors have companion speller programs they can offer.

Graphics software is a valuable asset in all areas of application, especially in proposal writing. Ideally, you should have hardware with at least a 16-bit microprocessor (and a 32-bit CPU is even better) and a 128K (or more) memory, and plotter for printing the graphics out. (However, you can get by with less, as witnessed by the graphics done here (Figures 4–6) with an 8-bit CPU, a 64K memory, and a daisy wheel printer.)

Other samples, tips, and how-to help will be offered later in these pages, as reference material (which you are welcome to copy on your system and store in your files).

Charles Stallworth DCASR Chicago Attn DCASR Chi-A/ O'Hare IAP P.O. Box 66475 Chicago IL 60666 312/694-6610
H -- ACTUARIAL CONSULTANT SERVICES for period 1 Oct 84 thru 30 Sept 85. Sol. DLA8CH-84-R-0002 The primary actuary must be a fellow of the Society of Actuaries. The actuary must have experience with Federal acquisition regulations and cost accounting standards. It is necessary that the resulting contract be awarded to a Contractor that will not pose a conflict of interest problem to the government by performing actuarial services for any Contractor and at the same time for the government. A RFP will be forwarded to those interested parties who submit a written request within 30 days from the date of this notice. (220).

General Service Administration, Real Property Contracts Division (TPPB), Rm 702, John W McCormack POCH, Boston MA 02109, Attn: J Bernstein, Tel 617/223-2716.
● H -- APPRAISALS to estimate the fair annual rental rate of GSA operated buildings. (The fair annual rental rate is the reasonable annual monetary amount expected for the right to agreed use of real and related personal property as established by competition in the rental market.) Location: 22 facilities in Boston MA and south suburban Boston—RFP IPPBB-84-58—Estimated issue date o/a 8/6/84—Proposal due date 8/24/84.
● H -- APPRAISALS to estimate the fair annual rental rate of GSA operated buildings. (The fair annual rental rate is the reasonable annual monetary amount expected for the right to agreed use of real and related personal property as established by competition in the rental market.) Location: 14 facilities west of Boston—Estimated issue date o/a 8/6/84—Proposal due date 8/24/84
● H -- APPRAISALS to estimate the fair annual rental rate of GSA operated buildings. (The fair annual rental rate is the reasonable annual monetary amount expected for the right to agreed use of real and related personal property as established by competition in the rental market.) Location: 15 facilities north of Boston—RFP IPPBNB-84-60—Estimated issue date o/a 8/6/84—Proposal due date 8/24/84
● H -- APPRAISALS to estimate the fair annual rental rate of GSA operated

Tennessee Valley Authority, Office of Nuclear Power, 1300 Chestnut Street Tower 2, Chattanooga TN 37401, Attn: Royce Maner, 615/751-4800
★ H -- DATA ANALYSIS AND PROVIDE TECHNICAL EXPERTISE NECESSARY TO MEASURE TRANSIENT RESPONSE TIMES OF PLATINUM RESISTANCE TEMPERATURE DETECTORS as required by NRC's Regulatory Guide 1.118. TVA will negotiate on a sole source basis with Technology for Energy Corp. See note 46. (207)

U.S. Dept of Justice, Procurement and Contracts Staff, Procurement Service, 10th & Constitution Ave, NW, Rm 6318, Washington DC 20530, Attn: Cathy D Coghill
❶ H -- TRANSCRIPTION SERVICES: Typing recordings of immigration hearings and judges decisions from cassette tapes. Interested firms should send requests for IFB JLOIR-84-B-0065 to the address shown above. Anticipated issuance date Jul 30, 1984 (206)

U.S. Dept of the Interior, Minerals Management Service, Procurement Operations Branch B, M/S 635, 12203 Sunrise Valley Dr, Reston VA 22091, 703/435-6415, Attn: James Mackay
H -- EVALUATION OF INDICATORS GENERATED FROM SOCIAL, CULTURAL AND ECONOMIC ANALYSIS. The objective of this study is to provide the Minerals Management Service with a more thorough understanding of the present state of community well-being in Alaskan villages, with special attention given to the areas of social, economic and cultural change that may result from outer continental shelf development. Reference RFP 3179 Est issue date Aug 1, 1984. Est closing date Aug 22, 1984. (207)

National Park Service, Valley Forge National Historical Park, PO Box 953, Valley Forge PA 19481-0953, Attn: Procurement Office, 215/783-7700, X32
H -- BRONZE RESTORATION OF THE NATIONAL MEMORIAL ARCH. All work is to be accomplished IAW the Conservation Code of Ethics and Standards of Practice of the American Institute for Conservation of Historic and Artistic Works (AIC). Only proposals submitted by contractors who are members of the AIC and are pledged to adhere to the AIC Code of Ethics will be considered. The RFP issue date shall be Aug 3, 1984. If interested, please submit request for a copy of Sol RFP-VAFO-4-01 prior to sol-closing date of Sep 4, 1984. Proposals received after the closing date will not be accepted. (207)

Naval Ordnance Station, Louisville KY 40214
H -- REVISE COMPUTER PROGRAM. Negs are being conducted with FMC Corp, Northern Ordnance Div, Minneapolis MN for Engineering Services to revised and update the 5"/54 MK 45 Mod 1 computer program design and performance spec. Note 22. (207)

U.S. Army Missile Command, Directorate of Procurement and Production, Redstone Arsenal AL-35898
H -- 7000 HOURS OF STINGER LAUNCH SIMULATORS (STLS) ENGINEERING SERVICES (RFP) DAAH01-84-R-A876 to be issued o/a 6 Aug 84 with a closing date o/ Sep 84—RFP is restricted to Brunswick Corp, Defense Div, 3333 Harbor Blvd, Costa M, CA 92626—See note 27 and 22—Point of contact H B Craig, address above, attn: DRSM IWE, 205/876-1159. (207)

Veterans Administration, Office of Procurement & Supply (93A), 8 Vermont Ave NW, Washington DC 20420, William S Stapleto 202/389-3125
H -- ASSIST THE DEPARTMENT OF MEDICINE AND SURGERY'S MEDICAL INFORMATION RESOURCES MANAGEMENT INFORMATION SYSTEM. Copies RFP 101-40-84 may be obtained 15 days after this notice appears. All requests must be writing. (207)

Naval Surface Weapons Center, Silver Spring MD 20910
H -- DEVELOPMENT AND MODIFICATION OF SPECIFIC COMPUTER SOFTWARE—Negs will be conducted on a sole source basis with Planning Systems Inc McLean, VA for continuated technical support for six months under N60921-83-C-0182. For additional information call Carlton Chase, 202/394-3770. See note 22. (207)

The Agency for International Development, James E Corley, Contracting Officer, C/O American Embassy, Tegucigalpa Honduras OR USAID/ Honduras APO Miami FL 34022
H -- HONDURAS: LONG-TERM ADVISORS IN HEALTH SYSTEMS LOGISTICS; HEALTH SYSTEMS MAINTENANCE; CENTRAL LEVEL HEALTH SYSTEM ADMINISTRATION; PLANNING, PROGRAMMING AND SUPERVISION. IN-SERVICE ADULT EDUCATION. Info System Development; Operations Research; and Chief of Party/Primary Health Care Expert. Short Term Technical Assistance particularly in family planning and project Management are also required. Sol Honduras 84-007. Opening date 15 days after publication of notice, closing date 60 days thereafter. Contract period 1 Jan 85 - 31 Dec 85 This will be an aid financed direct contract. (207)

H Expert and Consultant Services

U.S. Dept of HUD, 15 New Chardon St, Boston MA 02114, Attn: Richard E Weston, Contract Specialist, 617/233-4766
H -- CREDIT REPORTING SERVICES on individuals for HUD in the states of Massachusetts, Maine, New Hampshire, Vermont and Rhode Island. The Boston Regional Office intends to negotiate blanket purchase arrangements for use by all HUD offices in the geographic area. RFQ 053-84-023, closing date o/ a Sep 11, 1984. Firms interested in receiving requests for quotations should send info about their capabilities to the issuing office. (206)

Environmental Protection Agency, Contracts Management Division (MD-33), Office of Administration, Attn: M P Huneycutt (MCCM-S), Research Triangle Park NC 27711, 919/541-3024
❶ H -- DATA MANAGEMENT SUPPORT SERVICES. DU-84-A153 applies. The Environmental Protection Agency is soliciting proposals from small business firms for support and maintenance of EPA's Pesticide Document Management System, Pesticide Product Information-System and other related services. A limited number of copies of the sol is available to firms who submit written requests within the next 15 days. (206)

Tennessee Valley Authority, Division of Personnel, 305 Miller's Bldg, Knoxville TN 37902, Attn: Group Life Proposal, 615/632-2161
H -- GROUP-TERM LIFE INSURANCE PLAN for TVA management employees. Requests for RFP should be received by calling or writing Group Life Proposal within 15 days after the issue date of this notice and should reference Synopsis 62-84. (207)

B McWhirt, 202/692-6049, Naval Electronic Systems Command, Washington DC 20363
H -- TECHNICAL & MANAGEMENT SUPPORT FOR FMS CARE CLOSURE. Qty 2292 MH. RFP N00039-84-R-0589(S). NAVELEX plans to award a sole source contract to Booz-Allen & Hamilton Inc, Bethesda MD 20814. See note 22. (206)

Contracting Officer, USDA Forest Service, Federal Office Bldg, 324 25th St, Ogden UT 84401
H -- INDEXED BIBLIOGRAPHY TO STREAM HABITAT IMPROVEMENT. Provide

Administrative Office of the U.S. Courts, Procurement and Property Management Branch, Contracting Section, Washington DC 20544
H -- COURT REPORTING SERVICES. The Administrative Office of the U.S. Courts has reoccurring intermittent requirements for court reporting services for the U.S. District and U.S. Bankruptcy Courts at various nationwide locations. Experience requirement for each reporter is a certificate of proficiency equivalent to RPR and 4 years responsible courtroom reporting. Parties interested in being added to bidding lists should respond to this announcement within 10 days, stating specific geographical location for consideration. Reference Synopsis DCXOH-84-033. (207)

Defense Communications Agency, Contract Management Division, Code 680, 202/692-3083, Sharlene Capobianco, Washington DC 20305-2000
★ H -- DEVELOP MODIFY, AND CONDUCT TEST AND EVALUATION SCENARIOS AND TO ANALYZE/EVALUATE WIN SYSTEMS, WIN SOFTWARE RELEASES AND RELATED NETWORK PRODUCTS. The Defense Communications Agency will negotiate with System Development Corp for 104 technical staff months of effort. Acquisition of this effort will be accomplished by modification to Contract DCA100-81-C-0032. See note 46. (207)

Tennessee Valley Authority, Division of Conservation and Energy Management, 303 Power Bldg, Chattanooga TN 37401, Attn: Gregory A Helms, 615/751-7172
H -- PLACE TVA CONSERVATION PROMOTIONAL CAMPAIGNS AND ADVERTISEMENTS IN VARIOUS MEDIA throughout the Tennessee Valley. The proposed period of performance is one year beginning o/a Sep 1984. Requests for RFP should be received by TVA within 15 days after the issue date of this notice and should reference Synopsis 64-84. (207)

Contracting Officer, Federal Election Commission, 1325 K St, NW, Washington DC 20463
H -- PHASE II OF DESIGN OF GENERAL MODEL FOR COMPUTERIZED ELECTION MANAGEMENT INFORMATION SYSTEM. The Federal Election Commission is seeking organizations with technical capabilities to produce a set of guidelines and general functional specs for a computerized election management info-system. As the second phase of a three-phase effort, this project requires experience and expertise in election systems, computer technology and management info systems design. Period of performance is twelve months. Written requests for this sol should be sent to Mr James V Fare, Attn: IFB 84-2, NLT 15 days after publication of this notice. (207)

Chief, Supply Service (90C) Richard L Roudebush VA Medical Center 1481 West Tenth St, Indianapolis IN 46202, Carient Yeakle 317/267-8707
H -- CORRECTION: INDUSTRIAL HYGENIST SERVICES and technical equipment, materials and labor to perform asbestos sampling, air pollution control and monitors in coordination with project 83-1070. Asbestos removal and reinsulation of utility lines. Scope of work is modified to delete the requirement for testing of asbestos fiber content. Samples are to be taken by industrial hygenist for testing by VA under a separate contract. Offers will be considered from qualified firms within a 250-mile radius of Indianapolis. Sol 583-42-84. B00 7 Sep 84. (207)

David Taylor Naval Ship Research and Development Center, Bethesda MD 20084, Attn: F Reeves, Code 5322, 202/227-3476
H -- TESTING OF SYNTHETIC ROPE. Negs on a non-competitive basis with tension member technology Westminister CA. Test fixtures which simulate the RD-53D Helicopter winch is required. This synopsis is for info purposes only. Response must be received within thirty days of this notice. RFP N00167-84-R-0115. See note 22. (207)

Naval Surface Weapons Center, Dahlgren VA 22448
H -- ENGINEERING AND TECHNICAL SUPPORT IN THE DEVELOPMENT, TEST, AND EVALUATION OF THE MK 92 FIRE CONTROL SYSTEM PRODUCTION MODELS AND PHASES II AND III ENGINEERING DEVELOPMENT PROGRAMS--RFP N60921-84-R-4272--Naval Surface Weapons Center, Dahlgren VA 22448.--Contact Dave Plata, Code S125, 703/663-8391 for info regarding the RFP.--For copies of the RFP, contact Sherry Clark, 703/663-7490. (206)

Figure 7. Typical notices of government requirements in CBD.

GOVERNMENT PROPOSALS

The U.S. Government is kind to consultants: it offers them a great deal of business opportunity, whether they are large organizations, such as Arthur Young and Booz Allen, or self-employed, independent consultants. And the various federal agencies— thousands upon thousands of them—announce their needs in the *Commerce Business Daily* (CBD), published every day for this purpose. (See Figure 7.)

The publication is available by subscription from the Government Printing Office, Washington, DC 20402 at $81 per year for second-class mail or $160 per year for first-class mail (currently). But it is also available online, in an electronic edition, which offers a number of benefits, including on-time delivery, something you cannot get when you rely on the Postal Service.

Information on where and how to subscribe for online services will be presented later in this book, after we have discussed computer communications in greater detail.

CHAPTER FIVE

Capability Brochures

The growing complexity of almost everything about our society makes the capability brochure an increasingly important tool for marketing one's services.

WHAT A "CAPABILITY BROCHURE" IS OR OUGHT TO BE

The very reason for the importance of the capability brochure in marketing consulting services—the specific uses or areas of application, that is—are themselves indicative of what a capability brochure ought to be. Here are three of those reasons:

1. Because there are so many highly specialized fields today it is most difficult for many consultants to explain their special skills, abilities, and services in a few words. They need something such as a fairly comprehensive text to make prospective clients fully aware of everything they (the consultants) can offer.

2. Many executives and others have two serious problems today, vis-à-vis consulting services: they do not have a clear-cut view of what circumstances make the retention of a

consultant a wise move, and even after reaching the decision to turn to consulting services for aid, few know how or where to find the right consultant.

3.   Many consulting contracts, especially those for government agencies and other large organizations, are awarded only after reviewing competitive bids and proposals submitted by competitors for the contracts. And frequently the clients rely on capability brochures to establish which consultants they deem qualified to appear on the bidders' list and receive invitations to bid or propose.

A capability brochure often serves well as a general marketing tool, an introduction to what you have to offer, and even a general calling card, but it may also open new markets to you. In some cases, where the client requires such a brochure to admit you to competition for a contract, nothing else will do.

Those reasons should indicate clearly at least this about what a capability brochure ought not be: it should not be one of those tiny leaflets that fit in one's pocket, for it is not possible to do yourself full justice in that constrained format. It may be only two or three pages, but it may also be 20, 30, or even more pages. There are no "rules," except those of necessity—whatever is required to achieve the purpose. A capability brochure ought to be large enough to tell the full story—terse and efficient, but a complete text.

Yet, it must not go overboard in listing what you do and the benefits deriving therefrom, for fear of making yourself appear to be someone who claims to "do anything." That is deadly, in this age of specialists, for even if you are extremely versatile, it is an adverse image psychologically: clients expect consultants to be specialists, and if you appear to be a generalist, you do damage to that image as a specialist. (But there are at least two ways to handle the problem successfully, which we'll address shortly.)

THE CAPABILITY BROCHURE VERSUS THE PROPOSAL

Some people tend to regard a capability brochure as something that closely resembles a proposal. In a sense it does, but with this important difference: the proposal normally addresses a single problem or need, and focuses narrowly and sharply on that need, with all discussion, offers, and evidence of capability strictly in terms of that single problem or need. Even that section of the proposal in which you present evidence of your technical/ professional capability, experience, and other qualifications, you do (or should) focus all of that entirely on its impact on the problem or need the proposal addresses. Anything else is a distraction and weakens your proposal, instead of strengthening it.

The capability brochure, on the other hand, must be specific and sharply focused enough to establish your credentials as the specialist a client expects a consultant to be, and yet broad enough to establish your qualifications to handle a suitably wide range of problems and needs. (But there is an exception to this, too, which we'll turn to later in this chapter.)

For this reason alone, the capability brochure is in many ways far more difficult to write than is the proposal: the crucial focus is on establishing just that right compromise between those two extremes.

HAVING YOUR CAKE AND EATING IT TOO

If in fact your skills, services, and/or the kinds of needs and problems you address yourself to in your practice are unusually wide and diverse, you are facing that problem alluded to earlier—the problem of doing yourself justice, while avoiding that damaging image as a generalist. There are two ways to solve this dilemma:

1.   Create "departments" or "divisions" for the various sets of skills, services, or needs, even if you are an independent, operating alone most of the time, and be sure that your capability brochure clearly establishes these as separate divisions. (Note how large corporations do exactly this quite frequently.)

2.   If your various services are such that they are specific to different kinds of clients—that is, if they are such that no single client would be likely to be interested in all your services and capabilities—the logical answer is to create more than one version of your capability brochure—to have more than one capability

brochure, that is—and use that one which is most appropriate in each case.

You can even hybridize these ideas: even if you decide to have more than one department or division, as suggested in the first item, you may want to create a separate brochure for each.

CUSTOM CAPABILITY BROCHURES

You may, under certain circumstances, be compelled to create different versions of your capability brochure, or even prepare custom capability brochures—virtual proposals—if you pursue custom contracts from large organizations, especially from government agencies. Here's why:

Many organizations contemplating a future procurement of specialized services do not have a bidders list they consider suitable for the contract. In such a case, they can pursue the problem in either of two ways as follows.

1.   They can make the procurement a "two-step" procedure. In this kind of procurement, bidders are invited to submit technical proposals, sans costs. The client reviews the proposals, selects those consultants considered qualified for the second step, and invites those only to submit cost proposals, after which a winner will be selected from among those qualified for step 2—presumably, but not necessarily, the low bidder.

2.   They can invite interested consultants to submit capability brochures to establish their qualifications, after which only those deemed qualified will receive the solicitation and be permitted to bid or propose. Such requests for special capability brochures are published often by the federal agencies, usually, but not always, in the *Commerce Business Daily* (CBD) under the heading *Research and Development Sources Sought*, as shown in Figure 8. (Such notices may also be found occasionally under other headings in the CBD.)

Most often the second method is chosen when the program calls for unusual, rare, or extraordinary qualifications and the cli-

RESEARCH AND DEVELOPMENT
SOURCES SOUGHT

In order that potential sources may learn of research and development programs; advance notice of the government's interest in a specific research field is published here. Firms having the research and development capabilities described are invited to submit complete information to the purchasing office listed. Information should include: the total number of employees and professional qualifications of scientists, engineers, and personnel specially qualified in the R&D area outlined; and description of general and special facilities, an outline of previous projects including specific work previously performed or being performed in the listed R&D area; statement regarding industrial security clearance previously granted; and other available descriptive literature. Note that these are not requests for proposals. Respondents will not be notified of the results of the evaluation of the information submitted, but the sources deemed fully qualified will be considered when

Rome Air Development Center ATTN: PKRM, Griffiss AFB NY 13441, Tel: 315/330-3820

STRATEGIC AIR COMMAND INDICATIONS AND WARNING—Develop enhanced Indications and Warning (I&W) capabilities for the HQS SAC Intelligence Operations Center. A modern SAC Warning System (SACWARNS) will be developed and implemented. This effort will address the development of a data base, intergration of data into the data base and development of applications software and other ADP tools and equipment that support specific SAC & I&W functions. Primary functional capabilities to be developed are a SACWARNS interface to the SAC IDHS (Intelligence Data Handling System) Network, Event/Situation Monitoring, Indicator Status Monitoring and Reporting, Real-time Receipt for Elint and Imagery, Indications Analysis, and Enhanced Message Profiling and Screening. Development will occur in a contractor facility with integration and Air Force acceptance at HQS SAC. Respondees must have had experience in (1) indicator development, (2) knowledge engineering, (3) data base development for Indications and Warning, (4) major information system development, (5) development of open ended-information system specification from statements of requirements, (6) Cullinet software products, (7) IBM 3080 and 4300 series hardware and software products, (8) textual information processing including profiling; automatic dissemination and information extraction from text, and (9) development of expert systems for use in Indication and Warning. For additional technical information contact Lt. Kurt Schelkle, 315/330-3126. See notes 11, 49, and 68 (first paragraph only). Resonses must be received within twenty days of publication. Responses must referece Code I-5-4310-M.

TELEMETRY DATA ANALYSIS Establish feasibility of employing knowledge engineering tools for use in Exploitation of Foreign Instrumentation Signals (FIS). The effort will require a theoretical analysis of potential cognitive engineering concepts and will include a feasibility demonstration with experimental software using actual FIS data. Respondents must demonstrate expertise in the application of research and development in cognitive engineering and a thorough understanding of the underlying principles envolved in the exploitation of FIS telemetry data. SCI cleaance are required. See note 68 (first paragraph only). For additional technical information contact John Feldman 315/330-3038. Responses must be received within twenty days of publication. Responses must reference Code I-5-4014-M.

CATSS FUNCTIONAL SOFTWARE DESIGN Design software modules to support generic Air Force user requirements identified in completed CATSS analysis efforts. Common functions will be defined, unique feature identified, data requirements assessed and evaluations made of user system capabilites and fuctions. Validation of the functional design will be performed on RADC hardware. This acquisition is classified and the contractor will need access to or will generate classified information in performing this contract. Respondees must demonstrate specific extensive experience designing software modules. Responsesmust be received within twenty days of publication. See note 68 (first paagraph only). For additional technical information contact Major David Moulton, 315/330-7351. Responses must reference Code I-5-4779M.

CATSS DATA BASE STRUCTURE Design and develop an integrated digital cartographic data base structure. The structure will address the problems of storing and retrieving digital cartographic data to support preiously identified system requirments. The data base will be a combination of numerous DMA product data base files and willrequire the integration of digital cartographic data base maintnance concepts. The data base will be demonstrated for experimentation on RADC hardware. This acquisition is classified and the contractor will need access to or will generate classified information in performing this contract. Respondees must demonstrate specific extensive experience designing software modues. Responses must be received within twenty days of publication. See note 68 (first paragraph only). For additional technical information contact Major David Moulton, 315/330-7351. Responses must reference Code I-5-4780M. (231)

nesse, 313/233-2389.

TRAINING RESEARCH AND DEVELOPMENT APPLICATIONS SUPPORT. Exploratory development area PMRS 85-16. This effort will consist of research services in support of the Training Systems Div of the Human Resources Laboratory (AFHRL/ID) at Lowry AFB, CO. These will consist of continuing and short-term tasks to be assigned by letter of direction issued by the Air Force. The objective is to provide a variety of research activities in the general subject areas specified below, within an overall level of effort. (1) Resarch services will be performed within the following technical areas: educational technology; psychology; econometrics; computer and info sciences; engineering and electronics technology and statistics. (2) Efforts involve specialized research studies in areas such as training analysis, modeling, evaluation, instructional technology demonstration and hardware software support. Preparation and evaluation of experimental materials for use in training may also be required. Research services will include statistical analyses, system engineering analyses, design and breadboarding of computer-driven training devices, training research, experimental data collection and reduction in educational technology, and related activities. A significant portion of the effort will require the contractor to conduct a quick reaction "action oriented" studies and analyses based on task assignments which provide a brief statement of the problem. (3) In performing designated tasks, the contractor will use the following categories of people: senior scientist/engineer, junior scientist/engineer, research assistant/technician, with expertise in the subject areas listed above. Apportionment of effort among these categories will be by letter of direction. (4) It is contemplated that this will be a three year incrementally funded time and materials contract. (5) It is anticipated that this effort will require a minimum of one on-site contractor representative. See notes 31, 11 and the first paragraph of 68. Firms should indicate whether they are or are not a socially and economically disadvantaed business firm, and whether or not they are a woman owned business. The Air Force reserves the right to consider a small business set aside based on responses hereto. Offerors should ref SSS PMRS 85-16 in their response. Closing date for submission of response is 30 days from publication of this notice. Sponsor: Air Force Human Resources Laboratory, Attn AFHRL/ID, Gerald Walker, Lowry AFB, CO 80230. Tel 303/370-4387.

TRAINING DECISIONS SYSTEM (TDS). Exploratory development area PMRS 85-15. Advanced development of a computer-assisted decisions system to aid in developing overall training plans for selected Air Force career ladders. The TDS will consist of four subsystems to aid in "what-where-when" training decisions, with capabilities for (1) defining and analyzing alternative utilization and training (U&T) patterns, and determining management preferences; (2) allocating job training content to alternative settings, and determining the proficiency levels to be achieved in ea training setting; (3) estimating the training resource, costs and capacities required for ea U&T option; and (4) projecting the logical consequeences of training changes throughout the U&T system, and developing "optimal" training plans based on multiple objective functions. The contract will include enhancements of products from an exploratory R&D contract that extends through FY87; the development of system transition plans and advanced system specs; transition of TDS technologies to operational Air Force users; user training; TDS applications in eight Air Force Specialtiy areas; adaption of AFHRL software to operate on users' equipment; operational test, evaluation, and technical assistance to users; and state-of-the-art system advancements in utility and user convenience. Total length of the effort is est at 72 months. Respondents must submit evidence of expertise in Air Force job analysis, training research, operations research, decision systems, multivariate statistical models, computer sciences, optimization problems, and cost analysis. Respondents must also demonstrate in-depth knowledge of the structure and interrelationships of the Air Force manpower, personnel, and training systems. No special facilities are required. See notes 31, 11, 48, 49 and the first paragraph of 68. Firms should indicate whether they are or are not a socially and economically disadvantaged business firm, and whether or not they are a woman owned business. The Air Force reserves the right to consider a small business set aside based on responses hereto. Offerors should ref SSS PMRS 85-15 in their response. Closing date for submision of response is 30 days from publication of this notice. Sponsor Air Force Human Resources Laboratory, Attn AFHRL/MODJ, Dr Hendrick Ruck, Brooks AFB TX 78235. Tel 512/536-3648. (207)

Figure 8. Invitations to submit capability brochures to government agencies.

ent lacks a suitable bidders list. The two-step process would be entirely inefficient and wasteful, under the conditions cited, producing a great many proposals of little usefulness.

In several of these cases it is necessary to create a special capability brochure or at least a somewhat specialized version of your standard capability brochure. And even in circumstances where it is not absolutely necessary to do so, it is often highly desirable to do so—it would increase your prospects for success to do so. And this is an almost "tailor made" situation for computers and word processors: they can make it possible to create these special brochures when it would not be possible otherwise, or would at least be extremely difficult to do otherwise.

THE BASIC CAPABILITY BROCHURE

One excellent approach is to plan ahead, with the expectation of needing more than one capability brochure and also of the necessity to customize your capability brochure, requiring perhaps only one or two copies for some given special application. Here is a general plan for doing so:

1. Have a standard cover made up, useful for a variety of documentation purposes—proposals, brochures, reports, and other. It should be letter size—8½ x 11 inches—include your business name and address, logo, and other such matter (for example, a slogan or lines describing your services) with space for typing in whatever is specific to the application and use. Use white or a light color so that you will not cause the client eyestrain in reading it. (Light yellow is excellent for the purpose.) Some people prefer to use a cover with a die-cut "window" in it, so that identifying words and titles can be typed on the title page and read through the window. Or, if you prefer, you can get standard report covers in any good office-supply emporium, either with a window or with a space suitable for affixing a label with all the information on it.

2. Make up a standard title page. That's the first page, which carries all the identifying data about what is in the pages that follow.

3.   Make up a body of text that will serve as your standard capability brochure. But keep all the text passages short, by using lots of headlines or captions, and divide the brochure into as many sections as possible.

4.   Use as many simple graphics as possible, preferably graphics you have created with your computer and have stored in your disk files.

5.   Have all these text sections also readily available on one or more disk files in your computer, under your word processor program.

6.   Use some simple binding method to hold your brochures together—ring binders, staples, plastic spines, or others that you can apply easily in your office. (If you are in doubt, check with your office-supply store, where you can usually find a number of options available to you.)

You can, of course, have your standard capability brochure typeset, illustrated professionally, printed in quantity with some commercial binding, and even have it done on some expensive, glossy paper or light card stock. Unfortunately, a great many people will see this as having the significance of an advertising circular for some patent medicine simply because it is obviously prepared and distributed in quantity. In many ways, the capability brochure that has been done on a word processor and bound in your own office gets more attention simply because it is obviously prepared especially for each use.

CONTENT AND FORMAT

There is no standard format for a capability brochure. The general format for proposals, suggested in the previous chapter, may be followed as a general guideline, bearing in mind the admonitions and principles made earlier in this chapter. Bear in mind, especially, your objective. First of all, you are either trying to establish your capabilities—and that is itself something of a euphemism, really meaning *credentials* or *qualifications*. Secondly, you are trying to do so either generally, along the lines of your specialty, or specifically, in terms of a defined need. Therefore, you need to open with the traditional introduction—tell the reader who and what you are (name and technical or professional field, with the specific notation that you are a consultant, if your business name does not indicate that clearly), and give a brief indication of your general qualifications.

That should be followed with some detailed explanations of what you do, how you do it, what resources you can bring to bear in behalf of your clients, and your own résumé and those of associates, if you have associates.

Project histories should be offered, too, to validate your claims of experience and accomplishment. Preferably, you should identify the clients, if they will give permission to do so, for it's far more impressive and far more credible when you do so. (Don't do it without their permission.) Usually, a client will want to see the specific copy you propose to use before giving permission, and will often make permission conditional on the right to approve and even edit the copy.

Whether clients give you permission to cite specific projects you have done for them or not, you should try to get their permission to at least include their names on a client list, and you should include that list in addition to any project histories.

Project histories should be selected for their relevance to what you are trying to achieve with the brochure, and should be written up to maximize the relevance and the qualifying nature of the experience and achievement. Be careful to stick with the facts, however, since prospects may wish to call up the clients cited to verify your claims. And list projects in the order of their importance to your goals in writing up the brochure. Assume that many readers will not read all the project histories, but will read only the first two or three. Or perhaps they will read only the first few sentences of each project narrative. Based on such an assumption, make the first few sentences the most compelling ones, and be sure that they convey the main message immediately, so that you will make your point, even if you do not induce the reader to read to the end.

Many consultants list clients in alphabetical order. That's a mistake, for the same reason: many readers will not go over the whole list. List them in order of importance and prominence. If your client list includes General Electric, IBM, Blackstone Wholesalers, and Smith Die Works, be sure that General Electric and IBM get the top slots on the list.

WRITING STYLE

Writing style is important for more than one reason, the most important of which are these three:

1. Unless the reader fully understands what your brochure says, the effort is wasted. Clarity of expression is critically important.

2. Unless the reader is motivated to read all or most of what you write, your brochure cannot do the job you want it to do for you. Your prose, if not actually interesting, must at least not be stultifying.

3. Unless the reader believes what you write—finds your claims, statements, and explanations credible—your brochure cannot do its job properly. Your writing must be persuasive.

Follow the writing principles already covered earlier in the previous chapter. Minimize your use of adjectives and adverbs, and especially shun hyperbole. They militate against credibility, where nouns and verbs encourage belief. Quantify as much as possible, and do not use nicely rounded off numbers when you have precise numbers available. Quantifying, especially when you furnish precise numbers, is one of the principal tools in achieving credibility.

Be specific, not general. Explain what you do, how you do it, the resources you have, the results you achieve, and the benefits that result with as much precision as possible—use specific nouns and verbs and provide quantification.

Keep your language simple and uncluttered. Make each sentence address a single topic, each paragraph a single subject.

Know precisely what points you wish to make, and structure your language to build a case for each point.

USE HEADLINES FREELY

Help the reader follow your train of thought by using many headlines, and make the headlines *say* something precise, rather than refer vaguely to some general idea. Every headline you use ought to accomplish three things: it should help guide the reader to what the main message is or is to be, and so support clear communication and understanding of your copy; it should get some attention and arouse a bit of interest by not being trite and trying to be fresh and different; and it should help *sell* your message to the reader.

Here are a few examples of some typical headlines (left-hand column) that many people use, and along with them some more virile and interesting headlines (right-hand column) that could be used to freshen up your style a bit:

Trite, Dated, Headlines	Suggested Improvements
Introduction	What [Name] Does for Clients
	Who and What We Are
	This is [Name]
	An Organization for These Times
Discussion	How to Get a 20% Boost in Efficiency
	How We Save You Money
	How We Increase Your Profits
Qualifications	Pardon Us for Bragging, But ...
	Maybe We Know Something You Should Know
	Our Contribution to Your Efficiency
Staff	The [Name] Staff of Specialists
	Only the Best ...

Actually, even these are somewhat too generalized, although they are a considerable improvement. Some of them do make promises, or at least imply them, as they should. (The text following the headline should then provide the evidence to prove that the promise is made in good faith and that you can deliver on it.) But the headlines are even better when they are more specific and more sharply focused. And that can be done only after you have written the text and can summarize the most important appeal or point of each portion of text. So you begin with general headlines, in your rough draft, and then, in editing and revising, devise the final headline.

For example, suppose that you have written a description of some technical innovation of your own, such as a service that trains lay personnel in using the typical office computer. Your headlines should be as specific as possible in listing the specific benefits or major points of your service and how you achieve your results—workshop, hands-on training, on-the-job training, training in client's own office, training using client's own tasks, using the computer itself as a training medium (using special programs of your own design), or other such approaches.

For maximum impact, try to focus on the new and different aspects of what you offer. "Better" sells, but "new and different" commands attention to what you are saying so that you can sell. If you have nothing that has any new or different aspects, try to find new and different language to use in making your points. Even when you use colloquialisms, avoid the trite ones. Stay away, for example, from that already hackneyed phrase "user friendly." It simply is not new and fresh anymore, having been done to death already through overuse. Try, for example, to invent your own catch-phrase for user-friendly: perhaps "owner easy" or "operator simplified." Even if they are not very catchy, they are far better than using something that makes the reader groan mentally.

Go through your copy and study all those phrases that many of us use without thinking about whether they are old hat, whether they really say anything meaningful, or whether they are really what we want to say. One of the great advantages of the word processor is that it makes it so easy to try different words and phrases, trying to find the right ones or, at least, the best ones.

USE GRAPHICS

The purpose of writing is to communicate, explain, persuade, and otherwise get ideas and information across. No law, man-made or natural, says that a writer deals only in language. The most useful tool a writer has—perhaps even more useful than a word processor, in many ways—is the illustration. Go back to the previous chapter for a few ideas about illustrations, but do devise and use a few illustrations in your brochure. Illustrations are powerful communicators, if well conceived, and they do not have to be elaborate or costly; they can be quite simple and easy to contruct and yet do their job well.

A RECOMMENDED MODUS OPERANDI

Take advantage of the major attribute of word processing in this way: first, make an outline at least in general terms, although you really will write more efficiently if you work at writing, rewriting, and perfecting an outline until you have one that is thoroughly detailed and definitive. Then proceed to the rough draft manuscript.

When you are writing the draft, don't worry too much about most of these things said here about style and related matters, but do write with the taken-for-granted premise that what you are writing is only rough draft, that you will do a thorough edit and rewrite (at least once), and that nothing you have written is sacred—it can be changed without the slightest hesitation.

The reason for this is to avoid intefering with your flow of thought. During the creation of this rough draft, focus on ideas—information—and not on usage, spelling, punctuation, and so on. Get all the basic ideas and information recorded on disk. (Not on paper; you are definitely not ready for hard copy yet.)

Study your introduction carefully, if you have written one; usually an introduction is written last, but if you already have one, it will need extensive revision, in all probability.

Ideally, you should now do a second draft, and plan to do a third draft as well. This second draft should address the problem of organization primarily. Study your copy carefully for smooth flow of ideas, smooth transitions from one idea to the next, and orderly progression of thought from premises to conclusions (if technical argument) or from introduction of topic to establishment of main point (which should have been telegraphed at the beginning of a paragraph, page, or chapter). Use your word processor to reorganize as necessary. If your outline is not working well in practice—and they often do not—don't hesitate to make changes to the outline and the copy. Try to read from the reader's viewpoint, and see whether it all makes sense and *marches* in orderly fashion to the objectives. (Paraphrase of Murphy's Law: if it can be misunderstood, it will be.)

Once you have done the organization, added such transitions as you find necessary, and are satisfied that you have it all straightened out from the viewpoint of organization and transitions (you'll be polishing and improving transitions, but trying to write them in this first rewrite helps you detect problems of organization and judge how good your organization is), you're ready for the next step: editing.

Edit your copy for spelling, punctuation, clarity of expression, and the like. Study the headlines you have used and see if you can improve them, per the philosophy described here earlier. Simplify sentence structure, eliminate jawbreaker words and substitute simpler, more common ones.

Now you are ready for final polishing of your manuscript. Go through it now line by line, word by word, and polish it lovingly, remembering that special adaptation of Murphy's Law cited a few sentences ago. Try to determine whether anything you have said can be interpreted differently than what you intended. If it can be, you may be sure that it will, by at least some of your readers.

Only then should you fire up your printer and print out the hard copy.

CHAPTER SIX

Other Promotional Uses

Marvelous a marketing asset as word processing is, it is still only one of many uses of the computer in marketing.

MAILING IS A MUST

The use of your computer as a word processor to help you turn out effective proposals and capability brochures is a major asset in your marketing program, but it is not the only one. There are other ways your computer can support your marketing efforts effectively, both as a word processor and in other applications. One of these is in the use of mail as a marketing medium and tool. In fact, the heavy use of mail in a consulting practice is all but mandatory. Even if you did not wish to use the mails as one of your main marketing media, the normal course of business makes it necessary to use the mails extensively. However, the mails are probably among the best marketing media you can use, and are almost always necessary to supplement and implement those other marketing devices you may wish to pursue.

For example, suppose you wish to use a free newsletter as a

marketing device (which is, by the way, an excellent idea). There is no way you can do this with real effectiveness without using the mails extensively.

Or suppose you wish to do some public speaking, get letters to the editor and articles published in the right periodicals, send press releases out, and otherwise seek out various and sundry means to publicize your name and your enterprise: you will need the mails to get necessary coverage even for this.

THE THREE ESSENTIALS IN MAILING

There are three elements—things you must have and do—involved in using the mails effectively for marketing:

1. Getting and using mailing lists—the right names and addresses.
2. Getting and using the right literature to be mailed—something to bring results.
3. Doing the actual mailing.

MAILING LISTS AND LIST BROKERS

There are many list brokers, companies who rent mailing lists to those who wish to use the mails for marketing. These brokers have two general kinds of lists: house lists, or lists they own, and lists they manage. (Users of mailing lists sometimes use combinations of their own lists and rented lists, in which case they refer to their own lists as "house lists.") The term "managed list" requires some brief explanation:

Many people in business do at least some of their business by mail—publishers of periodicals, camera wholesalers, vitamin dealers, mail order houses, and a great many others. There are relatively few kinds of goods that are not sold by mail. Over time, these dealers build up mailing lists of customers (and mailing lists of inquirers, some of whom turn into customers, some of whom do not). These lists of customers are a valuable asset, for the names can be rented out again and again, at prices ranging from a low of about $35 per thousand names to highs of $75 to $100. A few of these dealers rent the lists out themselves, but the majority utilize an established list broker to "manage" their lists, which means to rent them out on a commission basis. Thus the owner of the list makes a tidy annual profit without doing much of anything for it.

Brokers keep their lists in large computer files, of course, and can summon up lists selected by any of various categories—zip codes, professions, businesses, size of previous sales, or any other parameter that has been stored with the names. So you can look over the broker's catalog—the larger list brokers offer quite elaborate and extensive catalogs—and order the kinds of lists you think will pay off for you—lists of banks, bank executives, engineers, engineering firms, manufacturers, retailers, or others. You rent the names for one-time use only, normally, and send mail to them.

Some people report good results with such lists. I am not personally one of them. I never got good results from rented lists, but that may be because I did not play the numbers—did not mail in huge quantity, where the probability statistics might possibly have worked for me. On the other hand, the conventional wisdom in that field is that compiled lists—lists compiled from directories, for example—do not work well at all. However, I got far better results from lists I compiled myself. (The message seems to be: try all the ways, and see which one works best for you.)

CREATING AND MANAGING YOUR OWN LISTS

If you use rented lists, you can get them in any of several forms, including those on gummed labels, magnetic tape, printout, and, probably, these days, on disk compatible with your own computer. However, if you compile your own lists from whatever sources you can find (directories, advertisements, or other), you'll have to make up and manage your own compiled lists—lists of prospects, that is. Moreover, you'll also want to maintain your own client lists that, hopefully, will grow and grow.

Using a database manager or even a simpler program, a file manager, you can do so with your own computer. In fact, you can handle the entire job with your computer:

☐ With a database or file manager you can compile, manipulate, sort, organize, and rearrange your own mailing lists.

☐ With your word processor you can, of course, create your literature, and for this use an individually typed and addressed letter is usually best, far better than a printed form letter and brochure, ordinarily.

☐ With a mail-merge program you can type an original copy of the letter on your letterhead, address each letter individually to whichever names from your mailing list you have chosen, and even address the envelopes automatically!

You can, or course, use this system in more than one way. The foregoing was addressed to mailing letters to prospective clients, but the same system can be used to send out press releases to newspapers, newsletters, and magazines, and you may wish to maintain special mailing lists or a set of lists for that purpose alone.

THE SUPPLIES AVAILABLE

The programs you need for all of this have been mentioned—a word processor, a file or database manager, and a mail-merge program. But to make it all work automatically for you requires the right kinds of supplies too:

Paper and Feed Mechanism

Probably the most popular and least troublesome hardware for doing all this is a printer with a tractor feed mechanism. Some users employ a sheet feeder, but probably the tractor feed is more versatile. (Sheet feeders are also relatively expensive.)

You can get paper for tractor feed printers in more than one format. First of all, you can get paper in at least three standard sizes, including regular 8½ × 11-inch letter paper. This paper has sprocket holes along the edges to fit into the pins of the feed mechanism, which draws it through the printer. The edges bearing the sprocket holes are perforated, as are the top and bottom edges of each sheet, so that the edges can be separated from the sheets, and the sheets from each other. However, there are those papers that leave a somewhat jagged edge after tearing off the edges and separating the pages, but it is possible to get paper that is "microperforated" and leaves smooth edges.

There is special paper offered with a colored border, suggested for use in proposal writing, and you can also get paper that is of double or triple thickness and treated to create one or two carbon copies of the original. You can also get your letterheads, invoice forms, labels, statements, notices, and all other kinds of forms made up in the same manner.

Envelopes are available, joined together for travel through the mechanism during addressing operations, and perforated for easy separation afterwards. (But you can, of course, use window envelopes and eliminate the envelope-addressing operation entirely.)

ONLINE SERVICE

An earlier chapter mentioned briefly the availability of "CBD Online." That is a service made available through licensing of commercial databases by the Department of Commerce, who are the publishers of the *Commerce Business Daily*.

The CBD is mailed every day from Chicago, where the Government Printing Office prints it for the Department of Commerce. Once, when the U.S. mails were being delivered efficiently, Monday's edition arrived on Monday, Tuesday's edition on Tuesday, and so on. Now Monday's edition will arrive on Monday once in a great while, having been mailed the week before, but it more often will arrive as much as a week later. Tuesday's edition will rarely arrive before Thursday or Friday, but may very well arrive after Friday's edition. It's a rare occurrence to get any issue less than 3–5 days late.

This leads to problems, sometimes in terms of learning about opportunities too late to take advantage of them effectively and quite often with regard to losing valuable time in getting a copy of the solicitations advertised and responding to them.

CBD Online is designed to correct that. By subscribing for the electronic edition you can get Monday's edition early Monday morning, Tuesday's edition Tuesday morning, and so on. Moreover, you can get all or only part of the edition—you need not subscribe for all of it—and save time and money, and you can even have the service organization do other things for you, such as ordering the solicitations you want. Of course, with suitable software—a communications program—you can "download" this information—transfer it to your own disk storage—in a few minutes, so you can read it at your leisure on your own screen or in hard copy printed out by your own system, instead of using the expensive online time for reading. (You pay by the minute, usually, for "connect time.")

Anyone interested seriously in pursuing government business is likely to find it well worthwhile to subscribe to the service. There are four organizations offering the service at present. Addresses and numbers are as follows:

SOFTSHARE/MCR Technology, Inc.
55 Depot Road
Goleta, CA 93117
(805) 683-3841 (Collect)

United Communications Group
8701 Georgia Avenue
Silver Spring, MD 20910
(301) 589-8875

Data Resources, Inc. (DRI)
2400 Hartwell Avenue
Lexington, MA 02173
(617) 863-5100

Dialog Information Services, Inc.
3460 Hillview Avenue
Palo Alto, CA 94304
(800) 227-1927 (outside CA)
(800) 982-5838 (in CA)

There are numerous online services available today, and they are growing steadily, both in number and in services made available. (In later chapters we will explore the online services in some depth and list a representative selection of them.) Here, in brief, are some of the marketing advantages online services may offer:

☐ Direct and swift communication with prospective clients. You can already cause your copy—letters, proposals, brochures, press releases, newsletters, quotations, and response to inquiries—to be printed out in another's system ("uploaded," when you are the sender; "downloaded," when you are receiving the copy) if the system is compatible with yours, via telephone connection, using a suitable modem and communications program. You can thus respond to a client or prospective client the same day, instead of waiting days for the mail to deliver your letter, proposal, or quotation. This can be a decisive advantage for you.

☐ The foregoing is equally true for other kinds of copy, destined to go to other respondents—press releases and articles, for example, going out to publishers, or anything else where time (speedy or at least prompt delivery) is important.

☐ Cables and telegrams can be sent directly from your office because most personal computers today, when suitably equipped, can link up directly with one of the national or international communications services and function as a telex. You don't have to leave your desk to send a quotation out to anyone almost anywhere in the world. The success of all the current express-overnight-services is testimony to the importance of speed today, and having the communications facility in your office can be an overwhelming advantage over competitors who are not so equipped.

☐ Huge resources of information are made available to you now, via online databases to which you can subscribe (and many free ones are also available, about which we will say more in a moment). These are invaluable aids in preparing proposals, finding addresses of potential clients, and supporting your marketing needs in a great many other ways. They not only save you a great deal of time in situations where you are hard-pressed for time (an almost inevitable condition in writing proposals), but also make information and sources available to you that would not otherwise be available.

MAIL LIST MANAGEMENT SOFTWARE ABUNDANTLY AVAILABLE

There is an abundance of software suitable for—designed especially for, in fact—such applications as the foregoing. Here are brief listings of just a few such programs, with the supplier's own descriptions, to illustrate this:

Accounting IV Mail List:

Mail list management for the small business; for IBM PC, Victor 900, Sanyo, CP/M, CP/M-86, MS-DOS

B.I.S. Micro-Mail List Processing and Bulk Mailing System:
Designed for aid to mass mailers; for CP/M, CP/M-86, MP/M

BusiPost:

File and mail list; for CP/M

Creatabase:

General-purpose file manager; for IBM PC/XT, Compaq, PC-DOS

List Handler:

Mail/merge database; for Apple

Datahandler-Plus:

File and mail management; for TRS-80, IBM PC

Demi-Mail:

Name/address mailing system; for TRS-80 I/III

The Disk Listmaker:

List maintenance; for TRS-80 I/III

Datafax:

File management; for Apple II/ IIe, IBM PC

Know Your Client:

File and mail list management; for IBM PC, Apple

COMMUNICATIONS SOFTWARE

Communications via computer requires software, as well as a modem, as all computer operations do, and there is an abundance of communications software available, some of it rather highly specialized. The following sampling will illustrate both the diversity of communications software available and some of the many things you can do vis-à-vis communications with a computer and proper software.

Gram-A-Syst:

Telex, electronic mail; for IBM PC, Apple, Victor 9000, KayPro II, TRS-80, CP/M, MS-DOS, TRS-DOS

The Apple-IBM Connection:

Transfer files between the IBM PCs and Apple PCs; for IBM PC, MS-DOS

Micro-Link:

Send text in object and source codes; CP/M, CP/M-86, MS-DOS

MicroTLX:

Turns computer into intelligent Telex/TWX; for Morrow, KayPro II, Altos, Televideo, CP/M, MP/M, others using Z-80, 8080 microprocessors

Matrix-Express:

Electronic mail conferencing; for DEC, IBM PC

Intelligent Terminal:

Asynchronous communications package; for Altos, KayPro II, other CP/M, MP/M systems using Z-80 and 8080 chips

MicroEZLNK:

Interface with Western Union's EasyLink service; for Morrow, KayPro II, Altos, CP/M, MP/M, others using Z-80, 8080

Matrix Transaction Exchange:

Electronic mail conferencing; for DEC Professional

NewsNet:

Database with 150 online business newsletters, UPI, PR newswire; for most computers and systems

Information System:

Networking; for IBM PC

FREE SOFTWARE

Software is expensive. Programs of the types listed here for file management, mailing list handling, communications, and many other kinds of applications generally run from about $100 and up, with most programs in the "up" category. And "up" usually means several hundred dollars, often well into four figures, in fact.

Many computer manufacturers are today selling their systems

"bundled," which means with several software packages included. (At their list prices, the software packages often represent more dollars than the computer itself costs!) In some cases, you can select the software of your choice from among options. But there is another way to get free software: there is an abundance of good software in the public domain.

PUBLIC DOMAIN SOFTWARE: HOW TO GET IT

Many hobbyists, government agencies, nonprofit organizations, and others who may be simply public-spirited are today creating software programs and making them available free of charge to everyone, with the sole proviso that the user must use the software for his or her own purposes—and they can be business purposes—but may not sell the software or copies of it.

The software is made available in a variety of ways, but the main avenue is via downloading from online databases and electronic bulletin boards—"BBs." Many—perhaps even most—of these BBs are operated by individuals, sometimes as the individual's hobby, sometimes to promote the individual's business enterprise. Many others are operated by computer clubs (there are a great number of these, and it is advantageous in many ways to belong to one), by various organizations, and by government agencies. (The latter appears to be growing in numbers, and one individual has written and published a rather large directory/guidebook to free information, which includes lists of such BBs whose files are available at no charge to anyone interested.) A few charge a nominal sum for registering with them and being assigned an identification code and log-on procedure, but most are entirely free of charge. And most ask only, in return for permitting you to download the available software, that you upload such public domain programs that you acquire elsewhere which are not already in the BB's library.

In some cases, local dealers can, under certain circumstances, make such software available, too. The dealer from whom I purchased my own Morrow system makes a communications program available to buyers of modems for the cost of the disk only. However, a more common route to acquiring this software, for those who for whatever reason find it difficult to download it themselves, is the computer club. It is through the local Morrow computer users group, to which I belong, that I acquired my free communications, mailing list, and much other public domain software.

OTHER USEFUL, FREE INFORMATION

Software is not the only class of free material available through these BBs. One local BB, operated by a government agency, provides a calendar of computer shows and related events, which is a useful reference for anyone wishing to attend such convocations to make good business "contacts," an objective of many who do attend these conclaves. You can also make some of your "contacts" through these public databases by participating in discussion groups conducted via telephone and computer, either "live" (spontaneous) or via files, to which you can add comments at your leisure. And you can also do some PR—public relations work—for yourself by being active in these online groups of enthusiasts.

CHAPTER SEVEN

Practical Principles and Admonitions

There are right and wrong ways to do everything, and using a personal or desktop computer is no exception. A few practices and principles adopted as standard operating procedures can save you a great deal of grief and regrets, while greatly increasing the rewards of computer use.

WORD PROCESSING: NUMBER 1 USE

According to all surveys reported publicly, by far the most popular use of desktop computers in offices is for word processing, despite the fact that word processing programs are outnumbered by accounting programs offered in the marketplace. However, the popularity of word processing is understandable, since many small businesses entrust all their accounting to a public accounting service, and most large firms have a centralized accounting department, so the many and sundry other offices of the firm have no need or use for accounting software. On the other hand, it is a rare office, large or small, that does not have the need to produce correspondence and many of the other uses already discussed; hence the popularity of word processing: virtually every office has the potential to benefit from it. (Unfortunately, relatively few really do benefit to any significant extent, as we shall see in a moment.)

WHO SHOULD WORK AT THE KEYBOARD?

The help-wanted advertising pages of any large-city daily newspaper will reveal, almost any day of the week, several columns of appeals to "word processor operators," as office after office installs computer hardware and word processor software. At the same time, word processor operators have become probably the most sought-after class of office temporaries, according to an article in *Office Administration and Automation*, August 1984 ("Need a Pro? Try Temporary Help," by Josephine Flamingo), which reports that at least one office-temporary service provides *only* word processing operators, but that all providers of office temporaries find a heavy demand for experienced word processor operators, as typewriters are increasingly being abandoned in favor of the new technology.

That is good news, but it's also bad news. The good news is that more and more offices are using word processing. The bad news is that most of them are also misusing word processing and deriving far less benefit than word processing can and should provide.

"Word processor operator," it soon develops, is a euphemism for typist, and the word processor is treated as though it were merely a supertypewriter. Little has changed in these offices, except the typist must now learn how a word processor works and master the control signals for the specific word processor in use. Instead of typing the handwritten drafts or copy on dictating-machine belts at an electric typewriter, the operator types them on a keyboard and has them printed out on the system's printer.

There is some slight gain in efficiency, especially if a speller program is used to help in proofreading copy. Many errors are corrected on-screen, before printout; changes made after printout—requiring insertions, deletions, and other electronic cut and paste—are entered more easily, so that retyping by human hands and subsequent proofreading by human eyes is only partial, confined to that which is new or revised copy. But that is only a small part of the many benefits to be derived; many other, potential, benefits are not being realized.

THE COMMON MISUSE OF WORD PROCESSING: A SCENARIO

Despite the many benefits of (a) electronic cut and paste, (b) search and find and search, find, and replace functions, (c) instantaneous copying, (d) proofreading help and, (e) the many other aids to the drudge work of the editorial functions, even greater benefits result when the creators—writers, editors, reviewers, and managers—work at the keyboard. All too often today, writers—who may be engineers, medical technicians, or any of many other classes of professional specialists and managers, rather than professional writers—labor at their desks scrawling manuscripts on lined yellow legal pads. Typists/word processor operators keyboard and print out hard copy. Editors labor over that hard copy, mark it up, and send it back to the writers for rework and/or the word processor operator for rekeyboarding and the next generation of hard copy. After several such cycles and much time wasted sorting out the confusion created by the extravagant oversupply of printed paper in several generations, the final draft is identified and sent on to management for review and final comments. Finally, the last round of rewriting, editing, keyboarding, and printing hard copy is entered.

At this point relatively little has been gained by using word processing. In fact, there have been losses in efficiency, resulting from the basic approach to the work. In this scenario of the typical use of word processing, the whole cycle is based on the old-fashioned method of words on paper through many cycles of editorial work. What happens all too often today is that instead of a benefit resulting from the word processor, an evil results: it has become too easy to print copy on paper, so a ludicrously extravagant excess of copy results. Even the slightest editorial changes are the trigger for cranking out yet another copy, and soon enough it becomes nearly impossible to determine which is the latest draft or which are the latest changes, with subsequent tremendous waste of time and energy. In this situation, the word processor has by this time become a monster, instead of a benefactor.

UNDERSTANDING WHAT WORD PROCESSING IS— WHAT IT *REALLY* IS

The major causes of the problem described can be attributed to two human foibles:

1. The almost instinctive resistance to change.
2. The misunderstanding of what word processing really is.

In fact, these two causes are related and are probably really a single cause, for the misunderstanding about word processing is the result of almost automatic resistance to change. So many users of word processing insist on fitting it into their already fixed view of what their normal office processes are, rather than viewing it as a new way of doing things. That is, it is a force-fit, making the word processor conform to an old pattern rather than changing the pattern—the practices and procedures—to fit word processing. Word processing is not automatic typing. It is not automated editorial production. It is not electronic cut and paste. That is, it *is* all these things, but they represent a minor theme, and if you think of word processing in these terms, you see the trees but you miss the forest. Word processing is a *new and different way* of creating correspondence, manuals, brochures, proposals, reports, and all other written documents. It is a *better way*, a *far better way*, of doing so—if used properly. And "properly," in this case, means *creatively* and *differently* than typewriters are used. The system itself must be changed, with principles and procedures changed to reflect a proper understanding of what word processing can do. That, in fact, is the key: word processing, used so as to utilize it to greatest advantage, contributes even more to the creative end of the editorial processes than it does to the production tasks. It is a tool for the writer and editor, and even for the reviewer, that makes each one's job easier to do well, and results in a far more efficient and more effective operation overall.

A BETTER SCENARIO

The proper scenario for gaining all the blessings word processing has to bestow is (1) to have all the key people involved in the creative end—writers, editors, and reviewers—working at keyboards and (2) to reprieve the printer: give it a rest; it's being greatly overworked. Far too much paper is being generated, and paper is the very antithesis of word processing in all the early stages of generation. With regard to editorial processes and older practices, word processing reverses the logic of words of paper: when you use word processing, paper is the result, not a means. Rough drafts do not need to come to life on paper, and they should not. They have lives all their own on disk and screen, and they should be allowed to live those lives out before being reborn on paper. They should appear on paper only after all changes have been made, and final drafts are needed in the form of hard copy.

This means that writers work at keyboards creating their drafts, and editors do their editing at keyboards, working on a copy of the original file. (The originals are always kept safe until it is certain that they are no longer needed, at which time they can be wiped out and the disks reused.) Writers rewrite and revise, as necessary, at the keyboard. Reviewers (and that includes those technical specialists reviewing for technical accuracy and managers reviewing for whatever managers think they must examine and evaluate) should work at monitors or terminals, making their observations either as comments on the disk (which are not printed) or perhaps by memo.

This does not mean that there will never be a hard copy printed out before all of this is completed. Managers may balk at working in this manner, or someone may wish to take a copy on a trip, to read en route. But it does mean that this is the ideal, a goal to aspire to, if word processing is to be used well. It does not mean, however, that the creative end of the work will benefit only from the obvious increases in efficiency. In fact, the quality of the writing ought to improve considerably, for this reason alone:

Extremely few writers, even experienced professionals, write acceptably good first-draft copy. The essence of good writing lies, usually, in rewriting. However, most writers, even professionals, hate to rewrite—it is usually drudgery of the most distasteful kind—and those who write in typical offices are most often not professional writers. Consequently, many do not rewrite at all, with predictable results so often lamented by others. And even when forced by executive edict to rewrite, they often confine that rewriting to the minimum changes, which are hardly more than self-editing of the lightest kind.

Word processing makes rewriting quite easy. It is child's play to make deletions, insertions, and move whole pages—even whole chapters—around. Consequently, writers working at keyboards tend to do far more self-editing, rewriting, revision, and polishing of copy than they do when working by older writing methods.

A most common fault in writing is in organization. Editors can patch up leaky spelling and punctuation and shore up faltering syntax, but they usually can do nothing about massive misorganization, especially when the copy concerns technical or other highly specialized subjects. Word processing capabilities make reorganization quite easy, of course, as already noted. (This very chapter is itself an insert between two chapters written earlier because this proved to be a far more logical place for it than the one originally conceived for it, and it is so easy to move it from there to here!)

Add to this the ease with which writers can summon up reference materials readily accessible in computer files and even copy materials directly into the new manuscript, and you begin to see the inducements to writers and editors to think more intensely about the copy and to work more intensely at improving it.

This does not mean that there is no place in the office for the "word processor operator." There is ample work for such skilled office workers to do, even in publications work, where they will normally be charged with producing the final hard copy, especially if it is to be camera-ready—the copy from which the printer makes plates and prints the end product or the copy that goes to the office copier for duplicating. But there are many other chores, such as working from dictating masters, to produce correspondence and various interoffice and in-house records.

ARCHIVING OR "BACKING UP"

For many years it was—and still is, to some extent—a common practice to make at least one carbon copy of every letter and other document of value for one's files. Later, when office copiers became a commonplace in even the smallest offices or were conveniently available as public facilities nearby, most offices did away with the inconvenience of carbon paper and made file or archival copies this new way.

Things haven't changed a great deal, in principle: it is still necessary to have file copies, even though the original copy consists of many thousands or hundreds of thousands of tiny magnetized spots on the surface of one or more floppy disks. But there is this difference: whereas a piece of paper stored away in a metal cabinet is unlikely to deteriorate, except over a number of years or in case of disaster—fire or flood—even slight mishaps can lead to the loss of information archived on a computer disk or diskette. Here are some of the ways those magnetized spots that represent a file copy can become damaged or destroyed:

☐ Accidental punching of a key while the data is still in memory and not yet transferred to the more permanent storage of a disk file can wipe out hours of work by "dumping" everything in the memory circuits.

☐ A momentary power failure, one of even a second or two duration, causing barely a flicker of your lights, can wipe out your computer memory entirely, with everything that is in it, as described.

☐ A power surge or spike, which can result from even the minor effect of starting an appliance somewhere, as well as from other causes, such as lightning striking or static electricity discharging, can dump your computer's memory and may cause even more serious effects, such as damage to your computer.

☐ But even saving the data by transferring it to disk is no guarantee that data will not be lost: accidental punching of the wrong key, while the disk is in the logged drive, can wipe out part or all of a disk or a file on the disk or jumble the file.

☐ Placing the disk under the telephone or too near some other source of electromagnetic radiation can accomplish the same effect as punching the wrong key while the disk is in the logged drive.

☐ A bad spot on the disk, such as a flaw or worn spot in the magnetic coating (which can exist in even a new disk, but is relatively common in a disk you have used over and over for some time) can dump part of the contents of a file or cause a program to "crash," with a similar result.

☐ Inattention while entering data can cause a disk to become overloaded—overfull—with loss of some of the data. (Most software warns you that you are out of space, but you should leave yourself a margin of safety and not rely on getting that warning in time. Moreover, full disks are far more likely to "crash" than those having some room to spare.)

☐ Physical problems with a disk drive—dirt particles, or a "head crash," for example—can cause damage to disks, and a physically damaged disk is generally a total wipeout of everything on it, since it is probably hazardous to the health of your disk drives to use it again.

Because of these many hazards to your data, it is good advice to make archival copies of everything, including copies of the disks containing your original programs, and the instruction manuals you get with your computer and with your software almost invariably make a point of so advising you. The first thing you do with program disks is to make at least one working copy and store the original ("distribution" copy) away in a safe place.

You should do something similar to that with all your disks: unless you really do not care about the file, you should make at least one backup copy. (I generally make two, to play safe.) But don't wait too long, expecially if you are creating a lengthy or voluminous file: stop periodically to "save" or "write to disk" what you have entered into memory, but which is not yet stored on disk. Then that momentary interruption in power will result in a much smaller loss of data. If your area is afflicted with frequent power interruptions, as some areas are, do your "saves" often. And you might wish to consider installing a "constant voltage" or "uninterruptible" power supply as a safeguard against data losses.

It's also a good idea to have a surge protector. That's a device that suppresses those voltage surges or spikes and protects your equipment from them.

If you want to play safe with disks and files you intend to keep as permanent records or will use often to read from, and prevent accidental erasure by inadvertently writing over the data already on them, you should cover the write-protect notch. Figure 9

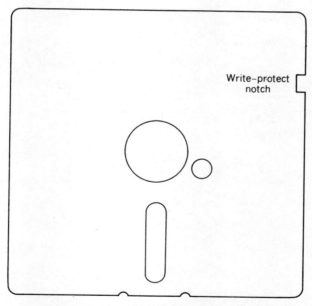

Figure 9.   Write-protect notch of disk.

illustrates where the notch is on the disk. If you cover this with a piece of tape or one of the self-sticking tabs provided for that purpose with every batch of disks you buy, the computer will be unable to write to (on) that disk, thus preventing accidental erasure in that manner. That, of course, is why it is called a write-protect notch.

PART THREE

The Computer as a Consulting Tool

The computer can contribute as heavily to your professional effectiveness and efficiency as a consultant—to both the range and the quality of the services you provide clients, that is—as it can to the marketing of your consulting services. In fact, the division of the subject into the separate categories of functions in the following pages is somewhat artificial, contrived to help you assimilate the considerable amount of new information you need if you are to make maximum use and derive maximum benefits from your computer, rather than because such categorizing is inherent in computer functioning. In short, the attributes that make the computer so valuable in marketing your services are the same ones that make it an equally effective servant in expanding your professional abilities and efficiency as a consultant.

In fact, this part of the book focuses on the computer as a contributor to your success in two different ways: one, it will help you carry out your tasks more efficiently; and, two, it will enable you to prepare better—and therefore more pleasing—reports and presentations to your clients. And for still another thing, it will help you produce highly professional products and services that will be additional income centers for you, and make their own direct contributions to your marketing success, while they are also earning income for you.

PART THREE

The Computer
as a Consulting Tool

CHAPTER EIGHT

The Computer as an Aid to Analysis

Charles Babbage, inventor of the first digital computer over a century ago, did not call his invention a computer; with prophetic insight, perhaps with greater insight than his successors in that field, he called it an "Analytical Engine."

CONSULTING IS NOT (NECESSARILY) PROBLEM SOLVING

Analysis of some sort is an inherent function of consulting in most applications, whether or not the service which you have been called on to render includes solving a specific problem. And consulting is not exclusively a problem-solving activity, nor are consultants always called on because clients are faced with problems they cannot solve alone. Perhaps that was true at one time, and perhaps it is still largely true in some highly specialized professions, such as medicine, but the modern business and professional world employs consultants for many other purposes. The temporary-help industry, for example, has grown from early "Kelly girl" origins to a $4 billion industry that now supplies writers, illustrators, engineers, scientists, and technical/professional specialists of all kinds, many of whom justifiably and understandably consider themselves to be consultants, even when employed as temporary help. The growth of the industry has been phenomenal, despite recessionary periods, from $431 million in 1971 to $3.48 billion in 1981, with a projected $4 billion for 1984, according to the *Office Administration and Automation* article cited in the previous chapter. Although this article is slanted primarily to office workers and to suppliers who focus primarily on office workers of various kinds, it does make the point that technical people and those with computer skills are most in demand. What it does not report on is the large but highly specialized group of engineering–consulting firms who specialize in furnishing stress analysts, engineers, scientists, programmers, designers, technical writers, and many other highly specialized professionals. Virtually all of these regard themselves as consultants, although they are most often employed to augment the client's own staff of technical/professional specialists, as a special kind of temporary, either because the client does not have enough qualified personnel to meet the needs of the moment or because the client does not have the right technical/ professional employees to satisfy the need. Often the need represents a relatively short-term peak requirement arising out of a special contract the client has undertaken: an entire industry of technical/professional temporaries has arisen out of "high-tech" government contracts for such things as modern weapons and space projects.

Still, whether employed in that special category of technical/ professional temporary or as an independent consultant, no doubt all must solve problems daily, in carrying out their duties— and clients, paying the premium rates for these specialized consultant/temporaries, expect these pros to solve all daily problems without delay. But whether or not you are called on to solve problems, analysis is always a part of the job that must be done, and the computer is an especially valued companion and helper for that kind of work.

THE THEME IS VERSATILITY

The computer's capabilities in mathematical manipulations—
"number crunching," in computer vernacular—are well known, of
course, because they are inherent in the nature of computers, and
were the prime purpose for their original development. And that
capability for handling pure mathematics extends to examining
quantitative relationships in a wide variety of applications, in addition to the obvious one of accounting and payroll management, for
many of these fields and functions do represent, in fact, problems
in quantitative relationships. But even when the essence of the
function has nothing to do with numbers, human genius has devised ways of using the computer's capabilities for countless other
functions that are not by nature mathematical functions, to wit:
digital computers function on the principle of a binary—two
digit—number system, and the heart of the computer lies in its
ALU—arithmetic logic unit—which is the chief instrument for
manipulating the strings of 1s and 0s that represent the two digits
of the binary system. Those two digits can stand for many other
mutually exclusive values other than the numerical ones. They can
represent true and false, up and down, black and white, stop and
go, high and low, or any other pair of opposites that are mutually
exclusive and must be one or the other, with no compromises or
other states permitted. However, a de facto standard exists in the
form of a group of eight of those 1–0 bits (each digit is a "bit")
strung together (e.g., 10011010) and called a *byte*. There are 255 different combinations of eight bits possible. And if each of those 255
combinations (bytes) is assigned to represent a number, alphabetical character, special character, or symbol, it becomes possible to
do a great many other things with a computer than calculate taxes
and payrolls. It becomes possible to add enormous power to human capabilities for control and management of virtually all fields
of human activity. For example, just one class of software alone includes programs for database management, designing and developing databases, and organizing information generally, a large application area in itself, but yet only one area. Computers perform
countless other sophisticated and useful chores for their users,

and we have touched on only a relative few in earlier pages. Following is a small sample of some other areas in which the computer can support you with its tireless and speedy capacities for drudge work, and for which management and control applications software is abundantly available:

Inventory	Scheduling	Project management
Financial planning	Sales & marketing	Mail order
Communications	Decision support	Graphics
Telemarketing	Education & training	General administration
Legal services	Banking	Science and research
Architecture	Entertainment	Publishing
Astrology	Government services	College administration
Teacher aids	Marketing research	Real estate
Property management	Transportation	Travel services
Wholesale trade	Retail trade	Distribution
Membership organizations	Social sciences	Visual arts
Photography	Statistics	Sports & leisure
Health care	Menu planning	Weight control
Personnel management	Music	Hospitality

TYPES AND CLASSES OF SOFTWARE

When we speak of what the computer can do for you, we are really referring to the software—the programs—for it is the software that is designed for and geared to various applications. The hardware—the computer itself—is "merely" the mechanism for operating the software.

Software can be and is classified in many different ways, but we are interested here, for the moment, in only one general classification and its two subcategories: we are concerned with applications programs, but we must recognize that these are subdivided into general applications programs and industry- or professional-specific applications programs.

Programs have been designed and developed to serve the specialized needs of bankers, broadcasters, physicians, dentists, contractors, writers, photographers, astrologers, association executives, teachers, administrators, publishers, real estate brokers, investors, speculators, printers, veterinarians, farmers, sheep raisers, musicians, composers, and countless others, and new programs are appearing almost daily.

There are, for example, many accounting programs, all of which can probably be adapted to your own needs. And they are quite different from each other in a variety of respects. For example, many are designed for large corporations, while others are designed to serve the needs of small business. On the other hand, there are many accounting programs designed specifically for certain industries, businesses, and careers. Here are a few examples:

MICROBASE AD AGENCY SYSTEM.   Accounting and billing for advertising agencies.

AG COUNT.   Accounting and cash flow for farm management.

ARCHITECT'S BUSINESS MANAGER.   Project and financial management for architects.

But of course the programs are not confined to accounting. There are industry/career-specific programs for many other purposes:

REACH AND FREQUENCY.   Radio/TV ratings advertising sales proposals.

CONSTRUCTION MANAGEMENT INFORMATION SYSTEM.   Accounting and information control for construction industry.

CONSTRUCTION ESTIMATING.   The title explains itself.

FIRE SAFETY POINT ASSESSMENT.   Assigns points to fire department
concerns—finds problem areas.

GL-PLUS.   Critical path scheduling.

PERFORMANCE ANALYSIS OF PASSIVE SOLAR BUILDINGS.   Calculates
solar and backup energy used each month.

FAULT CURRENT ANALYSIS.   Engineering and economic evaluation
analysis and design.

Another way that software aids and supports analysis is via the
many graphics programs. These are programs that convert data
into such graphic representations as pie charts, bar charts, curves,
x-y plots, and sundry other graphs and plots, which can be presented on paper, film, or other media, as well as on-screen. This is
itself an analysis, as well as a graphic representation of the results,
and is of itself a great aid. Here are just a few such programs,
whose names are so definitive that no comments are required:

4-Point Graphics	ACCUCHART	GRAPHEASE
ATHENA/graph	AUTO-GRAPH	Charts Unlimited
Apple Business Graphics	Auto Graphics	Demografix
Autograf Images	BPS Business Graphics	Diagram-Master
Business Analysis	Business Graphics	EZ*Bargraph
Chart Pro	Chart-Master	Ed A Sketch
PC-Draw	Master Plot	The Prime Plotter

ORGANIZING AND MANAGING INFORMATION: DATABASE MANAGEMENT

Perhaps the very heart of analysis lies in the art of organizing and
managing information. Certainly, no sensible analysis is possible
without examining the available information and organizing it on

some logical basis, from which sensible correlations can be made and logical inferences—conclusions—drawn.

One useful tool for this is the database management system, a type of software program. But before exploring this useful software and what it can do for you, let's first define what we mean by a "database," for that is a very much used and abused word and, indeed, some professionals draw a distinction between the words "database" and "data base," although it is rather unclear just what that distinction is, and some prefer to spell it "data-base," although all appear to agree on the use of "DBMS" to stand for database management systems. In any case, as much as some professionals tend to obscure and bury the definition of a data base in arcane jargon, the definition of a database is simple enough: it is any accumulation of data that has some common theme or any reason at all for being accumulated or assembled in one place. A card file of your telephone numbers or a set of pamphlets describing how to prepare your favorite dishes is a database—if you want it to be. You decide what information represents a related set, and it can be as large or as small, as uniform or as diverse, as you wish it to be. And it can be in any form you wish: a card file, a tape, a floppy disk, a notebook, or a sheaf of papers. (Of course, if you wish to computerize it, you must get it into some kind of "machinable" form, such as tape or disk—most likely disk, of course.) You can also consider it to be a single database or several databases: only you need make the judgment. Only you *can* make the judgment, in fact, for only you know whether the data has some common binder.

KINDS OF DATABASE MANAGERS

There are many database management programs. Some are quite sophisticated, designed for major databases and mainframe computers, but there are many intended for use on a more modest scale, and there are two kinds of database managers, the so-called relational database manager and the file manager, with the relational DBMS (also called by some a "high end" database manager) the larger and more sophisticated of the two. In fact, every relational database management system includes within it a file manager program (which is called by some a "low end" system, of course). And here, again, there seems to be some dispute, with some professionals insisting that all these programs are database managers, while others are equally vociferous about distinguishing database managers from file managers.

To put it into the simplest possible terms, the file manager permits you to store and organize your information—your database(s)—and retrieve any of it from any file, in toto or selectively, at your pleasure. But you cannot have more than one file open at a time, although presumably you can combine files, within whatever the limits of the system are. (You may find exceptions, but this is the general truth.)

On the other hand, the more sophisticated relational DBMS permits you to access more than one file at a time and to combine information selected from different files—to use *related* information or to have the program relate the information (hence the epithet "relational").

The advantages of the relative flexibility of the relational DBMS over the more rigid structure and capability of the file manager are many. A simple example will illustrate: suppose you run a book club with a file manager. You would set up a file for each member, and you would provide space in the file for whatever you thought necessary—perhaps for listing three books per month, along with their prices and other relevant data. Now if the average member bought only one book a month, you would waste a great deal of file space, which might become a severe handicap, in time, for most systems have no storage capacity to spare. On the other hand, you would be faced with a dilemma whenever a member ordered four or five books, for the file manager is unsuited to handle exceptions to the rule, or aberrations; it's a simple-minded program, a program with a one-track mind.

The relational database manager is better educated and more flexible. With it you would not have the problem because you can create for each member a file just big enough to serve the needs of the occasion, but no bigger, by using two files, one set up to make up orders, the other to retrieve customer information for making up the order. No space is wasted, and there is no upper limit to the number of books the member may order and be billed for. All you need is some cue to the commonality—the relationship—of the data in each file, such as a customer i.d. code, and the interactive or "lookup" function in the program will connect the data in each file. For example, as soon as you enter the customer's i.d. in the new-order file, the program will search the related file and write in the relevant data, such as name and address, while making up the order form and invoice.

Of course, you can do many other things with the relational database manager because of that flexibility. You can do all sorts of analyses of the files—what part of the country a given title sells best in, whether there are seasonal patterns and what they are, what kinds of members tend to order what kinds of books, and sundry other studies, limited only by the data you have on each member and by your own imagination in devising studies.

Now perhaps you begin to suspect why applications and questionnaires often ask all those "dumb questions" that appear to have no bearing on the situation; they are building a database for future analyses that will be most helpful in running their enterprise successfully. (And, of course, you can do likewise, and use your database manager to help build your own practice, as well as use it to serve clients' needs.)

Of course, there are many database managers, and they vary in different ways. One way in which they vary is in degree of difficulty: some are quite easy to use—extremely "user friendly," as they like to express it in the trade, to indicate that a program is easy to learn and use—while others require far more knowledge and study to learn and use. But that is not the only way in which they vary from each other.

Like accounting and many other types of software programs, database managers can be general-purpose systems, adaptable to most uses, or they can be special-purpose systems, designed for specific industries, professions, or situations. Typically, you can use such a program to design forms and reports, to generate and produce reports, to manage mailing lists, and to handle a host of such tasks.

The question may arise here as to why anyone uses a file manager, since the database manager is so obviously superior in so many ways. The answer is that some needs are simple enough to be satisfied by a file manager, and it is therefore senseless to introduce the complication of a full-scale database manager. If, for example, you want only a mailing list manager you need not waste the time and money on a database manager; it's neither good economics nor good management to do so.

A FEW DATABASE TERMS

Of course, you can't escape without learning a few new terms, beside DBMS, database manager, and file manager. You will need to become acquainted with these too:

FIELD.   Each single entry item of data, such as "name," "address," "city," and so forth. The database manager allows some maximum number of fields per record, from as few as a dozen or less to as many as thousands and, in some cases, without limit. Most database managers tend to accommodate the higher numbers, but the practicality of this is limited to the storage or file space your system can make available.

RECORDS.   Each unit of data, made up of related fields, such as a single order, a part description, or other item that has some number of fields making up the record.

FILE.   A set of records stored together, usually related to each other, with information on how they are to be stored and displayed.

INDEXING.   The capability of the program for indexing fields for searching, which varies from one program to another.

SORTING.   Organizing and/or reorganizing the data according to some index, such as name or address. The more sorting you wish to do, the faster a program you must have, or the sorting will be so slow as to be impractical.

DATA IMPORT.   The ability to read information developed with or under another program, such as a word processor. (You should make sure of compatibility of data and formats among all your programs.)

DATA EXPORT. The opposite of data import, the capacity to write information from your program in some format that can be read by another program, such as a word processor or spreadsheet, or a different database.

MENU. List of selections on screen, with identification of all possible options and commands to exercise each. Some programs will enable you to create your own menus, while other limit you to the standard ones furnished with the program.

PASSWORD. A secret code assigned to users of your database manager to prevent unauthorized access to what is presumably confidential and proprietary information.

BATCH PROCESSING. The ability to process several routine tasks sequentially without the need to tend the machine and order each batch processing individually. This can save much of your time and let you turn your attention elsewhere while reports are being printed out.

The usefulness and popularity of file managers and database managers is demonstrated by the large number of software programs available for each. Some are general in application, while others are specialized for such applications as (mailing) list management, text management, schedule management, and many other applications. This diversity is often reflected in the name of the program, and just studying the names is itself an education in this kind of software and its intended use.

Following are representative listings of both types of programs, separated by category. In some cases the separation and assignment of category is arbitrary, since the distinctions are not always clear-cut.

Computer models, operating systems, and, in some cases, microprocessors are listed, to the extent that the developer has made the information available. The listing of several systems, however, does not mean that the program will fit any of these systems but, rather, that the developer has made versions of the program available for the various systems. This means that you must be sure that there is a version available for your own system and that you get the right version, if and when you order one of these.

File Managers

Program	Computers/Systems/Other
Aladin DMBS™	IBM, Apple
Accounting IV Mail List	IBM, Sanyo, CP/M, CP/M-86, MS-DOS
Agenda	IBM PC
Automated Telephone Directory Mailing List	IBM PC
B.I.S. Micro-Mail List Processing and Bulk Mailing System	CP/M, CP/M-86, MP/M
The BENCHMARK® Mail List Manager	IBM PC, NEC, Sony, Victor, North Star, CP/M, CP/M-86, MP/M, MS-DOS, PC-DOS
BusiPost	CP/M
Cardfile	CP/M, CP/M-86, PC-DOS
Catalist	IBM PC/XT, Compaq, Eagle, Columbia, MS-DOS
Condor Series 20	Z-80, 8080, 8085, 8086
Core/Pack	IBM PC/XT, CP/M, CP/M-86
Creatabase	IBM PC/XT, Compaq, PC-DOS
DATA-TRAC (Database)	Altos, Onyx, IBC, Dynabyte, Oasis
Datahandler	TRS-80, IBM PC
DCM™ Document Control Manager	IBM PC
Data Master	IBM PC
Data-File Manager	TRS-80 I/III/IV, TRS-DOS
Datasafe	CP/M, CP/M-86, MS-DOS, PC-DOS

File Managers (*Continued*)

Program	Computers/Systems/Other
Deluxe Addresser	Commodore PET
EZ*Maillabel	IBM PC, MS-DOS
MAILTRAK	IBM PC
PACE (Programmed Assignment of Client Engagements)	CP/M
Page 1	IBM PC/XT, Columbia, Eagle, Victor 900, Compaq, MS-DOS, PC-DOS
Records Manager	IBM PC, NEC, MS-DOS
Synopsis	CP/M, MP/M
pfs: FILE*	IBM PC/XT, PC-DOS
pfs: REPORT	IBM PC/XT, PC-DOS
AE Database Development	Apple II+, Franklin ACE-1000, DEC, Xerox 820, Eagle, Televideo, CP/M, MP/M
Accent®	DEC
Advanced DB Master	IBM PC/XT
Autoindex	IBM PC, Victor 9000
Baseline	CP/M
Custom File—Data Base Management	IBM PC, MS-DOS
DATAEASE™	IBM PC/XT, Victor 9000, DEC Rainbow, MS-DOS, CP/M-86, PC-DOS
DataStar™	Z-80, Apple, CP/M
ESQ-1	CP/M, MP/M, TURBO-DOS
FMS 80	Apple, IBM PC, CP/M
File Fax	Atari, Apple II/II+/IIe, Osborne, NEC, Commodore
Information Management	IBM PC/XT
LOGIX	UNIX

File Managers (*Continued*)

Program	Computers/Systems/Other
MASTERFILE™	PC-DOS, MS-DOS, CP/M, MP/M
Merge Master: Text Merging/ Manipulating Software	IBM PC
Notebook	CP/M-86, PC-DOS
Omnifile—The Professional's Information Management System	IBM PC/XT, Victor 9000, DEC Rainbow, Compaq, Wang, MS-DOS, CP/M
Promot	CP/M, MP/M, TURBO-DOS
dBase II Utilities	CP/M

SPREADSHEET SOFTWARE

Another class of programs that can be a great aid to analysis is that known as spreadsheet software. A spreadsheet program is one that enables you to devise theoretical or hypothetical models and make a series of trial fits, on the basis of "what if?" assumptions. By entering a series of known factors and then trying different variations, you can make projections of the results of electing certain alternatives. For example, you might wish to determine the probable effects of raising your prices on your annual profit and loss statement. You will probably lose some business by raising your prices (that is a reasonable assumption, although sometimes the reverse turns out to be true, surprisingly enough). Perhaps you wish to estimate how much business you could stand to lose, raising your rates by different percentages to see the net effect of each hypothetical increase. By making several trial fits, you can soon arrive at a reasonable estimate of what increase will provide the income you need, with the smallest hazard to your practice (or whatever trade-off you wish to project and calculate).

Such programs can be used in many ways, and some of the more recent "integrated" versions also provide you with graphics capabilities, which are themselves great aids to analysis, since they translate quantified data into graphic representations.

Following are some spreadsheet programs, with brief descriptions, as reported by their developers.

Income & Expense Spreadsheet IV (P): Income and expense accounting, with graphs and full spreadsheet functions.

1-2-3™: Combines electronic spreadsheet, information management, and graphics in a single, fast, easy to use software package.

Supercomp-Twenty: Spreadsheet.

Calc Result: Three-dimensional electronic spreadsheet.

D-CALC™ Financial Analysis System: Spreadsheet.

Eagle-Calc: Electronic spreadsheet with "what if" capabilities.

SOFTWARE FOR PLANNING AND DESIGN

Analysis is a component of design and planning, and there are many software tools designed for that, too. Here are a few samples of such software programs:

MicroGANTT XT: Project planner.

Financial Planner & Asset Management: Professional financial planning service program as client service.

Investments Records Management Aid: Investment planning.

Auto-Load for Finite Element Analysis: Engineering and economic evaluation analysis and design program.

Call Vendor for Information: Structural analysis and design.

Commercial Building Energy Analysis Program: Engineering applications building design.

Critical Path Method Analysis Program: Engineering applications—building design.

Domestic Water Service Supply Program: Engineering applications—building design.

EarthWork/Road Design: Complete road design—cut/fill, balance.

Electrical Distribution Circuit Analysis: Power systems design.

Engineering Applications (CAD) Consulting and Custom Software: Engineering.

SOFTWARE DESIGNED SPECIFICALLY FOR ANALYSIS

File managers, database managers, spreadsheet software, and many other kinds of programs are aids to analysis simply because they are designed to facilitate the organization and handling of information, either generally or for some specific industry, business, or profession. However, there are also many programs which are designed specifically for analysis per se, and so stated by their developers. These programs can save you a great deal of time, as well as lead the way in analyzing many situations that you will be confronted with in your practice; they actually guide you and perform much of the analysis. And even when a program is not a perfect fit, it may very well give you a model and/or methods that will "travel well"—be amenable to adaptation for other situations and uses. In fact, it will be relatively rarely that a program will be a perfect fit, but it will almost always be easier and more efficient to adapt a program to fit your need than to start from scratch to design one.

Following, in no particular order, are some examples of such programs, with the developers' own words describing the nature or objective of the program:

Pro-Forma: Property management and analysis.

PANDEX: Multiple lease—analysis of commercial real estate.

B.I.S.Sourceware—User Access and Tracking Module: Mainframelike user tracking statistics and analysis.

BETA™: Billing and employee time analysis.

BMDP Statistical Software: Data analysis.

Business Analysis: Examines and forecasts data—produces charts.

Business Analyst: Business management.

Business Cycle Analysis: Stores graphs on cycles and trends that aid in decision making.

Business Forecast: Business programs decision support.

Micro-DSS™/Finance: Financial modeling and analysis.

Speedstat: Business analysis.

Graphical Analysis: Use graphs to find relationships between variables.

Powerful Business Software: Integrate O/E, invoicing, inventory control, A/R and sales analysis.

Job Estimator/Cost Tracker: Job estimation, cost tracking, cost analysis.

Questair: Generates customized surveys and analyzes data.

TRANSPORT PC™: Planning tool for distribution/warehousing— provides analysis.

B.I.S. Sourceware—Sales Analysis Module: Analyzes sales by vendor, product, department, profit center, and so on.

CyberKalman: Time series analysis and forecasting.

The Fundamental Investor™: Fundamental securities analysis.

The Intra Day Analyst: On-line "tic by tic" technical analysis of stocks/commodities with graphics.

The Investor's Portfolio™: Portfolio analysis.

The Mortgage Calculator: Yield to cash flow analysis and amortization schedules—mortgages.

Active Circuit Analysis Program: Circuit analysis.

Beam Deflection: Structural analysis.

Grade Beam Analysis: Structural engineering.

Heat Transfer Analysis: Mechanical engineering.

CHAPTER NINE

The Computer as an Aid to Reporting

No matter what your reporting needs are, large or small, formal or informal, there are software programs that are just right for the purpose.

DATABASE MANAGERS VIS-À-VIS REPORT GENERATION

One of the requirements of most consulting projects or assignments is the development and presentation of reports to the client, and one of the many features of database management systems is their facility for generating reports. Of course, that should come as no surprise, considering that the inherent role of the database manager is handling data—organizing, reorganizing, sorting, ordering, reordering, and otherwise manipulating it. In fact, some of the basic functions of database management are designing forms and reports, entering and organizing data (building databases), and generating reports therefrom. The basic nature of the database manager—its very reason for existence, in fact—lies in the presumed need to handle masses of data that must be assembled and organized into coherent patterns. The design presumption is not only data that has a "relational" nature—data that appears to be heterogeneous, perhaps, but has some common threads or basis for interrelationships—but data that is voluminous enough to require and justify the help of a powerful computer system for its management and effective utilization.

There are many database management systems offered—a few were listed in the previous chapter—and they differ widely in their specific characteristics and capabilities. Personal Pearl™ is a relatively simple system, with ample menu and help-screen support, for example, while some others, such as dBase II, offer little in the way of on-screen help and require considerable expertise to use effectively. Also, as you read in the previous chapter, some file managers and database managers are quite general and can be applied to almost any use or situation, while others are designed especially for specific applications, such as bulk mailing, financial management, or the needs of the medical practitioner.

Among the strengths of database managers, in addition to automating and otherwise supporting the sorting and organizing of information, is their ability to handle data on a statistical basis and to select data selectively for reporting. This latter ability is one of the great strengths of relational database managers, in fact, for sometimes the job of analyzing the data and drawing conclusions therefrom is an even bigger job than gathering the data in the first place. However, this is not always the case.

THE INDEPENDENT CONSULTANT AND THE REPORTING NEED

Whether, as a consultant, you need something as elaborate as a database manager to help you meet your reporting obligations is another matter; not every consulting practice requires the handling and management of a great deal of data, at least not data on anything resembling a statistical basis or requiring massive correlations of data items, either informally or formally (via mathematical correlation or other statistical methods). In my own case, for example, a typical reporting need is to render a written and/or verbal judgment on the requirements and critical areas of a given request for proposals; this request includes a work statement and other documentation that requires study. In making such studies and analyses, I do voluminous note-taking, using my word processor to record my notes and observations, and I even construct simple listings, tables, and matrices in extracting and analyzing the important essence of the solicitation, but there is nothing in the process that would be especially aided by a database manager: Neither the bulk of the data nor the nature of the correlations and organizing of it justifies a database management system for my own work, in my judgment (despite the fact that I do have such a system).

This might not be so were I not an independent consultant, for then I might undertake much larger tasks—supporting clients bidding for billion-dollar projects—and the data-gathering would then necessarily be carried out by an entire staff and would result, hence, in a far larger database, probably justifying—even requiring—the use of a relational database manager. However, in my case, and in a great many others, where the practitioner is an independent consultant, the word processor is entirely adequate and far more useful for the task. You will have to judge your own situation for yourself, of course, but if you are an independent consultant and your field does not require you to handle large masses of data, you would do well to consider a fully capable word processor as the principal computer aid to your report writing.

THE WORD PROCESSOR AS A TOOL FOR REPORTING

The word processor is a remarkably versatile and flexible software program, if you have one with full capabilities in both editing and formatting. In fact, many of the features, functions, and capabilities of a good word processor are similar to equivalent features in database managers and other software, while being remarkably open-structured, thus allowing you a great deal of freedom in how you use the features. Here are some of the features in WordStar™, which is a typical full-featured word processor. (In fact, as a pioneer program that has over one million copies in use today, WordStar has been used as a model and/or a standard to be improved on by other developers.)

Files

You can have as many files as your storage permits, and you can name them according to any system you choose, within the constraints of the operating system. (CP/M, for example, permits a prefix of up to eight characters, followed by a period and a suffix of up to three characters, such as WILLIAMS.LTR or BROWNCO.BID. So you can code your file names by types or groups (suffix), with the prefix the unique identifier.

The files can be as large as your storage permits, but floppy disk access is relatively slow, and you will find it agonizing to move around in lengthy disk files. I find it inconvenient to permit my own double-spaced text files to become longer than 15–20 pages, at least while writing. (It's easy enough to join small files later, to form larger files.)

COPYING

Copying anything, from a word to a complete file or even a set of files, is quite easy and can be carried out in an assortment of ways:

The word processor has its own file-copying commands, and you can use these to copy files. Typically, you would use this to "back up" a file—make a duplicate copy (on another disk) and archive it.

The operating system—CP/M, in my case—has its own commands for copying files and is even more convenient to use, for many applications, such as when you wish to copy a whole set of files, or even the entire contents of a disk. Using operating system commands, you can usually do that copying with a single command, whereas most word processors require a separate command for each file you wish to copy.

You can also delete files or any part of a file, and the same rules apply to using the word processor versus using the operating system commands to do so.

On the other hand, for many of the copying chores you will want to carry out, you can do things with the word processor you can't do with the operating system commands—copying portions of files or special items from within files, such as tables and drawings created with the word processor. With most word processors, you can mark the text you want to copy, and copy it as a block, within the same file, to another file on the same disk or to a file on another disk. And you can print out the copy, too, as well as reproduce it elsewhere, without disturbing the original, which will continue to be on record in its own file, ready for copying as often as you wish.

With WordStar there are several ways to do copying, according to what you want to accomplish. If you want a copy of the complete file, you need merely order the system to copy the file and advise where the copy is to be recorded. However, there is another way to do this: You can open a new file and order the computer to "read" the file you want to copy, whereupon the computer will copy the file it is to "read" into the new file you have opened. Or, if you wish to add two files, open the file to which the other is to be added and use the same command, using the cursor to tell the computer where to place the copy in the second file.

If you wish to copy just part of the file, you mark it, as explained, as a block, and move it to a new file. However, if you want to move it to an existing file, you must undertake another step, or else you will lose whatever is already in the target file. To avoid this, you move the copy to a temporary file, then open the file to which you wish to material moved or added, and use the "read" command to copy the material into the existing file. And you can do most of these things in less time than it takes to read these simple explanations.

EDITING AND FORMATTING

The editing and formatting features found in most word processors are extremely helpful in developing reports. But those who are not yet truly familiar with word processors have the idea that word processing is a help principally with the mechanical or production functions, whereas the fact is that the typical word processing features are equally helpful in the creative or generating functions.

Here are some of those mechanical functions and conveniences, several of which are illustrated in Figure 10:

Running Head.   In this case, the running head, which will be carried throughout the report, identifies the document: Report on RFP USDA-82-0056. I chose to make this head boldfaced and underlined, and the program will repeat that head on every page of the report without further instructions from me.

Running Foot.   The foot says "Introduction," and will appear on only those pages that are part of the section titled Introduction. Each time I start a new chapter or section, I will order a new running foot.

Underlining and boldface type are available in most word processors via what are referred to as "embedded instructions." These are commands to the printer, which appear on-screen but are not printed out.

Page numbering is automatic in most systems, unless you order otherwise.

Page numbers, chapter titles, figure legends, headlines, and whatever else you wish can be centered automatically, by a simple command. You need no longer count spaces or measure anything, if you wish something centered on the page.

You can vary margins, use one- or two-column copy, use right-justified or ragged-right copy, and you can vary this in your reports. And with some printers you can vary type fonts and use foreign characters and special symbols.

REMARKS AND COMMENTS

Not everything in the file need be printed. You can enter comments or remarks which serve you as notes and reminders, but which will not be printed out, if you code them properly. The

REPORT ON RFP USDA-82-0056

INTRODUCTION

A TRAINING REQUIREMENT

The Request for Proposals, RFP USDA-82-0056, is a training requirement. It calls for training selected members of the staff of the USDA (U.S. Department of Agriculture) FmHA (Farmers Home Administration) in real estate financing and related procedures, preparatory to an expansion of the FmHA activities and budget increases. It calls for this, in fact, in two major phases of work, which entails two major contractor duties:

Phase I: Training-program development.

Phase II: Training of USDA trainers to deliver the program.

Both are important facets of the requirement, and the client exhibits. in the RFP and statement of work, some anxiety concerning the contractor's expertise in the subject matter, as well as in training technology and staff to carry out Phase II.

In the pages that follow, we'll examine the RFP in detail and suggest the strategies that appear most suitable for winning the contract.

Page 1   Introduction

Figure 10. Some word processor features for reports.

notes will appear on-screen, when you summon the file, however, if you wish to refresh your memory. (You may also use this function to enter special codes to index portions of files for ready access via the "search" function discussed next.)

SEARCH FUNCTIONS

One of the most publicized features—and one that is most useful, in this case—is the search feature. This is a feature in which you order the system to search the file for a given word, term, or phrase. This is useful in several ways:

It is useful when you wish to go swiftly to some interior section of a file. Some word processors enable you to access the file by page numbers. WordStar does not. However, you can use any term you wish as a reference point, such as a figure number or headline.

You may want to use this feature as a convenient way of determining, when you are well into the writing of a report, whether you have or have not already introduced certain terms and information. It is sometimes difficult to remember later what you covered earlier, and in report writing this is especially useful also as a device to aid your research, when you wish to go back through your notes or reference files, to look something up, in the manner of using an index but far more convenient, since the program will "flip the pages" for you.

Most programs also have a "search and replace" version of the function, in which you can have the program go through an entire file and make changes, such as changing every "Blake Manufacturing" to "Black Manufacturing," or every "bear" to "bare." That's an editing function, of course, but useful nonetheless, and certainly a great time saver.

These are some of the mechanical features that make your job easier. But they also help you to create and generate reports, both directly and indirectly. They aid indirectly because they handle so much of the mechanical drudgery and leave you free to concentrate on the creative work. But they aid directly in that too, by providing easy access to the files you have built up and by helping to find the specific information you need.

REFERENCE FILES

Whether you do or do not have reference files, at first, you will soon build them up—or should do so. Here are the kinds of reference files you should accumulate over time, and perhaps some of them in the beginning:

Basic data, such as standards, mathematical tables, circuits, professional papers (proceedings), articles.

Your own file of reports prepared in the past.

Banks of data—relevant databases—acquired over time. (Even if you do not have use for a DBMS in the beginning, over time your databases may grow large enough to require and justify such a program.)

Notes and documents on the project in process.

Databases you have acquired via downloading information from online databases and information services. This is an especially important source of reference data for both immediate and future use, and should be discussed at some length.

ONLINE DATABASES

Online databases, which are banks of information—databases—available via computer-to-computer communication, using telephone lines and dialing the services in what are called "dial-up" connections, are a rich source of information. They can be valuable as an aid for report-writing purposes, as they are for marketing and many other needs—"CBD Online," mentioned earlier, for example. The earlier references were brief and fleeting, necessarily, and did not explore the subject in any depth. This is an appropriate place to explore it more deeply, as a readily accessible information source for reports and kindred uses.

There are many online information services, and their number is growing steadily. Probably the best way to offer a full appreciation of these services is via the following representative sample, with brief notes on what each offers. Studying these entries and the notes that accompany them will constitute a valuable education in online information services and what they can mean to you. Be advised, however, that this is by no means a complete listing nor are these comprehensive descriptions of the services offered. The listing was selected to give you a cross-section of the kinds of services and information being made available via these subscription services.

Be aware, first of all, that in some cases the online service offers access to its own databases—databases the service owns. In other cases, the service does not own the databases—or not all the databases it offers access to—but has made arrangements to provide subscribers with connections to databases others own.

They do this by connecting you to one of the many networks—Tymnet, Uninet, Telenet, or other. Or you dial-up one of these networks by dialing a local telephone number to gain access to the service, which may be at some distance from your own location.

Because online services sometimes arrange to connect subscribers to other people's databases, you may find that more than one online service can connect you up with the same database. Or, to put it another way, you may find that you can get the same information or database access via several services, so it would behoove you to investigate rather closely just what each service offers: You may be able to get a better service or the same service for a better price elsewhere.

You may even find that you can get direct access to a given online service, but that you can also gain access to it via another online service. For example, you can subscribe directly to NewsNet, but the Customer Service Bureau in Wyoming will also put you through to NewsNet. Therefore, we see the need to research and shop carefully, if you want to be sure that you have done the best for yourself that you can.

THE CHARGES

Charges for subscribers can include any or all of the following:

Initial charge: Some services, such as The Source and CompuServe, charge an initial regisitration fee.

Connect time: Most charge by the hour or fraction thereof (e.g., minutes)—or by the minute, which is the same thing—for the time you are connected to the service.

Many make additional charges, depending on what database you want to use or what service you want.

In many cases you must subscribe to the service generally and then to each individual element you want to use.

Many make a minimum monthly charge.

In all cases, when you are connected with the service via long-distance dial-up connection, you are paying the tolls. But in many cases, you are paying both AT&T tolls and a use charge for the network you are routed through. But even this does not tell the whole story, for the methods and basis for the charges vary even beyond these. Customer Service Bureau, for example, charges a membership fee ($5/month or $50/year), for which you are entitled to 20 "accesses" per month, plus 25 cents for each additional one. (The literature does not state how long an access you may have.) But there are also database charges and telecommunications charges made, the exact database charges not stated, but quoted on request.

Here, then, is the sampling:

Nielsen Business Services.   Offers Nielsen Retail Index, reports on consumer responses and purchases at point of sale for food, drug, health, and beauty aid products, based on reports prepared by Nielsen auditors. Offers insights into brand distribution, prices, and sundry related data.

ADP Network Services, Inc.   A division of Automatic Data Processing; provides subscriber access to several databases of business-oriented information, via network connections.

Customer Service Bureau.   Primarily a service that connects you to other databases or information utilities, including BRS, CompuServe, Dialog, Dun & Bradstreet, NewsNet, and several others.

BRS (Bibliographic Retrieval Services).   Covers more than 80 databases over many fields—sciences, education, taxes, law, finances, industry, investments, publications, and other.

Dialog Information Retrieval Service.   Offers access to hundreds of databases on business management, advertising, economics, politics, commerce, government, company finances, industries, corporations, investment, law, patents, medicine, agriculture, and computers.

LEXIS, Mead Data Central.   Online legal research service; user may search full text of federal cases and can find cases by various search terms—judge, court, date, place, counsel, statute, or other. Information available from *Federal Register*, *Encyclopaedia Britannica*, and other publications.

LEXPAT, Mead Data Central.   Full-text patent-search service: files on utility patents, plant patents, design patents, patent numbers with classification, manual classification, and index to manual classification.

NewsNet. Business-oriented information utility accessing many sources of investment and other business information.

NEXIS, Mead Data Central.   General news information service; provides subscribers access to many news publications in electronic editions.

On-Line Research, Inc. Access to databases through timesharing service, including Frost & Sullivan's Market Reports, U.S. Census for Agriculture, U.S. Census of Retail Trade, U.S. Demographics/town resident files, and others.

TRW Information Services Division. Financial reports and business credit reporting service. Also offers credit reports on individuals.

Westlaw, West Publishing Co. Law reviews, government updates, accounting and financial data, data on divorces, product liability, bankruptcy, and other legal matters.

These are just a few of the commercial online databases and information services; there are many more. But there are also many online databases and information services that are not commercial, or at least do not charge fees. There is a rapidly growing number of these databases who do not charge for their services or charge only nominal fees, many of them operated by government agencies, others by nonprofit organizations, and a few by for-profit organizations but making no charge because they operate the services as a marketing or sales-promotion device. But there is also that class of online systems known as "BBs"—the electronic bulletin boards introduced briefly in an earlier chapter as a source for free software. But the bulletin boards are also a source for information, too, and on occasion are quite valuable.

Electronic bulletin boards, you will recall, are operated by hobbyists, computer clubs, businesses, and government agencies. Clubs and bulletin boards are listed in several of the popular computer magazines—*Link Up, Micro Communications, Microsystems, Computer Shopper*, and others.

A great many of those who access the bulletin boards are relative newcomers to computers, but a great many are relative experts, too, some of them hobbyists who are more expert than the professionals. (A not unusual condition today.)

But there is another aspect to this, too: Many people use these bulletin boards as a medium of information exchange and even as a social outlet, conducting meetings, discussion groups, and other exchanges both "in real time"—spontaneously, while all are online together—and "offline"—leaving messages, to be read by others and responded to at leisure.

A great many of the people you will "meet" via such online connections are executives and professionals in their own right—in their own fields, if not in computer technology. So you may very well make contact, via the online connection, with highly knowledgeable people who can be most valuable contacts. Many fruitful relationships are established in this manner.

CHAPTER TEN

The Computer as an Aid to Presentations

The versatility of the computer continues to demonstrate itself, as it makes its valuable contributions to this additional arena of the consulting practice: preparing materials and making presentations, formal and informal.

PRESENTATIONS: WHY AND WHEN

For most consultants, making presentations is more than an occasional need. There are at least three occasions, generally, when the consultant must make a presentation or is expected to make one:

1.   Presentations are a key element in early or general marketing—in making your name, your presence, and your services known publicly–and in building an image and developing leads, as a general promotional (PR, public relations) activity, a critically important element of your marketing—that activity that precedes actual selling efforts, that is.

2.   Presentations are also a frequent must in selling—in making the actual closings of specific sales, especially for the more important contracts. Every close is inevitably and necessarily a presentation, whether formal or informal.

3.   But the need goes beyond sales and marketing, important though those needs are: Formal or semiformal presentation of progress and results, at both critical milestones and at the conclusion of projects, are expected by many clients, and are a good practice even when clients do not demand them. In fact, in some cases and for some kinds of consulting services, presentations are themselves actually inherent elements of the consulting service itself—the media or mechanism by which the service is rendered.

Much of what was said in the previous chapter about report writing has equal validity when applied to the preparation of presentations. In fact, some presentations are actually reports delivered orally, and the substance is the same, although the preparation involves other tasks and other products. But let's first examine each of the three listed occasions for making presentations first, and then look into how the computer aids in the task of preparing to make the presentations.

THE PR PRESENTATION: IMAGE BUILDING AND PROMOTION

It is usually as unproductive for the independent consultant to pursue consulting assignments by conventional advertising and sales promotion—"huckstering" methods—as it is for physicians, lawyers, and other professionals to do so. Even now that lawyers are permitted to engage in classical advertising in the media, few do, and no lawyer who pursues the "carriage trade" would dream of using commercial advertising, for fear of injuring his or her professional image beyond repair.

Like the physician, lawyer, dentist, and other professionals, the consultant's success in marketing to anything remotely resembling the equivalent of the "carriage trade" for consultants depends primarily on his or her image. An image as a huckster would be far more likely to repel the prospective clients than to attract them. Like the other professionals cited here, the independent consultant must pursue business in a different way, in a more discreet and more dignified way, not because law or professional societies dictate this arbitrarily, but because practical considerations—what works and what doesn't work—dictates this.

"TRUTH" AND "IMAGE" AS SALES ARGUMENTS

This is true because in any marketing, even when selling everyday products, "truth" is critically important. "Truth," however, is a word that must be qualified here: Truth is not an absolute quantity for anyone, especially not for the marketer. Truth, for the marketer, must be the prospective buyer's truth—the prospect's perception. That's the only truth or perception that counts, in marketing, for prospects buy according to their own perceptions, not to yours. And when it comes to professional services, you can read "image," in place of "truth" or "perception," for you will develop an image, and it is largely on that image that the prospect will judge you.

In discussing marketing earlier, the point was made that whatever you are selling—and often it is actually only a promise that you are selling—success in persuading the prospect to buy depends heavily on how much evidence you can provide that you can and will make good on the promise—that you will actually deliver what you promised. In selling yourself as a consultant, a large part of that evidence is your image: what the prospect sees in you. Obviously, you must work at creating an attractive and persuasive image, since it is you—you, personally, with your personal skills, sincerity, dedication, and integrity—that the prospect is asked to trust. Yes, buying the services of a doctor, lawyer, dentist, or consultant is investing in *trust*. In fact, the very success of the services provided by the professional may depend largely on the trust or what the patient/client *believes* he or she is receiving.

In light of this, a large part of your marketing must consist of doing the same things that these other professionals do to build their own practices: Engage in many activities that make you known to people who are likely prospects for your services and/or who are likely to send you referrals. These are some of the things you can and should do, along those lines:

Join as many of the right associations and professional societies as possible. Volunteer for committees, join special-interest groups, do whatever will help you widen your circle of business and professional friends and associates.

Attend the various conventions, conferences, and other such conclaves, and participate actively in them.

Speak to groups as often as possible, not necessarily for fees, but primarily for exposure.

Write books, contribute written articles to professional journals and other periodicals, write letters to the editor, and do anything else that either produces some PR itself or helps produce PR. (For example, such writings can easily lead to being invited to speak to groups and/or to join the groups.)

Do's and Don'ts of the PR Presentation

Bear in mind, in preparing PR presentations, what you are trying to accomplish. Or perhaps it is best to first list those things you are *not* trying to accomplish:

You are *not* trying to demonstrate that you are a silver-tongued orator.

You are *not* trying to demonstrate polemics—argumentative—skills.

You are *not* making a sales pitch.

You are *not* arguing the merits of your services, your field, or consulting per se.

What you *are* trying to accomplish includes these things:

You *are* trying to establish your credentials as a qualified consultant in your field, but indirectly, not directly.

You *are* trying to gain attention as a serious and competent specialist in your field, with something to say that is worth listening to.

You *are* trying to make your special services clear—discreetly—not blatantly.

You *are* trying to arouse interest in your field and indirectly in the kind of services you offer.

You *are* trying to be interesting enough to keep your audience wide awake and to encourage interest in inviting you back to speak again and/or invite you to speak elsewhere.

You *are* trying to be interesting enough and persuasive enough to encourage listeners to seek you out after you have left the platform, to engage you in follow-up private conversation.

That last-named objective deserves at least a paragraph or two of special discussion, because it is perhaps the most important objective in that it is often the one that most often leads directly to winning clients.

The Post-Presentation Discussion

When you have been sufficiently enthusiastic and persuasive—persuading listeners that you know what you are talking about and that the kind of services you specialize in are productive in terms of results—you will often find individuals from the audience seeking you out afterwards, at the first opportunity, to ask questions and pursue discussion. Each of these should be regarded as a good prospect, because many of them will be. (I have gotten many of my best assignments in this way.) If they know that you are a consultant—and you should see to it that they do, as we will cover in a moment—they may very well wish to explore the possibility of utilizing your services.

This is not to say that you may solicit business directly, when you speak, either in your presentation or in private discussion following. Using someone else's platform and audience for open solicitation is not only in bad taste, but is in violation of a generally accepted ethical code that you are someone's guest when you speak at someone else's meeting, and to use their platform for huckstering your own wares blatantly is a no-no. (Although it is acknowledged and recognized that this is your ultimate objective, the selling must be extremely low-key—indirect and discreet.) However, in meeting with individuals who seek you out, you may (and should) certainly exchange cards, and you may discuss possible assignments discreetly, schedule follow-up meetings and/or follow-up calls with the individual, and otherwise utilize the occasion. That, after all, is why you make the talks. But do all of this discreetly and in good taste: It is quite easy to offend others, when they perceive your actions as gross, unethical, or generally in bad taste, and so you defeat your basic purposes in making the presentation to begin with.

It's a Public Presentation

It is important to remember that in addition to being a PR presentation—that is its *purpose* —this is also a *public* presentation—that is its nature. It is a presentation made to an audience who, as a rule (although there may be exceptions), do not know you and probably do not know of you, either. Therefore, when making presentations of this kind you are generally introduced by someone, usually someone who is acting as the host.

This is where and how you do whatever selling and promotion are ethically and in the interests of good taste permitted you: whoever introduces you must explain who and what you are, provide some background, especially your credentials, and explain to the audience how fortunate they are to have the opportunity to listen to such an eminent expert as you.

Write Your Own Introduction

Professional speakers go off to their engagements fully prepared for this. (Many professional speakers are also consultants or engaged in other professional fields, and they want to be sure that audiences know what else they have to offer. They *make it a standard practice to write their own introductions.*)

In fact, you are likely to find that those who introduce you will often ask you if you have a prepared text to use in introducing you, because they have become accustomed to professional speakers having such a text.

The word processor is an enormous aid, in this respect, especially if you have different kinds of presentations to make on different occasions. But even if you are making the same presentation many times, you may want to vary the introduction some, for several reasons:

Your credentials may change, especially if you write books and serve in organizations, and you want to always include the newest and most impressive credentials in each introduction.

If you speak on different topics, that is likely to change the items you wish to have stressed in your introduction.

You may want to stress different kinds of credentials for different audiences. For example, if you write books, you may be invited to address one group of individuals about writing and publishing books, whereas you may also be scheduled to speak to a second group about the nature of consulting work and to a third group about the special field in which you consult. Even if you use the same basic information for each introduction, you probably will want to rearrange the order in which the information is presented and where the stress is placed in each case.

One word of caution: Resist the temptation to say too much in your introduction. Make all the important points—your main achievements—but try not to make it longer than can be typed on an index card, or you may find your host doing some serious editing of your copy to shorten it to manageable length.

Writing The Presentation(s)

Unless you are in a position to use the same presentation over and over—and eventually that must wear out and be replaced with something else—you will be writing new presentations frequently. Abraham Lincoln wrote his Gettysburg Address on the back of an envelope, en route to Gettysburg by train, according to what has now become a popular legend, but you need not be so handicapped: You can put modern electronics magic to work. And like the introductory remarks, you may be able to draw on the same basic information in each case.

Here, as in the case of report writing, you can draw on information you have resident in reference files, and use the legerdemain of the speedy electron to do cut-and-paste, trial fits, and whatever else you need to do to create the copy you want.

But that is not all the computer and word processor can do for you. They can also support your needs for presentation aids, such as posters, transparencies, and handouts.

Making Presentation Aids

Probably the most popular and least expensive presentation aid is the transparency or view-graph, an 8 × 10-inch acetate used in conjunction with an overhead projector to project a large image on a screen.

In fact, transparencies can be made on any office copier, by copying material onto an acetate sheet, rather than onto paper. And the copy can be prepared by typewriter or by any other means, including computer printer. However, the so-called letter-quality printer, which uses a daisy-wheel printing element, can produce copy only in the conventional typewriter-size fonts, although these will be magnified, of course, when projected onto a large screen. Also, you can develop tables, matrices, and simple graphics, such as those shown earlier as a form of "home made" graphics created with ordinary word processing resources.

On the other hand, dot-matrix printers offer much larger type sizes and even graphics representations that are somewhat more sophisticated than those shown earlier in this book. (See Figures 11 and 12.)

These are in black and white, but it is possible also to generate such graphics in color with some dot-matrix printers. However, even more professional transparencies are possible with plotters, which draw with pens and produce graphics of higher quality than either type of printer can.

At present, plotters are relatively expensive, and probably their

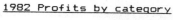

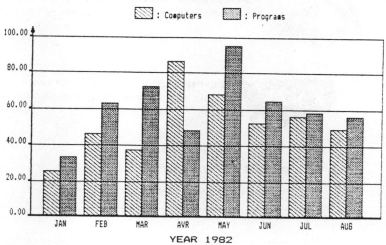

1982 Sales by products (thousands of dollars)

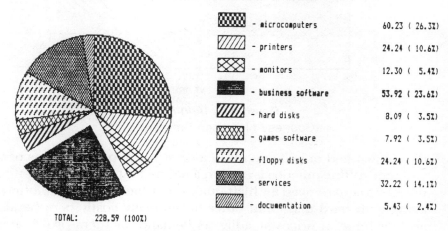

TOTAL: 228.59 (100%)

Figure 11.   Charts generated on dot-matrix printers.
(Courtesy of Krepec Software Inc.)

KREPEC Software INC.
5460 Royalmount, suite 208, Montreal, Quebec, Canada H4P 1H8 tel:(514) 735-4749

COMPANY XYZ Inc.
1000 blvd. Sunshine, Midtown, USA, 99999 tel:(000) 222-3333

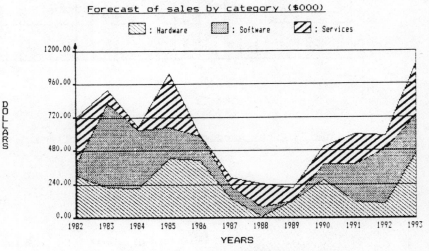

Figure 11. *(Continued)*
(Courtesy of Krepec Software Inc.)

cost is justified only if you make a great many presentations or if your consulting practice is of such a nature that you have a continuous or frequent need for high-quality graphics. However, plotters, along with hard disks and other traditionally costly peripherals, are declining in prices steadily, as demand for them proliferates and an expanding market enables manufacturers to begin to realize the economies of mass production. Hence, it is probably a good idea to stay in touch with the market for these almost-indispensable machines.

ABCDEF 012345

ABCDEFGHI 01234567

ABCDE 01234

ABCDEFG 0123456

ABC 012

ABCD 0123

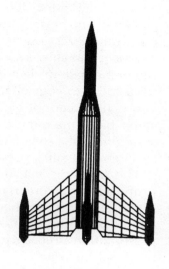

Figure 12.   Graphics and large type generated on Qantex dot-matrix printer.
(Courtesy of North Atlantic Industries)

SALES PRESENTATIONS: WHEN, WHERE, WHY

Almost everyone has need to make fairly frequent sales presentations, since it is relatively rare, in the consulting field, to win a contract or assignment without making a presentation before closing
the sale. What has gone before is prologue and has been the
means to generate leads—find interested prospects—but usually a
solid presentation is necessary before the sale can be consum-
mated. However, there are different situations surrounding the
sales presentation, as there are for other presentations, and to explore these and methods for handling each we need to digress
slightly and discuss the various sales situations first:

    First of all, there are many situations in which the sales presen-
tation is spontaneous and impromptu, made because an opportunity arises and it is necessary or advisable to make the presenta-

tion immediately, if you are to be able to take full advantage of the opportunity. It's true enough, usually, for the sizable project, that a series of marketing/sales/sales efforts must be made before the sale can finally be closed. But that is not generally true for small sales. For example, if you meet someone who turns out to be a good prospect and shows serious interest immediately, and especially if the immediate project is likely to be a rather small one, it may be destructive to your chances to delay making a sales presentation. You usually cannot close large sales without several preparatory steps, but quite often the small sales must be closed on the spot, spontaneously, so you must always be prepared to make informal, spontaneous sales presentations.

The large project, on the other hand, will usually call for a proposal—give you an opportunity to offer a proposal, that is—as noted in an earlier chapter. The proposal is itself a presentation, offered in written form, of course. However, quite often at least one presentation preceded the invitation or opportunity to write the proposal, and often a verbal presentation must follow it. In bidding to government agencies, for example, the contracting officials quite often call for formal presentations after the proposals are evaluated, before reaching a final decision, and proposers then appear before a panel or number of government executives and specialists to put on their "dog and pony show," as many describe this kind of presentation.

SOME SPECIAL SITUATIONS AND GAMES CLIENTS PLAY

Clients sometimes disguise their requests for presentations with other names, or describe the occasion as an opportunity to discuss the proposal, but in fact a more or less formal presentation is desired and is expected.

In some situations, all preliminary discussions and agreements have been made on a tentative basis with someone who must yet get formal approval from higher management in the organization. In fact, some organizations deliberately arrange things in this manner: To conserve the time of senior executives, less-senior ones do all the preliminary work of seeking out candidate consultants and handling all the preliminary discussing and negotiating, and only when the candidate has survived all of that—or when the executive has screened all candidates and chosen one—is the final approval given by the senior managers. Or, as a variant on this, several candidates may be accepted at the lower level, and the final choice among them made by the senior managers, after each of the candidates has submitted an acceptable proposal and made a presentation.

This means, then, that you may be making a sales presentation that is only a pro forma act, or you may be making a presentation that will be decisive in winning or failing to win the contract. You may be making a presentation to confirm all that has gone before—including a proposal—or you may be making one in competition with several other candidates.

Usually you have no reliable way of determining which is the case, so you are compelled to proceed on the assumption that the client is entirely sincere and honest in what he or she represents to you and asks of you. This may sound a bit naive, for we know that this is not always the case, but there is no other way to approach this that would not be self-defeating. And, in consequence, it is important to always make your best effort to be convincing and persuasive. But that is not all of it, either: Frequently these so-called presentations turn into inquisitions, in which you face a group of the client's staff, and are examined and cross-examined by them, in what has then become far more a stress interview than a presentation!

GUERRILLA TACTICS IN PREPARING THE SALES PRESENTATION

As in other situations, the computer, especially the word processor, is a great aid in several ways: In addition to all the help it can provide in preparing presentation materials, as described earlier in this chapter, it provides ready access to your reference files, enabling you to prepare and bring along a voluminous set of notes. These can be invaluable, of course, in fielding some of those questions that are thrown at you. However, the system can be used to create an even more effective defensive measure: Prepare an extensive presentation guide—a detailed and comprehensive set of notes and/or an equally detailed and comprehensive outline, for example—and make up copies for your listeners, as handouts.

This has a beneficial effect psychologically, in that it suggests strongly complete and intensive preparation on your part, and that discourages questions intended to "wring you out," rather than inspired by sincere desire for information.

Another effective defensive measure, in those situations when you are to make a presentation as a follow-up to a proposal, is to invite the client to suggest areas of coverage and, especially, to submit questions in advance. And if you succeed in eliciting specific response to these invitations, list each of those items prominently in your presentation guide and cover them as thoroughly as possible.

Take Advantage of Everything the Computer Can Do for You

For example, don't hand out poor xerographic copies of your presentation. Unless you are sure that you can get crisp, clear copies of your material, use your printer (hopefully, a letter-quality printer) to make as many *original* copies as you need for your audience, when making a sales presentation. (And even when you can get good xerographic copies, it is usually obvious that they are xerographic copies, and it is still a better idea to make all the copies "originals," as described. Make your presentation show clearly that you *care* about winning the contract or assignment, as well as that you know what you are talking about.)

Use Graphics Freely

Graphics are even more important here, when you are trying to close an actual sale, than they are in the PR presentation, when you are trying to generate leads and build an image and awareness of your existence. Charts and plots tend to make everything you present far more credible because they are *specific* and *quantified*. But don't reinvent the wheel: Use what you have already in files by adapting stored graphics to your current need, when possible. Review what you have, while studying your current need, and make a distinct effort to find as many appropriate graphics as possible. Presentations tend to be more impressive when you have lots of graphics, probably because they suggest that you have worked hard to develop a carefully crafted presentation.

Be Aggressive

Unlike the PR presentation, when you are the ultra-polite guest in someone else's domicile, in making a sales presentation you are clearly and definitely after the contract or assignment, and you should be entirely "up front" with the client about it, while still genteel and dignified. ("Aggressive" is not a synonym for "belligerent," although some people seem to be unaware of that when they are trying to close a sale.) One serious mistake some consultants make when trying to make a sale is an apparent reluctance to admit that they really want the sale!

They apparently do this as a result of confusion. Well aware as they are of the need to appear to be successful and not appear to be "hungry," they tend to exhibit a feigned diffidence about the contract, apparently believing that this shows their great success and resultant ability to be relaxed about winning new business. This is, of course, not the same thing at all. You can certainly make it clear that you are quite serious about wanting the contract, and that you are dedicated to winning it, not because you are "hard up" for work, but because winning and performing on such contracts is your profession, and you are a dedicated professional. Therefore, make it clear, *again and again,* as you present your material, that you *want* the contract and are fighting to win it. There must not be the slightest doubt in your prospect's mind about this, if you wish to be taken seriously.

PRESENTATIONS AS ONE OF THE CONSULTING SERVICES

Some years ago, having completed a project for the Postal Service Training & Development Institute, which many of the Institute's staff thought to be an ill-conceived waste of time and money, the consultant-contractor who had done the job was faced with a hostile audience when he was required to make a presentation of his final product. And it was a large audience, too, numbering over 20 men and women around a large conference table. Fortunately for the consultant, he was made of stern stuff and managed to survive this particular gang of wolves who tried desperately to prove that the project could not possibly have produced a useful result because they had decided in advance that it could not. Fortunately for most independent consultants, that kind of situation is far more the exception than it is the rule, although when a consultant must make a presentation of progress or results to a group of the client's staff, there are often occasional nonadmirers in that group who hope to skin the consultant.

This delivering the product and/or final results is just one of the several situations in which making a presentation is part of the consulting service itself. In this situation the consultant is expected to brief everyone concerned, explaining the result, answering questions, even conducting some informal indoctrination or training, which is what such presentations often turn out to be, in substance. But there are several variants of this, all situations in which preparing and making presentations are part of the consulting service.

Progress Reporting

In the case cited here, the consultant was asked to present the final results of the project to an assembled group of the client's staff, whereas throughout the project the consultant's liaison had been with the client's project manager only. In many other cases, the consultant must make several presentations over the life of the project, usually to report progress, discuss problems, and answer the client's questions.

Such presentations tend to be rather informal, requiring only that the consultant be ready to answer all questions and satisfy the client. Be aware, however, that while in most cases the client's staff tend to regard consultants with respect and even awe, as especially well qualified experts, in other cases the client's staff members see the consultant as an outsider and a potential threat to their own existence. The wise consultant will do whatever is possible to allay such fears and to win the cooperation and respect of the staff.

The final presentation of such a series is usually much more formal than are the progress review presentations. Now the staff wants to know what the final results are and be briefed in whatever those results mean to them. Here, a comprehensive handout—a detailed manual, for example—may have been required by contract, but even if it has not been, if the project is such that the staff will want to be briefed and ask questions, it is a good idea to provide whatever documentation you can.

Some contracts will call for formal training presentations as part of the required services. In such cases you will have to prepare such materials as are required, to include any or all of the following:

Lesson plan	Learning aids
Syllabus	Pre- and post-tests
Lecture guide	Study guide
Text (manual)	Completion certificate
Instructor guide	

CHAPTER ELEVEN

Computer Aid in Preparing Seminars

Seminars are or should be an important element in the independent consultant's practice. The computer can help substantially in the development of seminars and make major contributions to overall consulting success.

TWO "KINDS" OF SEMINARS

There are two principal ways in which you can utilize seminars commercially, as part of your independent consulting practice, to produce income. They are:

1. Offer seminars in a public place, with everyone welcome to attend, at a given fee for attendance.
2. Present seminars on a contract basis for clients, as an in-house program, offered as a custom consulting service.

Each of these merits its own discussion, but before embarking on that we must have a look at a few other matters, especially how seminars fit into the general picture of your activities as an independent consultant or how seminars can make their greatest contribution to your overall success.

WHAT DO/SHOULD SEMINARS REPRESENT TO YOU?

Seminars can be any or all of several things to you, as they are to many other practitioners, included the following possibilities:

1. They may be a single element of your regular professional services—a training element—including in some, if not all, of your consulting contracts.

2. They may be a separate service to clients, one of the services you render as a consultant.

3. They may be a separate enterprise, which you conduct as part of your overall practice.

4. They may be the principal element in your activities as a consultant, your main commercial enterprise.

5. They may be an effective marketing tool, used to make both PR and marketing/sales presentations. (Free seminars—usually miniseminars—are used by many consultants and other specialists as an effective PR and marketing device. That was not touched on in an earlier chapter discussing the computer as an aid to marketing, to avoid fragmenting the discussion of seminars, but will be discussed later in this chapter.)

In discussing the role of the computer in preparing presentations we touched briefly on the subject of training presentations, of which the seminar is an example. However, in terms of how these several factors affect what you do and how you do it, what we want to discuss in this chapter is principally the seminar as a direct income-producing element of your services, an element that produces income of itself, rather than as one of general consulting activities contracted for (although inevitably we will have to deal with all the factors, when we discuss seminar design, content, and other technical aspects). And, of course, we want to consider what the computer contributes or can contribute to this process. But first let us consider the two main ways in which seminars can be utilized as income-producers, for therein lie some of the main differences in what you, as the entrepreneur, must do to gain all the advantages of what seminars can do for you as a commercial undertaking. (And the differences also affect strongly how you will employ your computer to help produce, promote, and support seminar activity in various ways.)

SEMINAR ANATOMY

Before exploring in depth the subject of what seminars mean to the independent consultant and how they can be brought into play to contribute to your overall success, we need to be sure that we have a common understanding of what a seminar is. Like a great many terms, the word "seminar" is today employed to describe and refer to an event that rarely resembles or conforms to the dictionary definition or classical meaning applied to it.

A General Definition

In theory, a seminar is a small group gathered to conduct advanced study in some single aspect of a subject area, under the guidance or leadership of someone qualified to lead the group. (The leader is not necessarily the instructor nor the sole source of information, since in theory the group may be conducting discussion, introspection, brain-storming, research, and other discovery learning processes.) In practice, a seminar is a small group (but that word "small" is a relative term, of course, and may mean 10 or 15 people, but may also mean 150 or 200 people) being taught some presumably specialized subject by someone who is represented to have some qualifying credentials as an expert/instructor in the subject. However, in practice the subject may or may not be "advanced" study, and may or may not be in a truly specialized subject. In fact, seminars are offered today in a wide variety of subjects, such as speed reading, investing, real estate, office practices, word processing, proposal writing, marketing, salesmanship, multilevel sales, handling stress, management, legal specialties, and an untold number of other subjects, some specialized and possibly advanced, others relatively mundane and not truly specialized.

Length

Seminars can run to a fairly wide range of lengths, but they do generally fall between the extremes of one-half day to five days, with probably the vast majority offered as one-, two-, or three-day sessions.

Target Attendees

Intended registrants or attendees for such seminars varies as widely as do other matters, from the highly specialized technical/ professional expert, through the general executive or manager, to the midlevel managers and specialists, and to the general office worker. It is, in many ways, more useful to divide intended audiences into the two groups of those who attend at their own expense to gain personal benefits and those who attend at employers' expense to make greater contributions to the employers' organization. And even this definition is not quite as clear-cut as it may appear, as you will see eventually.

Content and Design

The basic design of a seminar is that of a series of lecture presentations, usually with visual aids and handouts, often with exercises for the attendees, to give them some hands-on or application experience, and presented by one or more individuals. Many, especially one-day seminars, are handled exclusively by one individual presenter/leader, while others offer presentations by several instructors or leaders. Many also include general discussions, for active interaction between instructors and attendees.

Costs

"Open registration" seminars—those held in public places, with everyone invited to attend, for a fee—vary somewhat in the fees they charge, but the typical fees, at the time of this writing, are approximately $200 per day—$595 for a 3-day seminar, for example— although the trend in fees has been steadily upward, climbing perhaps even more rapidly than are costs in general. The fees charged for offering seminars as in-house programs, on a custom basis, vary even more, so much so that it is almost impossible to suggest any typical rates here. However, we can note, in passing, that such fees range from whatever the consultant's normal daily fee is to special fees, depending on circumstances to be discussed later in this chapter.

PR/Marketing Seminars

These will be discussed in some detail later in this chapter, but it is worth observing here that since the purpose of such seminars is the dual one of PR (as in making presentations for PR purposes) and making direct sales, such seminars present mere "teasers" of whatever is being promoted and are structured to make direct sales—closes—and generate sales leads for subsequent closing. This will show up later, when we discuss these seminars more closely.

Now let us discuss each of these matters in greater depth.

SEMINAR SUBJECTS

The first requisite is a general subject for a seminar, and that subject must be such that it provides a *reason* for the seminar—a reason, that is, for attendance. On that point alone will hinge your success or failure as a seminar producer, to a large extent. And on that point alone will hinge, to a large extent, how much attendees will be willing to pay and whether the seminar must depend on individuals to attend at their own expense or whether employers will be willing to send employees, at the employers' expense.

To illustrate this immediately, consider the two seminar outlines shown in Figures 13 and 14. These are both samples of actual advertising brochures for seminars held as open-registration events, for which anyone can register and attend by paying the registration fees.

Study these for a moment and consider the intended audiences for each of these. Before you read further, make your own estimate of whether either or both of these appeal primarily to individuals who must pay their own registration (attendance) fees or to employers who would send employees at the organizations' expense. This will be a useful exercise, if only to provoke you to think about this. Then read on, and let's discuss this question.

In some respects the question has been a trick one because em-

---

SEMINAR OUTLINE

Proposals for Government Contracts
How to Develop Winning Proposals

8:30 a.m. - REGISTRATION, coffee and pastries
9:00 a.m. - Session Begins

I. The $160 Billion Market
   a. Understanding the market
   b. What the government buys
   c. How to sell to the government.

II. Locating Sales Opportunities
   a. How to uncover selling opportunities.
   b. Getting on the appropriate bidder's list.
   c. How to use the *Commerce Business Daily* as an effective marketing tool.
   d. How to use the Freedom of Information Act to market.

III. Proposal Strategy Development
   a. Why proposals?
   b. What is a proposal?
   c. What does the customer want?
   d. What must the proposal do?
   e. What makes a winner?
   f. Why strategy makes the difference.

IV. The Stages of Proposal Development
   a. Bid/no-bid analysis and decision.
   b. Requirement analysis—understanding the requirements.
   c. Indentification of the critical factor(s).
   d. Formulation of the approach and technical/program/pricing strategies.
   e. Formulation of the capture strategy.
   f. Establishing the theme.
   g. Design and presentation strategy.
   h. Writing the proposal.

V. Persuasive Proposal Writing
   a. What is persuasion?
   b. The art of persuasive writing.
   c. What makes others agree?
   d. What turns them on? And off?

VI. How to Write a Winning Proposal
   a. Writing to communicate.
   b. Writing to sell.
   c. Writing to arouse and sustain interest.
   d. Your proposal should promise desirable end-results.
   e. Your proposal should, preferably, be a unique claim, one your competitors can't match.
   f. Your proposal must be able to prove it's validity.

VII. Formats and Proposal Content
   a. Recommended format.
   b. Front matter and other elements.
   c. How to use format for best results.

VIII. Cost Justification in Proposals
   a. Understanding costs.
   b. What the government expects in cost proposals.
   c. Technical vs. cost proposal.
   d. Construction of the quote.
   e. How to make bids.

Figure 13.   Outline for seminar on proposal writing.

SEMINAR OUTLINE

I. Introduction
A. What Is a Consultant Today?
 Which Type of Consultant Are You?
 The Essential Elements of Consulting Services.
B. Marketing as the Key to Consulting Success.
 Are Technical Skills Enough?
 Mastering Sales and Marketing Skills.

II. Understanding the Marketing Process
A. The Three Elements of Marketing Successfully.
B. The Elements of Selling: Promise and Proof.

III. Marketing Your Consulting Services Generally
A. The Basic Need to Instill Confidence.
B. How to Gain Prestige and Build a Professional Image.
C. Developing the All-Important Leads.
D. Following Up Leads Correctly.

IV. Marketing To The Public Sector
A. Understanding Public Sector Markets.
B. The Skill of Proposal Writing.

V. Broadening The Base of Your Consulting Practice.
A. Expand Your Profit Centers.
B. Writing: How To Write and Sell Successfully.
C. Publishing: Including newsletters, reports, books, tapes.
D. Public Speaking For Profit.

VI. Open Discussion.

Figure 14.   Outline for seminar on consulting.

ployers might send employees to either one, but individuals also attend both as individuals. However, even in the latter case the individuals are attending as employees because they are generally self-employed or proprietors of small businesses. That is almost inevitable in the case of seminars dealing with business matters that are of as much concern to small businesses as they are to large firms. Still, if you study the outlines carefully you will note that the outline for the seminar on consulting (Figure 14) is clearly aimed at the independent consultant, rather than the large consulting organization, although the seminar promises information of interest to the larger organization, and such an organization might well decide to send some employees to the session.

On the other hand the outline for the proposal-writing seminar (Figure 13) offers no such hints, and since the government awards many huge contracts to supercorporations, as well as many small contracts to very small enterprises, the main appeal is to those large corporations who specialize in government work, but is still attractive to small and not-so-small organizations. Moreover, these are not necessarily for-profit businesses, but include universities, labor unions, and many other kinds of nonprofit organizations who undertake government contracts.

There are many seminars offered that are somewhat "ambiguous" in this respect: They are attractive to both the large organization and the small one, and that "small one" may include individuals, although not necessarily self-employed ones. As one example of such a seminar, consider those seminars on speed reading. A great many individuals attend these seminars for personal betterment, but many employers perceive it to be in their interest to train employees in speed reading, and so they send their employees. And in the case of large organizations with many employees they wish to train, they often decide to bring the seminar in-house, on a custom basis (a subject we will discuss in greater depth).

On the other hand there are many seminars offered that are clearly directed at either the individual or the business organization, and some which are clearly suited only to the large organization or to the small organization. Consider, for example, some of the following as seminar subjects, and try to judge the most suitable audience for each:

Typing with the Dvorak keyboard
Office automation and computer workstations
Contract administration
Word processing
Selecting the right computer
Handling stress
Management information systems
Making money with your computer
Marketing techniques
Contract negotiations
Buying real estate
Mail-order techniques
Home-based business

WORKSHEET 2

Now that you have previewed the categories, try actually working with them in the second worksheet (page 172). Study the categories further, think hard about them, and decide who would be the probable attendees for each of the seminars suggested and whether employers would be likely to pay for employees' attendance, in each case. Do this before you read further, to get the greatest benefit from the exercise.

NO SCHOOL SOLUTION

There is no "school solution" offered here, for none is really possible. If you have had a great deal of trouble making decisions, in completing the worksheet, don't be discouraged; that was the idea—to demonstrate how difficult it is to make such decisions if seminar subjects and titles are not defined and chosen with great care. If you were unable to decide who should go to these seminars and whether employers ought to pay for attendance, you can see that the public at large would have the same difficulty. You may recall that a few paragraphs ago I made the point that the

INSTRUCTIONS: Write your choices of intended participants for each of the seminars listed below, choosing from among the ten at the bottom of the worksheet, registering your first, second, and third choices. Also, check yes or no on whether an employer would pay for attendance.

Seminar Titles	Choices	Employer Pays?	
Typing with the Dvorak keyboard	___ ___ ___	Yes [ ]	No [ ]
Office automation and computer workstations	___ ___ ___	[ ]	[ ]
Contract administration	___ ___ ___	[ ]	[ ]
Word processing	___ ___ ___	[ ]	[ ]
Selecting the right computer	___ ___ ___	[ ]	[ ]
Handling stress	___ ___ ___	[ ]	[ ]
Management information systems	___ ___ ___	[ ]	[ ]
Making money with your computer	___ ___ ___	[ ]	[ ]
Marketing techniques	___ ___ ___	[ ]	[ ]
Contract negotiations	___ ___ ___	[ ]	[ ]
Buying real estate	___ ___ ___	[ ]	[ ]
Mail-order techniques	___ ___ ___	[ ]	[ ]
Home-based business	___ ___ ___	[ ]	[ ]

1: General executive	6: Private investor
2: Office worker	7: Computer programmer
3: Comptroller	8: Small entrepreneur
4: Marketing executive	9: Housewife
5: Engineer	10: General manager

Worksheet 2. Choosing a seminar title.

seminar subject must provide the *reason* for the prospect to attend. And if you substitute seminar "name" or "title" for "subject"—for that is the only way the prospect knows what the subject is to be—you can see more clearly what the point of this is. Except for "making money with your computer" and "home-based business"—and possibly "typing with the Dvorak keyboard"—it is almost impossible to do more than guess at the orientation of these seminars, and so to judge for whom they are or should be intended.

The two outlines shown in Figures 13 and 14 were for seminars titled, "How to Write Winning Proposals for Government Contracts," and "How to Succeed as an Independent Consultant." And if those are not the most imaginative titles in the world, they at least define the orientations of the seminar fairly well.

HOW TO DEVELOP SEMINAR IDEAS

Most subjects have within them the seeds of many possible seminars. You must remember that the basic idea of a seminar is that it deals with some highly specialized subject or, perhaps more accurately, with some highly specialized aspect of a subject, and offers information not readily available elsewhere. Let's take that seminar on proposal writing as an example. It evolved out of a more generalized seminar on marketing to the government, and is today often presented as part of a larger seminar that does deal generally with government marketing. However, experience showed clearly that proposal writing was one area of government marketing where even the largest corporations felt they were always open to learning more. No matter how confident they were about all other aspects of their government marketing efforts, they seemed to tend strongly to the feeling that it was always worthwhile to increase efforts to train their staffs in improving their proposal-writing skills. That is, they generally responded much more enthusiastically to solicitations to attend seminars in the highly specialized art of proposal writing than they did to solicitations to attend seminars in the far broader field of government marketing.

In fact, you can brainstorm ideas all by yourself on any topic by doing a simple exercise: Take any topic in your field and try to develop variants. Following is an example of how you might develop some of those titles we used to focus them more sharply on targets—both kinds of people who should attend and what they would learn or how they would benefit. Here are some examples, using the first few items from the list we have been working with:

Old Title	New Title
Typing with the Dvorak keyboard	Increase typing efficiency with the Dvorak keyboard
Office automation and computer workstations	Office automation with computer workstations: for managers
Contract administration	Administration of government contracts: for comptrollers
Word processing	Word processing: for typists
Selecting the right computer	Selecting the right computer for the small office

Try rewording the remaining names for yourself, and try different combinations or different kinds of prospects, to get the full idea of this. Take a subject and try "slanting" it to specialized people and/or situations, (especially in fields you know well and relate to your own consulting specialty) as in the following example:

Original Wording	Variations
Handling stress	Stress and the general manager
	Stress in the busy law office
	Handling stress in everyday living
	Special stress problems of the construction industry
	The psychological implications of stress
	Surviving stress interviews
	Designing stress interviews

I could go on and on developing new ideas out of the idea of stress, focusing on various situations and people (prospective attendees). The objective is to identify the most viable ideas by remembering something about the laws of supply and demand, while also bearing in mind that a seminar is by nature coverage of a highly specialized subject. It is that which justifies the relatively high cost of a seminar: The attendees pay to get information and guidance not easily available—ideally, not available anywhere else at any price. In terms of your services and seminars, this means that you must try to come up with a specialized subject and/or unique coverage, a subject that is of importance to a large number of prospects, and important enough to them to justify the cost and time required to attend a seminar. (All these conditions must be met to achieve success in a seminar.)

To do this, you must think hard about all the possible applications of your own knowledge and skills. Ask yourself the following kinds of questions, to start the ideas flowing:

What are the common and serious problems of many people, in connection with your own field?

Who, specifically, are these people?

How can you help these people in a seminar setting?

What is different and special about what you can do for these people?

What are the specific benefits of what you can do for them?

Are the benefits strictly personal, or do they make the individual a better employee?

Would their employers pay for this help? (That is, would the seminar training benefit the employer?)

USING THE COMPUTER TO HELP

Once you have become accustomed to working at the keyboard and screen, you will find that there is no other way of recording ideas that is as satisfactory, as convenient to use, or as helpful in organizing your thoughts. This is true for at least the following reasons:

You can set down thoughts as they occur, and you never have to rewrite them, as you do with pencil and paper or via conventional typewriter, because the word processor and other programs enable you to sort, organize, reorganize your lists, and change your wording at your ease. You can delete, make insertions, change the

sequence, group related ideas into sets, and do many other manipulations at the press of a few keys.

You can print out hard copy (paper copy, that is) whenever you
wish, if you find it helpful to stare at information on paper, but you
can also discard it and go back to the screen with new ideas whenever you wish. The ability to move words around on the screen so
easily and spontaneously is itself a great help in thinking ideas out,
trying new combinations, comparing titles, and otherwise priming
your mental pump. It's a computer/word-processor version of
doodling, but is far more productive of useful results.

HOW TO EVALUATE SEMINAR IDEAS

Develop as many ideas as you can, and use some criteria to measure or evaluate each idea against the others. Try to find the idea
that offers these advantages:

The greatest number of prospects (largest market).

The most unusual program.

The greatest or most attractive benefits.

A program/benefits you are especially qualified to deliver (can
show outstanding credentials/qualifications for).

Kinds of benefits that are least readily available anywhere else.

Benefits that most people would be willing to pay for.

Benefits that most employers would be willing to pay for.

MARKETING THE SEMINAR AS A PUBLIC EVENT

The two ways to market your seminar(s) have been mentioned
briefly already: marketing them as public, open-registration events
and as custom, in-house programs for clients. We'll deal with the
first type first:

To market your seminar you will have to first decide who will be
the main body of buyers: individuals attending at their personal
expense, or employers sending employees to attend. Why is this

important to establish in advance? Primarily because it tends to dictate your marketing strategy and even your marketing and sales methods, for several reasons.

The Promises of Benefits

The benefits you promise must be the benefits that accrue to the buyer, who is the attendee in one case, but not in the other. If the attendee is to pay, then the promise must be directed to personal benefits, usually. But if the employer is to pay, then the message must focus on benefits to the employer as an employer, whether the employer is among the attendees or not. Therefore, we see the absolute need to know who is to be our prospective attendee and who is to be our prospective customer, especially if they are not the same.

Reaching Prospects

Generally speaking, seminars are sold most efficiently and effectively via direct-mail solicitations. One reason for this is that direct mail gives you the best opportunity to "rifle shot" your sales appeals—direct them to a given audience. With organizations as prospects, this is relatively easy: You can rent or compile lists of the right kinds of organizations—those that are the "right kinds" for your purposes, that is—and mail your literature to them.

When the prospects are organizations, that is relatively easy to carry out, using mailing lists you have rented or compiled, because such lists are usually available. But it is difficult, often impossible, to get mailing lists of individuals, as individuals, that would enable you to select the addresses on the basis of some reason to judge them good prospects for your seminar. Instead, you are compelled to go to some broad medium, such as newspapers or radio and TV (and/or free miniseminars, as many promoters do) to reach your prospects and solicit their attendance. This is a relatively inefficient way to do the job because it must "buckshot" the population at large, to find that tiny percentage of good prospects for

your seminar. And even the free miniseminar suffers from this because you must use the buckshot approach to announce that free
seminar and get the right prospects to attend. (There are, of
course, some exceptions to these "rules," but the exceptions are
just that: exceptions.)

The Literature

As a rule a different kind of literature is needed for each of the situations. Using direct mail you need a direct-mail package—
generally some kind of descriptive brochure, a letter, a registration
form (which is usually part of the brochure, perforated for easy removal), and a return envelope. (Many mail-order experts insist that
the return envelope is an important part of the package.) You must
bear in mind that the package bears virtually the entire brunt of
the burden for selling your product to the addressee, and so it
must be ample enough to carry the sales wallop it needs. And, of
course, the mailing must be in sufficient quantity to implement
the basic strategy of probability statistics.

On the other hand, if you are relying on media advertising
and/or free seminars, you do not need a great deal of literature,
since those who respond will be well-qualified prospects, prospects who have shown a definite interest in your seminar, and you
should be able to close a good percentage of them.

Note: It is a good idea to get advance payment (but call it "advance registration") for more than one reason:

1. It commits the prospect while enthusiasm is high, and cuts
   down the number of "no shows." (Even with advance payment you are likely to get a few no-shows.)
2. It provides operating capital.
3. It helps you plan by providing a good estimate of the number of attendees. (You still get some paying at the door.)

Most seminar producers charge more for payment at the door,
although some represent prior registration fees as discounted for
advance payment, and most guarantee refund if the registrant

cancels within some time-limit in advance of the seminar date (usually a week or two). But you can avoid refunds, if you do seminars on a regular basis, by giving cancelers a "rain check" to attend a future seminar, instead of a refund. That helps both parties.

ADMINISTRATION: COMPUTER ASSISTANCE

The open-registration seminar represents an administrative burden, with its need to arrange preparation and printing of literature, advertising, mailing, registering, cancellations, arranging for meeting rooms and coffee service, and sundry other details. Here again, the computer is a great aid in many ways. You can get programs that are especially designed to cope with such problems, but any good database manager would be almost ideal for this use because all this administrative labor in fact creates a database—setting up and maintaining the register, along with credits for advance payment, notices of cancellation, and other notations; scheduling, payments received and payments due; running accounts; keeping track of critical dates in the program; keeping a register of speakers, if you are using others; and otherwise relieving you of much of the paperwork burden. And your database program can be used also to help you design the forms you need and generate the reports and records you should have, just as your word processor will be valuable for developing the literature.

If you are running your own accounts, you can set up special ledger sheets for seminar activities, but if you are running seminars on a regular or frequent basis, you will probably do well to establish a special ledger for the activity, treating it as a separate profit center or even as an independent enterprise.

PROFITABILITY

There is no doubt that this type of seminar is almost always the most profitable one for the independent consultant, despite the fact that it is also the one that requires the greatest amount of work. Consider the gross income from a one-day seminar at a typical (and yet relatively modest) fee of $195 per registration:

Number of Attendees	Gross Income ($)
10	1950
15	2925
20	3900
25	4875
30	5850
40	7800
50	9750

Running such a seminar with only 10 attendees is marginal, since your expenses, on even the most modest promotional budget, are likely to be well in excess of $1000. Still, it demonstrates the low risk involved, since even with a meager enrollment of only 10 you run little risk of losing money, and with 20 or more you can be reasonably sure of enough profit to make the venture viable. And my experience has demonstrated that a modest mailing campaign, carried out with enough vigor and care to rifle-shot it accurately, can produce enrollments of 50 and more.

COSTS

Costs will vary widely, according to many factors, but here are some typical ones, as broad guidelines:

Meeting rooms (e.g., in a local hotel)	$50–150/day
Coffee service	$15–25/gallon
Printing	$150–500

Newspaper advertising and radio and TV time vary so widely as to make "typical" rates impossible to cite, but there are ways to keep these costs minimized by running small "inquiry" advertisements and announcements, with just enough copy to arouse curiosity, if not interest, and furnish a telephone number to call for more information, which can be a verbal presentation by telephone, if you wish, getting names and addresses to mail literature to, or even inviting callers to a free miniseminar, if you prefer. (This is one way to combine the two ways of reaching prospects, in an attempt to get the best of both worlds.)

CUSTOM, IN-HOUSE SEMINARS

All seminars can be candidates for presenting on a custom basis, as an in-house program for some organization. Obviously, if you offer a seminar that employers are willing to send several of their staff to, there is an excellent possibility that employers will consider having you present the seminar to their staff exclusively. But even those seminars that are normally addressed to individuals as individuals, although not usually as viable as the business or professional seminar, can often be sold in that manner, under a variety of circumstances. And since selling that latter type of seminar on a custom or in-house basis seems the less-likely prospect, let's discuss that first.

Let us suppose that you have a seminar on how to land the job you want—write a dynamite résumé, learn special techniques for getting your résumés into the right hands, master the art of dominating the interview, and other priceless information. There is the possibility that a large corporation forced to lay off a number of employees might retain you to present the seminar to employees being terminated: Some employers do go to expense to try to help laid-off workers to find other jobs. It is always worth considering such possibilities as this.

However, there are at least two other avenues open for presenting the seminar on a contract basis: regular or permanent associations of various kinds and ad hoc groups formed for a single purpose, such as sharing the costs of a seminar in this manner, with the result that each attendee saves a good amount of money; and such conclaves as conventions and conferences, which often include seminars as part of the proceedings.

Associations

Probably no other society in the entire world has as many associations as does the United States. We are a nation of "joiners," with thousands of organizations assembled as trade associations, professional societies, fraternal groups, protest groups, political action committees, neighborhood teams, and sundry other peer groups, clubs, and other associations. Thick directories of associations are published every year. For example, it is reported that there are 71 associations of consultants alone!

Many of these associations arrange seminars as special events and as part of their own annual conventions or conferences. As special events sometimes the association chooses to make the seminar a fund-raising event, and they charge their own members a full fee to attend, although the association decides what that will be, and makes a separate arrangement with the consultant presenting the seminar. In other cases, the association sponsors the seminar as a service to members and makes no charge or keeps the charge as small as possible. An association may therefore sponsor seminars that are of interest to members only on a personal basis as individuals and have little or no relationship to the common purpose of the organization. Therefore, virtually all seminars are potentially suitable for such arrangements. Members of societies may be interested personally in learning how to use makeup with professional skill, operate a word processor, decorate a home, cook with a microwave oven, find money for college, or quit smoking, regardless of the reason the association exists.

Conventions and Conferences

Associations and other trade groups are not the only sponsors of national conventions and conferences. Other organizations, such as publishers, sometimes organize such convocations. *Training* magazine, for example, organizes and stages its annual Training and Consulting Conference in New York City during the first week of December each year and has taken to staging the event also in

Chicago and on the west coast, offering a great many seminars at each such conclave.

Ad Hoc Groups

A group of individuals might wish to participate in your seminar, but might be unwilling or unable to pay the price you charge for open-registration presentations. But because you have no marketing expense and little other costs in presenting your seminar, you can afford a fixed-price presentation. And if the ad hoc group is large enough, you can turn a good profit on perhaps only $50 per attendee. But you do not have to wait for such groups to form spontaneously: You can make it a matter of policy, known to all, that if anyone wishes to assemble such a group you will negotiate a custom presentation of your standard seminar. In fact, if you wish to promote this method, you should prepare a brochure, explaining how to get such a group together and what to do next, and see to it that the brochure gets widespread distribution.

At this point it becomes necessary to examine more closely what that word "custom" means. The word is an adjective, and I have been using it here to modify the word "presentation" and not the word "seminar." What's the difference? Just this: There is a vast difference between a custom *presentation* of your *standard* seminar and a presentation of a *custom seminar*. Rather early in the business of presenting my seminars in-house for client organizations I came to that realization in this manner:

When I began to receive spontaneous requests to quote a price for the presentation of my seminar on proposal writing to in-house groups of some rather large corporations, I assumed that I would customize the seminar itself to the individual interest of the client, and I quoted prices based on that assumption. And closed zero orders.

I soon came to the realization that even the largest corporations were not eager to pay the necessary price to prepare special seminars for them. (I should have known this from earlier experience in the training and education field.) I then began to quote such contracts on the basis of presenting my standard seminar, possibly with minor, spontaneous customizing, at my normal consulting rate. I immediately began to close virtually all such leads, at which time I began to realize that I was underpricing the market (I was providing my own special manual and other materials) and gradually adjusted the price upward to more realistic levels. I now charge nearly double my normal consulting rate for such presentations, without meeting serious resistance, and have since been informed by some clients that they would be suspicious of the value of my seminar if I charged less.

Therefore, be careful that you have a complete understanding when you are responding to an inquiry about custom presentation of your standard seminar. You may be able to do a little spontaneous customization, as you speak, but it is necessary to have a clear understanding of what you have agreed to do. (Of course, sometimes a client does want a completely custom seminar, developed especially for the client's own needs, and is willing to pay enough to get one. (I have had such clients, too, but I have learned to prepare a simple proposal for client acceptance, to be sure that we both have a mutual understanding of and agreement to what I am to deliver.)

Of course, you can sell your seminar presentations on any or all of these bases, for they are all viable, insofar as your seminar is appropriate to the arrangement. In fact, it is probably a good plan to attempt all of these methods and avenues of marketing, and thus determine by actual trial which is/are the best market(s) for your seminar. Or you can tackle the marketing problem from the other direction by deciding which markets you prefer, and then fashion your seminar for that/those markets(s).

THE PR/PROMOTIONAL SEMINAR

Seminars are an excellent marketing tool for independent consultants, even those seminars where the attendees pay full rates, if the attendees are such that they are legitimate prospects for your consulting services. If, for example, they are senior employees or executives of organizations who are good targets for your services, they are often in a position to bring you into the company for consulting work. It's a good idea to bear this in mind, as you make seminar presentations to such audiences, and this will often pay off with subsequent consulting contracts.

Of course, as in the case of the ad hoc group to whom you may be able to sell a custom presentation, you can wait for such lightning to strike, or you can cause it to happen. That is, you can give free miniseminars of an hour or two each, designed specifically to develop sales leads—clients.

One organization currently doing this around the country is the Lowry group, headed by real estate millionaire Al Lowry, who boasts that he was a supermarket butcher before he learned how to make millions in real estate. His organization runs a weekend seminar in his methods, offering what appears to be a rather thick and comprehensive course manual that is to become the learner's "bible" later. The individual who conducts the seminar and explains how one can learn the secrets of getting rich in real estate by attending the Lowry course and gleaning all of Lowry's special methods assures the listeners that little of what is in this vaunted manual has appeared in any of Lowry's several successful books on getting rich. He also explains that there is no way to get this manual, except by attending the seminar. Later you learn that the price for the intensive weekend course is $545, discounted to $495 for attendees who sign up immediately, but the discount is also offered in a follow-up solicitation sent out several days later to those who have not signed up for the seminar at the first meeting. You get a second chance to win that discount, although it was originally offered as good only to those who sign up immediately.

The "literature" offered at the free seminar (which is advertised heavily in local newspapers and on TV and radio) is surprisingly skimpy and cheaply printed, a mere few pages of offset printing. And the follow-up literature is of the same caliber. Not at all impressive. However, the seminar presentation itself is dynamite, given by people who are alleged to be successful graduates of Lowry's program and who are certainly excellent speakers and skilled sellers.

The Evelyn Wood speed-reading school also uses this as their principal marketing device, offering a free speed-reading lesson at the free seminar, and making all efforts to sign up attendees for the regular course of study in the art of reading at high speed.

Generally, such free seminars last from one to two hours, are held at local hotels during evening hours, after working hours for most people. Almost anything can be sold by this method, but the method is relatively expensive, and economics dictates that the method is best suited to selling "high ticket" items such as seminars and training courses. The method definitely focuses sharply on skilled salespeople on the platform and tends to use high-pressure methods. Whether it will work in the hands of a less-than-fully professional individual skilled in selling in this manner seems somewhat doubtful, at least if the objective is to sign up buyers on the spot. Salespeople who work in this manner generally work on a percentage, and presumably the salesperson does quite well in selling the Lowry weekend seminar. However, make no mistake about it: It requires a great deal of selling skill, normally, to persuade people to commit themselves to sizable financial commitments spontaneously, without at least a few days to ponder the matter. It is not a profession that just anyone can pursue successfully, at least not without a great deal of experience and special training.

On the other hand, there is a way that the method can be made a useful one for the independent consultant who offers seminars more or less regularly. And depending on to whom the seminars are offered—individuals or employers—the sessions should be held in either a local hotel (to reach individuals) or at a convention or conference (to reach companies and other organizations).

The purpose of such a free seminar is to build a prospect list for immediate and future reference. In time, the list will grow, and if you mail solicitations to each name on your list, it should ultimately be worthwhile in the results it produces.

Of course, the computer has among its many attributes a well-developed capability for managing mailing lists and assisting in several other ways with preparing and sending out sales letters and other direct-mail elements.

ADDITIONAL INCOME OPPORTUNITIES

Many consultants who present seminars of their own and even those who speak at other people's seminars for a nominal fee (honorarium) or sans fee use the occasion to realize additional income from the sale of their books, reports, tape cassettes, and newsletter subscriptions. In fact, for some the income from such activity is even greater than that from the registration fees, so they keep the (registration) fees as modest as possible, to encourage maximum attendance. However, there is still another aspect to this, one that has a double benefit:

In mailing out literature soliciting registration, even a good rate of response—orders received versus literature sent out—is on the order of one to two percent. But at least some of those who fail to respond do so not because of a lack of interest in or lack of desire to hear what you have to present; many are just unable to attend for various reasons. If you have other things to sell—books, tapes, newsletters, and so on—at least some of those addressees will respond with their orders.

In my own case I often managed to get enough orders via responses to my original mailing to more than pay for the entire mailing, making the seminar a substantial contributor to my bottom line, as well as increasing the sales of those other products through which I sold my information, counsel, and instructions in the gentle art of writing contract-winning proposals.

A FINAL NOTE

It is important to put seminar presentations in proper perspective, vis-à-vis your consulting activities generally. It is easy to forget what seminars represent, for the independent consultant, and to thus lose contact with your main professional mission. In all this discussion of how to conceive, prepare, market, and turn a profit on seminar presentations, even to the extent of making it a main or separate enterprise, don't lose sight of the fact that the seminar *is* a logical and legitimate consulting service. It is, in fact, a *medium* for delivery of consulting service, and you may even consider it to be a form of *group consulting,* in which those who cannot afford to buy your services on a direct one-to-one basis can afford your services as one of a group. For that reason alone your seminars ought to include for attendees the privilege of posing direct questions and eliciting your opinions, given spontaneously in response.

CHAPTER TWELVE

Computer Aid
in Newsletter
Publishing

The computer can take most of the "pain" out of newsletter publishing, even for the experienced newsletter publisher.

HOW NEWSLETTER PUBLISHING FITS THE CONSULTING ENTERPRISE

As a consulting activity, newsletter publishing parallels seminar presentation in several ways, especially in its basic applications and in the many ways it can contribute to your success overall as an independent consultant. Here are some of the major applications and benefits of newsletter publishing to the independent consultant which parallel the benefits of seminar presentation:

1. It is very much a fit (compatible with your mission), as a medium for delivering consulting services to your clients.

2. It can be a major income-producing element of your consulting practice, or even a separate enterprise, and can even become a source of true wealth.

3. It can be used effectively for PR, to publicize your services, make yourself known to those you consider your prospects, and generally to support marketing and sales of your consulting services.

4. It can be used to help defray the costs of marketing seminars, while producing additional income at the seminar presentation itself (as explained in the previous chapter).

5. It can be used as an effective aid in marketing other products of your consulting practice; it is an excellent medium for that.

A BRIEF LOOK AT THE NEWSLETTER: WHAT IS IT?

The newsletter derived its name early on from that which was, in fact, a *newsletter*. Today, however, the term is as the word *computer* is to that bit of modern electronic wizardry.

Marvin Arth and Helen Ashmore observe in their excellent book, *The Newsletter Editor's Desk Book* (Parkway Press, Shawnee Mission, Kansas), "A newsletter is a private newspaper that conveys specific information to a specific audience." That, of course, is true for a great many newsletters which do, in fact, deal primarily with news per se, albeit news of a specialized nature and/or about highly specialized subjects, such as personnel management, battery technology, or construction activities. But many newsletters deal far less with news, even highly specialized news, than they do with rendering advice, reporting what they represent as being "inside" information and stories, how-to information about specialized subjects, and many other varieties of such non-news coverage.

Newsletters vary enormously, to both extremes of a broad spectrum in all parameters—formats, coverage, audiences, types of publishers, frequency, prices, number of subscribers, and any other element of comparison you can name. Some are extremely expensive, formally typeset, and published on glossy paper; some are also typed on old mechanical typewriters—and even hand printed, in a few cases—and printed by the least expensive means on the least expensive paper. They range from a 4½ × 6-inch format to newspaper-sized 22 × 35 inches and from a couple dozen subscribers to hundreds of thousands of subscribers. They are produced in offices and facilities ranging from an expensive suite in a plush office-building tower to a corner of the publisher's bedroom. They are published by major corporations to publicize products and win customers, by associations serving members, by politicians wooing constituents' votes, by moonlight publishers trying to earn some additional income, by activists promoting causes in which they believe passionately, and by publishing organizations making a serious business of the activity. Here, for example, is a listing of several newsletters, with some information about them, to illustrate some of this enormous diversity. These examples are drawn from *The Newsletter Yearbook Directory*, Third Edition, published by The Newsletter Clearinghouse and edited by the well-known newsletter specialist and publisher of his own newsletter, Newsletter on Newsletters," Howard Penn Hudson. But, first, to give you a quick appreciation of the range of topics, here are just a few of the listings from the "Index of Subject Categories":

Accounting	Banking	Carpets	Dental
Ecology	Fabrics	Gas	Health
Insurance	Jewelry	Labor	Machinery
Nursing	Oceanography	Packaging	Radio
Science	Taxes	Urban Affairs	Warehousing

And here are a few of the newsletter titles, with a few bits of information about each, including circulation figures (in parentheses), when the publisher chooses to supply them. (Many do not.)

"Motorcycle Business Newsletter," twice monthly, $96 (500)

"Aerospace Daily," daily, $520

"The Computer Marketing Newsletter," monthly, $60 (3600)

"Speechwriter's Newsletter," twice monthly, $82

"The Food & Drug Letter," biweekly, $335

"Immigration History Newsletter," twice yearly, $3 (650)

"Adoption Report," quarterly, $5 (5000)

SUBSCRIPTION FEES

Note the nominal fees charged in some cases; in some others, not listed here, there is no charge at all, not even a nominal one. These are newsletters operated for purposes other than profit, sometimes by profit-making organizations, using newsletters purely for PR and marketing/sales promotion, and in other cases by nonprofit organizations dedicated to some cause considered worthy and supported, usually, by contributions. In fact, in many cases the newsletters are used as media for fund-raising appeals, which is a specialized form of PR/marketing application. Moreover, some of the newsletters for which substantial subscription fees are charged today began existence as free or nearly free newsletters published for PR purposes, but proved to be equally viable as producers of income. (I receive a free newsletter every couple of months from Clinton Computer, from whom I bought my own Morrow MD3 system, and something a bit more elaborate, virtually a magazine, from Morrow every month, also free and unsolicited by me.)

The practice of charging a nominal fee for the newsletter is not entirely for the purpose of defraying its actual cost—even the most modest newsletter represents several dollars a year cost per recipient, for production costs alone, without counting your own time and labor. However, people tend to value things by what they cost, so that they tend to regard a free newsletter as being nothing more than pure advertising literature. In fact, if you do intend to distribute your newsletter free, in the interest of getting wide circulation (at least initially), it is a wise move to inscribe an annual subscription fee on the masthead, whether you do or do not actually charge subscribers. But let's go back to the beginning of this chapter, to the main points made there, and consider them more carefully.

THE NEWSLETTER AS A CONSULTING-SERVICES MEDIUM

In the previous chapter the point was made that a seminar may be considered to be a means for providing consulting services on a group basis, for situations where the client either cannot afford your personal services or believes that retaining you for such direct consultation is unnecessary to his or her need. Very much the same point may be made here, with respect to newsletters: The newsletter itself can be a consulting medium. Through it you can offer advice and service to readers (who can be considered to be clients in a special category) if you structure your newsletter to implement that idea—that is, if you design your newsletter for that purpose. In fact, even if you adopt the newsletter idea as a PR device, you can and should still bear that kind of objective in mind, to permit it to serve as a sample of what you have to offer.

In either case, what you must do is include features in your newsletter that provide consulting services—counsel, guidance, information, and instruction, indirectly if not directly. Among the features that will make the newsletter a medium of your consulting service are these:

Service Articles—"how-to" pieces on relevant subjects

Letters column—comments, ideas from readers (group discussion)

Q & A column—answers to readers' questions

Guest articles by qualified specialists

THE NEWSLETTER AS AN INCOME SOURCE

Like the seminar, the newsletter can be both a direct and an indirect source of income—direct through the sale of subscriptions and indirect through its great influence as a medium for selling your consulting services, seminars, and other products—books, reports, cassettes, or anything else you produce.

As a direct source of income through subscription fees—not advertising—a newsletter can be highly profitable. For example, consider a monthly newsletter that you build to a circulation of perhaps only 1000 subscribers. At a typical annual subscription price of perhaps $48 a year, the gross income is, of course, $48,000, and the gross profit—not counting the salary you pay yourself or the costs of other labor—is on the order of $42,000. Even after paying for the help you need in mailing the letter out every month and paying yourself some kind of salary for the several days a month you spend in writing and assembling the letter, you have a substantial portion of your income deriving directly from the publication. And it is possible that you will achieve a greater circulation, too, and earn even more income.

Not all your subscribers have to be individuals. In some circumstances, you can sell bulk subscriptions to organizations—large corporations and associations, for example—although you will usually have to negotiate special prices for such things. You might even sign a contract to permit the organization to distribute the letter as their own publication, and have a quantity printed up for them every month, with their own identity and title. (Many deals of this kind are made by newsletter publishers, where the conditions are right for them.)

Newsletters do not ordinarily accept advertising, although there are some exceptions to that. But because of space restrictions, for one, and because one of the subscriber's motivations is to get an all-"meat" periodical—no advertisements or fillers, but all directly relevant and useful information—advertising is generally taboo in newsletters. However, many newsletter publishers use their newsletters to sell such other products and services.

Usually they do this in any or all of several ways:

Direct and unabashed advertisements in the newsletter.

Editorial stories about the other offerings, describing them and explaining them, sometimes with an order form, sometimes by inviting the reader to send for more information.

An advertising enclosure in the newsletter, either represented as a "special supplement" or presented frankly as an advertising circular.

A separate literature package mailed to the entire subscriber list (and usually to others as well).

Your subscribers constitute a customer list, of course, and such a list generally produces a good response, usually far better than any other list does. That customer list is itself a valuable property, both for marketing your own services and products and as an asset that can earn income for you through rentals to others.

Once the newsletter is built up—has an ample circulation—it becomes a valuable property in itself. There are some newsletter publishers who produce several newsletters, and some highly successful newsletter publishing entrepreneurs have sold their businesses for seven- and eight-figure prices.

In short, while the newsletter can do a great deal for your bottom line, a truly successful newsletter can often do even more for your net worth.

THE NEWSLETTER AS A PR/MARKETING/ ADVERTISING TOOL

The newsletter is the almost-ideal tool for publicizing and marketing your service. Handled properly—with dignity and a high degree of professionalism—it makes you known rapidly and gives you a proper image. It will be read, whereas a brochure is often discarded without even a glance. You can mail it, hand it out, leave supplies in selected public places, post it on bulletin boards, and use small advertisements ("inquiry" advertising) to offer a free copy or complimentary subscription to anyone who requests it.

This latter idea is a most helpful one. While you can rent mailing lists of individuals or organizations along the lines of almost any qualification or specifications you can prescribe, the best list to use is your own customer list, and the next-best list is your own up-to-date list of inquirers. And while you can't normally promote a consulting service effectively through media advertising, you can use inexpensive media advertising to induce inquiries for your follow-up.

The keys are proper wording and proper medium—the right offer addressed to the right audience. That is, you must know who you are trying to reach—who your best prospects are—and you must then create a newsletter that will appeal to that group and find an advertising medium that will reach that group with your offer.

Ordinarily, the popular media—daily newspapers and general interest magazines—are wrong for this purpose. Every industry and profession has its own special journals, tabloids, magazines, and other periodicals—some are annual directories, for example—that have relatively limited circulation because they are circulated to only those in the given industry or profession, but the circulation is concentrated, and you can select the exact audience you want. There are many thousands of such publications, usually several for each industry, business, or career field, covering various aspects of the field and/or addressed to different individuals in the field—general managers, comptrollers, marketing directors, production managers, and other. Here, for example, is a mere sprinkling, to convey the idea (some of the titles explain themselves, without other comment):

Meeting News (for meeting planners, convention managers, etc.)

Cashflow (for corporate treasurers and financial managers)

Advertising Techniques (for advertising executives)

Farm Supplier (for farm supply dealers and managers)

The Antiques Dealer

Modern Tire Dealer

Airport Services Management

Lighting Dimensions Magazine (for lighting designers in entertainment)

In Business (for entrepreneurs and home-business builders)

Builder Insider (for architects, builders, home owners)

Business Software Magazine (for corporate decision makers)

Dental Management (dental practice management)

Cable Marketing (for cable TV managers)

Florist (for retail florists, wholesalers)

Produce News (for growers, shippers, distributors of vegetables)

Once you have selected your audience and publication, you can offer a free copy of your newsletter or even a free subscription to anyone interested. Include in your advertisement enough information—an idea of what the newsletter is about and what kind of information it provides—to make its value to the reader clear. For example, if your target audience consists of high-level managers and executives who are responsible for buying computer software, you might use such a periodical as *Business Software Magazine* and such copy as any of these:

FREE SAMPLE COPY of newsletter, "The Business Software Letter." Write _____

150 sources of free business software listed in "The Business Software Letter." For FREE SAMPLE COPY: _____

LEARN WHERE/HOW TO GET FREE BUSINESS SOFTWARE in "The Business Software Letter." Complimentary (3 month) subscription FREE. Write of call: _____

Keep up with the latest developments in software by reading "The Business Software Letter." FREE trial subscription. Write: _____

Many small advertisements of this type are likely to produce better results than a few large ones. Moreover, by using many small ones, in different media, at different times, and with different wording, you can soon determine what works best for you and concentrate on that. (No matter how expert you become, your estimates and judgments are never as effective or as reliable as actual testing is. Always *test*, to be sure.)

Of course, when the inquiries arrive you must respond promptly with the sample copy of complimentary subscription and a letter (individually addressed and printed out on your computer) inviting the reader to subscribe, offering a free subscription, or whatever you wish to do. But don't forget that you are a consultant, too, so be sure to explain your consulting services, seminars, and/or whatever else you offer.

THOSE OTHER PRODUCTS

Reports, books, seminars, tape cassettes, and other such byproducts of a consulting service and newsletter publishing enterprise are highly profitable items and can help keep your consultancy comfortably in the black. Those report, or "folios" as some call them, can be quite simple typed documents turned out on your printer and duplicated by the same firm that prints your newsletter, using your letterhead as the "self-cover"—first page, which carries all the title information, copyright notice, and date, and other such information—or you can use a special cover, which your printer can also make up for you. Such reports can cover virtually any subject that is relevant to your consulting practice and your subscribers/clients' interests—how-to-do-it, where-to-find-it, latest developments, new ideas, or whatever else you think merits a special report. Depending on size and other circumstances, such reports can be priced from $5 to $40 or more.

Tape cassettes sell well: Many people would rather listen to a tape than read a book or manual. Therefore, many seminar leaders record several of their seminar sessions, get professional help in editing all the resulting tape down to a set of tapes—usually three or four, although sometimes even more—that in the composite represent a good seminar session, and sell the tapes, along with an instruction booklet or manual, suitably packaged, for anywhere from $75 to $300. It is major business in itself today.

THE MANY COMPUTER CONTRIBUTIONS

Your computer can make a great many contributions to your newsletter and to any ancillary products you sell. Of course, the word processor in your computer can handle all the editorial chores, just as it does for proposals, but you will generally do your proposals in single column copy—each line extending from the left-hand margin to the right-hand margin—and you may choose to run your copy "ragged right" or unjustified, and even double spaced. But you are likely to want to be a bit more "cosmetic" with your newsletter, since the word processor makes it possible, and do your copy as two-column, right justified copy, as though it were formally typeset.

The word processor makes this easy to do, although the specific procedures will vary, with different programs. Using the popular WordStar, the progression goes as shown in Figure 15. First the copy is double-spaced, while being developed as draft. After editing into final copy, you can run it single-spaced and justify it as either single column or double column, as shown. With any good word processor, the choice is yours, and any one of the choices is as easy as any other, so you need not be influenced by any fears that one style is more difficult or requires more work to achieve than any other.

I constructed all three examples in Figure 15 from an original paragraph of my manuscript without retyping a single word, by using the copying functions of the system, with its other capabilities. I merely pressed certain keys to cause the program to copy that paragraph and reformat it into the two samples shown in the figure. Moreover, I "goofed" several times in making up the figure, and so merely wiped out what I had done with erase commands and did things over. (This was easier and faster than fixing mistakes.) The whole thing, even making and correcting mistakes, took only a few minutes and was far easier on my nerves and schedule than such mistakes would have been were I forced to retype the copy several times and manipulate copies with scissors and paste pot.

Even so, WordStar, unfortunately, is not as good on two-column copy as are some other word processors because of some weak-

The word processor makes this easy to do, although the specific procedures will vary, with different programs. Using the popular WordStar, the progression goes as shown in Figure 15. First the copy is double-spaced, while being developed as draft. After editing into final copy, you can run it single-spaced and justify it as either single-column or double column, as shown. With any good word processor, the choice is yours, and any one of the choices is as easy as any other, so you need not be influenced by any fears that one style is more difficult or requires more work to achieve than any other.

[Double-spaced, single-column, rough draft]

The word processor makes this easy to do, although the specific procedures will vary, with different programs. Using the popular WordStar, the progression goes as shown in Figure 15. First the copy is double-spaced, while being developed as draft. After editing into final copy, you can run it single-spaced and justify it as either single-column or double column, as shown. With any good word processor, the choice is yours, and any one of the choices is as easy as any other, so you need not be influenced by any fears that one style is more difficult or requires more work to achieve than any other.

[Single-spaced, single column, justified final copy]

The word processor makes this easy to do, although the specific procedures will vary, with different programs. Using the popular WordStar, the progression goes as shown in Figure 15. First the copy is double-spaced, while being developed as draft. After editing into final copy, you can run it single-spaced and justify it as either single-column or double column, as shown. With any good word processor, the choice is yours, and any one of the choices is as easy as any other, so you need not be influenced by any fears that one style is more diffi-cult or requires more work to achieve than any other.

[single-spaced, two-column, justified final copy]

Figure 15. Evolution of rough draft to final copy.

nesses in its printing-command format. (For example, microjustification has to be turned off when formatting for two-column copy.) However, with a little care in hyphenating words, it is possible to achieve a good professional appearance in the final copy.

The same philosophy applies to those reports and manuals you can and should consider turning out as adjuncts to your newsletter and also applies to other elements of your consulting enterprise. They, too, can be prepared as double-spaced rough draft, and then printed out as justified single- or double-column final copy, ready for the printer.

But that is not the only way the computer can help with the publishing end of your consulting venture; there are many other areas where the computer will be a great help, both in editorial functions and in other chores that must be performed.

THE EDITORIAL "SAFE"

Some months (that is, for some issues, assuming that you publish on a monthly schedule) you have more material than you can use, while in other months you don't have enough good material for the issue. But all material falls into certain categories. For one thing, material is either time-sensitive or it is not. That is, some material is useful only if you run it in the current or upcoming edition, but will have to be discarded if you do not because it will be of no value next month. And some material is seasonal, and even if it will work for the same season of any year, if you fail to use it at the proper time, you will have to discard it or save it for next year. But some material will be useful whenever you choose to use it.

These are factors that should affect your decisions as to what to use for each issue. You want good material, but you also want to use that "perishable" material while it is still good. You can do so by saving nonperishable material, when you have more than you can use, for future issues. Editors keep such material in desk drawers or elsewhere, which some refer to as their "safes."

Once you have a computer, that computer—a floppy disk, that is—becomes your editorial safe, or should. It is wise to enter as much material as possible into disk files and save the material in files on those little plastic disks, ready to be summoned up, in toto or in part, any time you need them.

This is a great help to an editor in more than one way:

For one thing, it is the most convenient and most readily accessible storage imaginable. Since your files are now such that they can be kept readily at hand on your own desk, you literally have all this material at arm's length. (I can reach out and select any of more than 40 disks, each holding more than 150 pages of material, without leaving my seat, and there are as many more I can reach by simply standing up.) You should never again have any great trouble finding anything, if you make proper notations on the sleeve labels of those disks. Of course, you will still keep a great deal of paper around because much of your material is in paper form, because it is not practicable to automatically enter every-thing into disk files, but you will soon have far less paper in metal file cabinets or desk drawers than you did before. At the same time, you will get a great deal of material via online communica-tions with databases and possibly with contributors, and that will go straight onto your floppies as it arrives. Later, you can select from it, and edit and cut as much as you wish.

Some newsletter publishers write all of every edition them-selves, some accept contributions for which they pay only in free copies of the newsletter, and some pay contributors. If you find yourself able to afford to, the latter is the best way to publish. It's too much of a burden to handle it all yourself, and contributors, especially those who get paid for their contributions, will often come up with good material you would not have gotten otherwise. Let such publications as the *Writer's Digest*, *The Writer*, and *The Newsletter Yearbook Directory* know that you want and will pay for freelance contributions, and you'll soon be getting plenty of material to review and buy, if you like it.

REVIEWING MATERIAL ON-SCREEN

I find it much easier to review material on-screen than on the typed page, and you probably will to, after you have become com-fortable with your system. You can flip through the material more quickly, juggle paragraphs around for trial fits in different patterns, and do this with copies of the material, so that you do not run the hazard of destroying original material by changing it beyond re-pair. You can cut and paste electronically to your heart's content, and discard anything that does not work out well. And you can do all of this on-screen, and never print anything out until you are sure that it is what you want. The ease with which you can do this is economical of both your time and your emotions: You need never again have severe bouts of frustration suffered in trying to fix up stubborn copy. You can cut and fit as much as you want.

COPY FITTING

That extends to copy fitting, too, and there the ease of on-screen cut and paste is among the most satisfying benefits of the word processor. With a newsletter you are working to a fixed format, usually four or eight pages. But even if it is six or seven pages, you are still working with a fixed page length, and your typical make-up problem is fitting the copy so that you end up with a full page, with no "air" (blank space) in any column, and no copy left over.

In the old-fashioned way, all copy had to be prepared in "galleys," long sheets of single columns, and then literally cut up and pasted together. Editing this material to end up with exactly full pages was difficult, and traditional reporting style was designed to permit an editor to cut a story as soon as he ran out of space, and still have a story. But even then he had problems of cutting in the middle of a sentence, and to this day newspapers and magazines have columns that have little notes ("fillers") at the bottom, saying such things as "The blue whale is the largest mammal on earth," to avoid that deadly "air" in the column.

With electronic copy fitting, that can usually be avoided, because you can fit the copy on-screen, and trim (edit) the copy until it is an exact fit, before you print it out. You need never have air or fillers in a column.

PROOFREADING

"Speller" programs or electronic dictionaries are now quite common, and probably everybody who uses a word processor has a speller program, which does two things for the user:

1.   It helps with spelling, by checking the spelling of a word and calling your attention to words that are not in the electronic dictionary, or by giving you dictionary help (at your option) by showing you a portion of the appropriate section of the dictionary on-screen.

2.   It helps with proofreading via this dictionary function, although it doesn't do it all. But it is a distinct help and will catch many errors you miss in checking by ocular scanning alone.

FILE COPIES

The observations about disk files versus paper files applies to file copies of all back issues of your newsletter. By keeping those back issues on disk, as many newsletter publishers do today, you can always summon up a back issue for review and/or printing out a complete copy or some portion of it. This is, again, a great convenience and a most efficient way of filing material.

In connection with that, the search function found in most word processors is a great aid for searching out some story or item that was published in an earlier edition. That alone can save you hours of time otherwise spent in searching back issues.

MAILING

Of course, you will use your computer to help with the mailing— maintaining the mailing lists, printing labels or envelopes, and keeping track of the status of each subscription. You can have the computer search the list each month to identify all subscribers whose subscription is due to expire soon or which will expire with the current issue, and even automatically type out reminder letters that it is time to renew. Do be careful, though, because your computer is really not very smart. If you have a subscriber listed as Jones Tool & Die, Inc., your computer is perfectly capable of addressing a letter, "Dear Mr. Tool & Die, Inc." or "Dear Mr. Inc."

CHAPTER THIRTEEN

Computer Aid in Managing Your Practice

"Management" is a vague noun. It needs some definitive adjective, such as "general," "technical," or "business" before it begins to take on useful meaning. And only then can we begin to discuss its true meaning and relate it to your success as an independent consultant.

THE TWO FACES OF MANAGEMENT

There are two kinds of management, technical and business management. Most of what we have examined and discussed so far has concerned technical management, that is, the management of the many technical and professional functions of your consulting practice, including marketing, seminars, writing, and publishing. It concerns establishing, maintaining, and marketing the many services and products that constitute the modern consulting practice of the independent practitioner. Managing these functions well means that you have a sound basis for a highly successful consulting practice. But that isn't enough, of itself, to ensure that you will have a successful practice. For that you must take steps to bring about good *business* management also. And that means sound fiscal management, seeing to it that you have an accurate and detailed profile of all costs, income, profits, and other such financial matters so that you can consider and make the right decisions about all of these—about the general conduct of your practice.

Of course, this is easy to say, and it doesn't take a great deal of wisdom to say it; the truths are rather obvious. Doing it is another matter; that is rarely easy. And it is especially difficult for the independent consultant who is usually a technical expert in some field and highly capable in that field, but untrained in business management and too busy to take the time to learn all the details of business management while conducting a demanding practice. And even turning the problems over to the professionals, such as a firm of certified public accountants, is only a small portion of the answer, which sometimes produces more new questions than it does answers. The CPAs can keep your books, balance them, calculate your tax obligations, and write up your various accounting reports, but that doesn't answer most of your questions. It might tell you whether you are earning profits or losing money on your seminars, for example, but it won't usually tell you what to do about losing money—whether you should cut the costs of producing them, raise the price, advertise differently, run them at different locations, or abandon them entirely. You will find it difficult to get this kind of information from a public accounting firm for the simple reason that they do not understand the technical side of your business and therefore are not in a position to design a system that will produce all the right kinds of information, the kinds you need for the successful conduct of a consulting practice. Yet, somehow, you must get this information to make sensible management decisions.

WHAT IS MANAGEMENT?

A great many management gurus have spent a great many hours of energy writing about management, trying to define it and trying to determine what it is, what it is not, what is good management, what is bad management, how to become a good manager, and countless other facets of and thoughts about the subject. Moreover, the universal solvents—promised panaceas—and contrived acronyms offered to achieve good management have been almost innumerable: management grid, zero-based budgeting, critical path method (CPM), program review analysis technique (PERT), planning, programming, budgeting system (PPBS), Theory X, Theory Y, and Theory Z, the one-minute manager, management by objectives (MBO), and still others, without end. We have been assured that management is getting things done through other people by (1) making other people want to do things they should do; (2) making them do things you want them to do; (3) making them want to do things you want them to do; (4) giving people praise and providing positive reinforcement; (5) making sure that they get satisfaction; and (6) structuring work so that the individual does a whole job, with a recognizable result, instead of a meaningless rote task; and through countless other theories and dogmatic pronouncements, offering cures for all managerial ills and transgressions.

All of these are based, paradoxically, on the relatively narrow view of managers in the larger organizations, where management is concerned with planning and directing the efforts of others, and where managers bear responsibility for the outcomes of other peoples' efforts. But the case under consideration here is that of managing the independent consulting practice, where the efforts are entirely or almost entirely your own, and the real essence of management is easy to state, at least in general terms. It is this: Management is the act of utilizing available resources to achieve specific objectives. And if that appears to resemble any of the cited ideas or management tools, such as MBO (management by objectives), the resemblance is purely superficial, for this is not management by objectives, but management to *achieve* the objectives. In MBO the fundamental idea is that all management should be geared to stated objectives established beforehand. In what is suggested here the fundamental idea is to manage all available resources for maximum results, hopefully to exceed the objectives, rather than to be constrained by them, to aim above the objectives, regarding them as the absolute minimums acceptable.

Note here that the measure for judging the quality of the management is built into the definition: The quality of the management is measured by the success of achieving and even exceeding the objectives. It is based on the notion that there is never enough time, money, help, or other resources to get the job done; managers are the people who get the job done anyhow, despite the lack of adequate resources. (The corollary is that anyone can do the job with ample resources.) It is that ability that is the measure of a manager, and defines the individual as a manager. It is that which you must do, in managing your own enterprise successfully. And you are likely to find that it is only when you do not have enough of anything—time, money, and other resources—that you manage to operate at a profit. Somehow, when everything goes smoothly and there seems to be enough of everything, you tend to discover that you overbudgeted and are either losing money or fighting to avoid doing just that. And that gives rise to another idea: Perhaps good management is the art of deliberately underbudgeting and then "making it happen" anyhow!

MANAGEMENT VERSUS ADMINISTRATION

Many people tend to confuse management with administration, and there is a hazard in this confusion. Of course, the two have some relationship (even profit and losses have some relationship to each other!) but they are not the same thing at all. Administration is primarily the handling of relatively routine functions, calling for a modicum of good judgment but concerned primarily with exercising certain well-defined skills and knowledge. And as long as it remains relatively routine, it remains in the domain of administration.

Management is concerned with decision making, the making of important decisions, usually decisions based far more on human estimates and judgment than on any established discipline or methodology. (Were methodology available for all decision making, we would no longer need managers, but could do quite well with technicians instead.) Deciding what software to use for accounts payable is an administrative decision, for example, but deciding that the time has come to install a computer is a mangement decision. Handling inventory is administrative functioning, but deciding whether to stock up on certain items or to keep the inventory slim on those items is a management function, to further illustrate the difference.

It is also fair to say that management decisions tend to be ones that call for a combination of experience, judgment, instinct, and even a gambler's courage, more than on knowledge and practice of technical disciplines or established management tools. The many facts a manager collects before making an important decision are a large part of the basis for making the decision, but they do not dictate it: In the end the manager must gamble on experience, judgment, and instinct, although basing the judgment in part on the indications suggested by the collected evidence.

This is not to minimize the importance of those facts, for the management decision should be an estimate, not a guess. Those facts are important; they are the basis for the decision. And that is why accounting is so important—not because the IRS and other government agencies demand records and tax payments, but because accounting is the main source of the information that goes into managerial decision making. And that is why the public accounting firm generally cannot do the accounting job properly for you: They do not (ordinarily) know what special information you need to manage your enterprise most effectively, but know only that general information that most proprietors need, which accountants furnish as standard routine reports.

WHAT DO YOU NEED TO KNOW?

What you need, in general terms, is both reportorial and diagnostic information. You need to know the status and results of all elements of your enterprise in enough detail so that you can determine *why* something is doing well or not doing well. It doesn't help much to know that you lost money overall last month, nor does it help very much even to know that your seminars have not made money, if you can't determine why they did not make money. Nor can you simply raise prices, to overcome a deficit, unless you are sure that raising prices is the correct answer.

Here, for example, are some of the things you want to know when you conduct a mail campaign:

When was the mailing (date, season)?

To whom was the mailing (what list, description of it)?

How big was the mailing?

What was the result—how many orders and how many of each kind, if more than one possible?

What was the percentage return?

What was the dollar return?

What was the ROI (return on investment)?

How did this compare with other mailings?

You should have parallel information for all other kinds of business operations, to get a true understanding of what you are doing, right and wrong, and what you can do to get better results.

On the other hand, suppose you want to run inquiry advertising to build a mailing list of interested prospects for newsletters, seminars, or other purposes. You want somewhat different information:

When was the advertising run (date, season)?

Where [in what publication(s)] was it run?

What was the result—how many responses (inquiries)?

What was the percentage return?

What were the patterns of responses, if any (from what kinds of people, what areas, etc.)?

How did this compare with other mailings/advertisements?

And later, after follow-up mailings and/or other efforts to close, you want to add this information:

How many orders, finally?

What was the dollar return?

What was the ROI (return on investment)?

How did this compare with other mailings?

How did this compare with other mailings/advertisements?

Finally, after all data is in, you want to summarize it on some kind of spreadsheet, where you can make those comparisons called for and make all relevant correlations, to enable you to determine the relative merits of different kinds of copy, different mailing, lists, different offers, and other variables.

HOW TO GET THE INFORMATION

There are two ways to collect this information and to organize it, for the purpose of making those correlations and drawing suitable conclusions for future reference. One way is to design your own system and actually write your own programs. Once that would have been necessary. Today it is not, for there is a superabundance of software readily adaptable to this need. Today you can get any of a variety of accounting programs and other software that will do the job. Actually, you can design your own system, in that you choose the software—the array of programs—that you want, because there is such a variety of choice today that you can usually find standard programs that are suitable to your needs. But before going into that, you should understand some accounting basics:

ACCOUNTING FUNDAMENTALS

Accounting may be complicated in its execution and in the jargon that accountants use, but it is not complicated in its basic truths. They are these:

There are two kinds of dollars in an enterprise, those you take in and those you pay out. Each is classified and subclassified in many ways, but that does not change their nature. Dollars you pay out, whether they are for salaries, rent, telephone, supplies, or other such items are the cost of doing business. Dollars you pay out to buy furniture, fixtures, inventory, and many other items are not costs—not yet. They are merely conversions of the dollar into another asset. You will pay out or spend those dollars only as you use up the inventory and write off—depreciate—the other items. Call them fixed assets, fixed expenses, variable expenses, or by any other term, but you do not change these basic facts. And, for tax and other purposes, you can count these costs as incurred when you make the purchase, or you need not count them as costs until you actually pay out the money. You are allowed that choice, according to what kind of accounting system you use (that is, what kind of accounting philosophy you choose to follow).

You can do the same with dollars in. Income—money in—can be counted as income either when it is due you—is "receivable"—or is actually paid to you. You can set up your system either way, according to which is best for you.

Don't allow yourself to be confused by accounting terms. It is necessary to do all this work for management purposes—to provide the information you need as a manager to understand what is going on (causes and effects) in your enterprise, as well as to pay the taxes you are obliged to pay your several governments, but bear in mind these fundamental principles that do not change, no matter what jargon is applied to them or how mystical the manipulations of the accountants and the legislators.

Small entrepreneurs, such as independent consultants, usually have a single set of books—even a single ledger—for all aspects of their accounting, whereas large organizations have many books, and keep separate ledgers and journals for different accounting operations. You can easily see this in reading listings of computer software programs offered for accounting operations. But you can also see many specialized programs offered, directly to special kinds of businesses and industries.

Following are some listings of different kinds of accounting programs offered. These were chosen from among many thousands of the same general types, as a mere illustrative sampling:

General ledger	Accounts receivable	Accounts payable
Payroll	Asset ledger	Purchase order journal
Inventory	Sales invoicing	Professional time record

Service billing	Small purchases	Rental accounts
Debit ledger	Investments	Budget ledger
Depreciation schedule	Order entry	Cost of sales
Checking account	Telephone accounting	Client write-up
Client record	Commercial contractor	Construction job costing
Project costs	Distributor accounts	Cost accounting
Financial management	Financial modeling	Fixed asset accounts
Leases ledger	Job cost system	Invoice control
Loan amortization	Order tracking	Tax schedules
Payables journal	Receivables journal	Petty cash journal
Project diary	Expense account ledger	Other direct costs journal
Econometrics	Fixed asset management	Engineer's business manager

There are a great many more of these same types. But there are also others, more highly specialized and designed to help managers analyze and plan. Here is a sprinkling of these:

1-2-3, ABS 86, and BPT.   These are all spreadsheets, designed to enable the manager to analyze detailed data and to project a variety of what-if hypotheses by trying different numbers (e.g., different selling prices) to gauge the probable effects.

Bizpack, BMDP Statistical Software, and Cable-Plan.   These are budgeting and forecasting programs, to facilitate analysis and planning.

Context, MBA, The Executive Package, and Financial Analysis.   These are integrated software packages, including a variety of programs for analysis, forecasting, recording, budgeting, and planning. One includes 40 typical business problems, with tools for solving them.

DATABASES AND DATABASE MANAGEMENT

Database managers have been mentioned before as well-suited to many needs, including these. But it bears mentioning again because these kinds of programs, especially the full-fledged database managers, are especially appropriate to your needs, vis-à-vis the kinds of problems we have been discussing in this chapter. Your entire business system is your database or, perhaps more accurately, your set of databases. And, like many other databases, yours are not static, but are dynamic: they keep growing, as you add clients, job records, marketing results, and other information you gather in the normal course of doing business. And that is of great significance. To quite a large degree your success will be the outcome of your decisions, and your decisions are only as good as the information upon which your judgment is based; they cannot be any better than that, except by chance, and chance is no basis for building an enterprise or a career.

Here are some of the databases you should have begun to acquire and build, and which you should keep adding to and maintaining—keeping up to date:

Mailing Lists.   Keep building your mailing lists of prospects and clients. If you begin with rented lists, you can use them only once for each rental fee paid, although the names of any who order from you become your own, to be added to your client list, the very best mailing list ordinarily, which should be kept separate from the others. (When a prospect buys from you, move the name from the prospect list to the client list.) Keep records of rented lists and how they produced for you, so you know what to order, should you wish to use them again. (Mail-order experts agree that the right mailing list is one of the most important factors in mail-order success.)

Results Data.   Keep adding data gathered with regard to the results of mailings, and keep making correlations on the basis of the growing mass of data. The larger the database, ordinarily, the more reliable are the correlations as indicators or forecasters of future results. It's a statistical—probability—discipline, which is always sensitive to the size of the database.

Orders.   The client list should be matched with a record of the items clients have ordered—newsletters, reports, manuals, tapes, seminar registrations, consulting services. Again, the size of this database is important. As it grows, you will be able to make correlations and determine the indicators that tell you who the best prospects are for the different services or products you offer.

Interests.   Keep track of the items—kinds of articles in your newsletter, types of tapes and reports, and so on—that attract the greatest interest and enthusiasm and, of course, the greatest numbers of orders. These kinds of data take much of the guesswork out of decisions with regard to the directions one should take in future efforts.

Patterns.   The idea is always to find patterns, as well as specific and direct results information. You should study the demographic data and try to correlate it with results, to detect the patterns and trends—remember that a pattern may vary, reflecting a trend of the moment.

A good database manager is a must, for best results with the preceding items. There are many database managers, some of which we'll look at in Part Five of this book.

MISCELLANEOUS OTHER FUNCTIONS

What I write here today will be already dated by the time this book is in print. What is visionary projection today will be accomplished fact within months, history in a year or two. Such is the extraordinary dynamism of the computer industry, proliferating exponentially—at an ever-faster rate—in sophistication, as well as in numbers of units and users. Still, much of the future in applications technology is quite certain and has begun to appear already. Banking from your home via your personal computer, for example, is already an accomplished fact in a number of places and will be more and more commonplace in the future. For this you need communications software, and there are many inexpensive programs, even some public domain—free—ones, available. Soon you will have to visit your bank only occasionally and be able to handle many of your banking transactions without leaving your office. And soon enough you will be able to handle many other functions at your desk. For example, it is already technically feasible to send copy to your typesetter or printer by computer-to-computer telephone link, and this is being done in many offices and print shops. You can communicate with just about anyone anywhere who has a terminal, modem, and telephone, and you can record that information on disk and print it out, to create a permanent record, as well as view it on-screen.

You can make purchases in this manner. Many of the public database services and online bulletin boards maintain "electronic malls," wherein they describe offerings and prices via computer-to-computer links and accept your orders, for shipping subsequently. You can send purchase orders in this manner, but of course you can set up your own electronic mall and accept orders for whatever you offer—newsletters, tapes, reports, manuals, or other.

More and more you will find your own clients utilizing their computers and modems for communications and transactions that can be carried out this way. When you are part of that network of businesspeople doing business in this manner you provide a certain convenience for your clients and prospective clients and present yourself also as a modern, successful, and sophisticated consultant, a favorable image.

PART FOUR

Selecting the Right Computer for Your Practice

In the extraordinary outpouring of computer books for the lay citizen, there have been quite a large number purporting to make computers as easy to understand and use as a TV or videocassette recorder/player. Extant are such titles as *Computers for Everybody*, *Without Me You're Nothing*, *Computer Programming for the Complete Idiot*, and *Computers Made Simple*, among countless others designed to allay readers' fears and encourage purchase of the books.

Perhaps it is possible to make computers "really simple," as one author puts it in his own title. However, because the computer is essentially an *interactive* device, which requires you to take an active role in using it, as compared with the passive role you play in using a TV or VCR, it cannot be quite as simple to use even the most "user friendly" computer and software programs as it is to watch a videotaped movie or football game.

Still, it is not *that* difficult to learn how to use a modern personal computer, if you select one that is suitable for your own needs and purposes. In Part Four you will find some guidance to help you in doing that, with an all-out effort on my part to keep the information free of technical fog.

CHAPTER FOURTEEN

Does Software Come First?

Conventional wisdom changes, as circumstances change, and the "software comes first" wisdom is not an exception.

THE PROBLEM OF NO STANDARDS—OR IS IT ONE OF TOO MANY STANDARDS?

One of the outstanding complaints about the computer industry is that it does not conform to any uniform set of standards. This is not to say that there are no standards; quite the contrary, there are too many standards, so that you always have the problem of seeing to it, before you buy computers, peripheral hardware, software programs, and/or supplies, that what you are buying is compatible with whatever else you are buying or have already bought. From the beginning each manufacturer designed and built computers to the manufacturer's own, usually unique, specifications. Peripheral equipment that worked with one manufacturer's computer would usually not be compatible with or even adaptable to Remington-Rand, RCA, Philco, Honeywell, Burroughs, or the computers of any other early birds in the computer industry. In fact, so individual were were all these pioneers of the computer industries that it is perhaps remarkable that anything at all ever became standardized across the industry, as a few things did. (But that may have been because those few things were so "right" that they were clearly the only way to go—for example, the binary system itself.)

SOFTWARE AND HARDWARE ARE MUTUALLY DEPENDENT ON EACH OTHER

Much less was the software—computer programs—interchangeable among the various computers. All software suitable for any given computer was either supplied by the computer manufacturer or written to order by or for the computer buyer, which helped give rise to the large custom-software-development industry, companies who undertake major programming jobs under contract. (This is a well-populated field, with a great many small- and medium-sized companies and a few rather large corporations in it.) And since all the early computers were huge and costly, in the beginning, only the large organizations bought or leased them (they were almost always leased to users, in the early days), and then they contracted with software developers to write programs (unless they had their own programming staffs, as some did). In general the problem then was that hardware was more abundantly available than was software. And what a computer can do depends at least as much on the software installed in it as on the hardware itself: Neither hardware nor software are of any practical use without the other.

THE "SOFTWARE FIRST" WISDOM

In that environment, it became wisdom to first be sure that the kind of software you wanted was available before you chose a computer: You first chose the software and then chose the hardware that was compatible—that would run the software. Hence arose the conventional wisdom, still regarded by many today as an inviolable rule and especially as the soundest advice for newcomers to the field. Again and again you read that software must come first, hardware second, on that theory that it is easier to match hardware to software than vice versa.

Some change came about gradually, especially after the microchips were developed, ushering the era of true microminiaturization of electronic equipment and giving rise to the pocket calculators and, finally, to desktop computers, soon enough referred to as "personal" computers. And it was then not long before those desktop/personal computers began to appear in great numbers. And in that environment of mass production of computers and a swiftly growing population of computer owners and users, the software industry also began to grow rapidly, producing software to be sold off the shelf.

SOFTWARE AND MARKET INFLUENCES

Two influences guide the development of that off-the-shelf software, for the obvious reason that these two factors identify the largest markets for various kinds of software:

1. The kinds of programs most popular and most useful—most in demand.

2. The makes and models of hardware (computers) most popular with the public—in use in the greatest numbers, that is.

Because the computer was originally conceived as a machine for "number crunching"—automating mathematical operations—it is not surprising that a great many accounting and payroll programs were developed almost at once, with other number-based programs also coming along rapidly for such things as inventory control, engineering calculations, and other such applications. And so it is not surprising that such programs appear in great abundance on every list of available software for personal computers.

Word processing has emerged as probably the most popular use of the personal computer, even more popular than accounting programs, and so we witness a great many word processing and related programs (such as spellers) also offered by a myriad of software developers. (A recent directory lists some 1600 such developers.)

A tremendous boost was given to the desktop-computer business by two young men who launched Apple Computers. Almost overnight a great many Apple computers were being sold. But soon enough the Tandy Corp./Radio Shack TRS80 computers appeared in the hundreds of Radio Shack retail stores and began to sell well. The Osborne, a pioneer in portable computers, followed soon after, as did a great many others, some well-known companies—NCR (National Cash Register), Zenith, and Hewlett-Packard, for example—and some lesser-known ones, such as Kaypro, Otrona, Altos, and Corvus. It should come as no surprise then that a great many programs have been designed for these popular machines and are offered as candidates for use in those computers.

PERSONAL COMPUTERS AND OPERATING SYSTEMS

One major difference among these many manufacturers and their equipment was in something called an "operating system," or OS. Each computer has a microchip called a CPU (central processing unit) or microprocessor, and this chip has a set of instructions built into it. However, the computer must have an operating system, which is a set of commands that utilizes the instructions built into the chip to cause the computer to execute program instructions, especially as far as operating the disk system is concerned. (In fact, in many cases the OS is formally titled a DOS, as in PC-DOS and MS-DOS, for disk operating system.) This operating system is the chief factor in hardware–software compatibility. A software program must be written for a given operating system, to be compatible with it and work in the computer.

Unfortunately, many of these manufacturers created their own, unique operating systems, in the hope that they would thus create captive customers, tied to their own hardware systems. The strategy backfired on many, for buyers followed the advice of choosing the software first, and there was little software available or under development for those computers that had not sold in large quantities. The software companies were, of course, writing programs for the more popular (and more populous) Apple, TRS-80, Osborne, and other computers. Some of these had their own unique operating systems, but that was of no consequence if there were enough of their machines being sold; only the size of the potential market was of significance.

THE FIRST DE FACTO STANDARD OS

Ultimately a de facto standard, CP/M (control program for microcomputers), a product of Digital Research, emerged. Osborne, Kaypro, and many others adopted the CP/M operating system, and before long there were a great many personal/desktop computers that incorporated this operating system. Not surprisingly, then, a huge library of CP/M-compatible software grew up, and soon there was a bigger library of software for CP/M-based computers than there was even for Apple, TRS-80, and a few other popular non-CP/M computers. Even today, with the library of PC-DOS and MS-DOS programs growing steadily, the array of CP/M programs is still far larger than any other. (In fact, a great many of the PC-DOS and MS-DOS programs are CP/M programs revised to work in PC-DOS and MS-DOS computers.)

IBM AND THE PC CREATE A NEW DE FACTO STANDARD

Still later—relatively recently, at the time of this writing—IBM appeared on the scene with the IBM PC (and later with some derivatives of the PC). For a time it appeared as though IBM would opt also to utilize CP/M or some variant of it, but for whatever reason (the industry buzzed with "inside stories" on the subject, for a time) IBM opted to have created for them by Microsoft, a software developer, the operating system known as PC-DOS, which is not compatible with CP/M but is also not radically different from CP/M.

Microsoft then created MS-DOS, its own proprietary version of PC-DOS (some believe it to be a clone of PC-DOS, while others point to some differences that prevent complete interchangeability with PC-DOS), which they license to many manufacturers whose machines are represented as being "IBM-compatible."

As a result of IBM's entrance into the PC (personal computer) market, with the enormous market power that IBM wields, radical changes took place in the market:

Until IBM entered the market with their original PC, personal computers were built almost entirely around 8-bit microprocessors, and CP/M and other operating systems were written for 8-bit machines. Machines using the newer 16-bit CPU were beginning to appear but had not assumed a dominant position in the market. The IBM PC changed that, since it is a 16-bit machine, and PC-DOS is an operating system for 16-bit machines. Most of the new machines now began to appear with 16-bit CPUs and 16-bit languages, such as MS-DOS and a 16-bit version of CP/M, CP/M-86. (The original CP/M is now sometimes referred to as CP/M-80, to identify it as an 8-bit operating system and distinguish it from the CP/M-86.)

So today we have a great many "IBM-compatibles" and a great many software programs for the IBM PC, for the compatibles, with their MS-DOS operating system, and for the many machines using CP/M-80 and CP/M-86. That is, there is already a large "library" of programs for these machines, as well as substantial libraries for most models of Apple and for Tandy/Radio Shack's TRS-80.

THE CONVENTIONAL WISDOM IS NOW A SOMETIME TRUTH ONLY

What this means is that the conventional wisdom about the necessity for choosing the software first is no longer true. At best, it is a partial truth and is entirely valid only if and when you consider buying a computer utilizing a less popular operating system than those already named here, for then you may, indeed, run into a problem finding the right software. But if you buy a machine with a CP/M-80, CP/M-86, PC-DOS, MS-DOS, Apple-DOS, or TRS-DOS operating system, especially CP/M and PC-DOS/MS-DOS, it is unlikely that you will have any difficulty finding appropriate software for any need you are likely to have. For all practical purposes—unless you happen to have some truly unusual needs—if you buy a computer with any of those operating systems you will almost surely find appropriate software for whatever you need to do.

SOME EXCEPTIONS AND CLARIFICATIONS

As all general rules do, this one has some exceptions. Or, at least, some factors that need to be considered in understanding compatibility of software and hardware with operating systems. One factor is this: Every operating system has more than one version and revision. Every software developer continues to update, improve, and revise the software, and software that is popular, as CP/M is, of course goes through many such revisions. The CP/M used in my system is CP/M Version 2.2 (known popularly as simply CP/M 2.2), Revision 1.5. Version 2.2 was, at the time I was upgrading my system, the latest edition of CP/M available from its developer, Digital Research. (Digital Research has since produced CP/M Version 3.0, which is largely, although not entirely, compatible with CP/M 2.2.) Revision 1.5 is the version of CP/M 2.2 that the hardware manufacurer, Morrow Designs, in this case, produced for use in his own machines.

That's typical. For any operating system, each manufacturer licensed to use the system must match it to his own computer, and thus produces his "revision" of the OS for his machine. And although most revisions of CP/M 2.2 (and of other operating systems) are largely compatible with each other, they are not entirely so.

That's not quite as hopeless as it seems. Although I could not run an Osborne CP/M or some of the other CP/M disks in this machine directly, the machine did come with software that permits running those other CP/M disks by making some minor adaptations.

So while there is little danger that you will not find suitable software for any of those machines and kinds of operating systems cited earlier, it is still a good idea to consider the software–hardware compatibility problem before finalizing your buying decisions. Nor can you be guided by the make and model alone, either, for although Apple and Tandy/Radio Shack have their own operating systems for most of the machines, both have used CP/M for some of their machines, and even IBM has used CP/M-86.

But that is not all of it, either. It would be wrong to infer from this that the hardware is unimportant, or even less important than the software. Even for the less costly machines, the investment is a serious one—usually on the order of $3000 to $5000. And even that sometimes only makes the buyer "pregnant," as one memorable corporate vice-president used to remark, and commits the buyer to a course of action that will soon enough require additional investments to gain full utility and benefit from the original investment commitment. For that is what the original investment is: a commitment. If you invest unwisely, as many do in their initial computer purchases, you will be forced to face the dilemma of whether to spend additional money to salvage the situation and make the best of it or to write the whole thing off as a loss. Unless you believe that you can afford to spend several thousand dollars as casually as though you were buying lunch, you must consider a number of factors quite seriously in reaching a decision.

FACING THE FUTURE

For one thing, there is the matter of looking to the future. Will the machine you buy today be useful for a few years to come or will this ultradynamic industry render it obsolete almost before you have learned to use it effectively? Will it be able to accommodate the software of the future? (And will it be possible to predict what that software will be?) If the history of the computer industry has taught us anything it has taught us that, in computers, last year is almost ancient history and that the future is only a few months from now. Obviously, it is difficult to plan very far ahead under these circumstances. Still, the commitment is too serious to undertake without giving some thought to where we are going, and there are, fortunately, a few factors and a few trends that portend the future and give us some basis, at least, for forecasting and anticipating where we are headed—what future computer capabilities are likely to be, that is.

What we do know is that the primary factors that affect those capabilities are memory and storage. As we proceed through Part Four of this book and examine the hardware side of the computer offerings you will come to understand that more clearly, and we'll begin to examine that aspect of computers and their capabilities in a moment. But first let's look just a bit further into the software side, for a few moments.

THE SOFTWARE TRENDS

We have discussed many aspects of the consulting profession and made frequent mention of different types and classes of computer software in the pages that preceded this. By now you should have begun to get at least a general appreciation of the many types of software available, and perhaps you have even been able to perceive the general trends of software over the recent years, for there have been at least two definite trends:

1. One major trend has been to make software more and more "user friendly"—easy to use. Some effort has been made to improve the quality of the documentation—the user manuals—but the primary focus of the effort has been to provide more on-screen help—menus, tutorials (even extended tutorials, which are virtual training programs), warnings, reminders of various kinds, programs to make keys "user defined" and to change two-key commands into simpler one-key commands, paper and plastic overlays to fit over keyboards and help you find the right keys quickly, and for some kinds of programs "overlays" of a different kind (software overlays, to help you use the programs more effectively and easily).

2. Another major trend is the trend toward amassing various programs "under one roof"—in a single program, in which you can go easily and swiftly from one program to another,

without exiting the first program, to take data from one program and supply it to another, while still in the main program, and even to establish "windows" on-screen, so that you can look at the contents of files in any of the several programs that make up the integrated software package you are using.

All of these trends in software add up to an ever-increasing demand for more and more memory and storage, especially for memory. But to get a complete appreciation of this, it is necessary to understand the basics of using a computer and even to review a few fundamentals. Let's take a more practical, hands-on look at what you must actually *do* to operate your computer.

MEMORY VERSUS STORAGE

Memory in a computer is internal, that is, part of the inner workings of the computer proper, usually in a microchip called "RAM" (random access memory). What you enter in the computer via the keyboard, a disk, or by any other input/output device goes to RAM and remains there until you cut power to the computer, whereupon it evaporates (in some quarters that is referred to as a "volatile" memory): The memory is wiped clean, erased completely, when power is turned off or when the system is "reset" by using the RESET switch. To save what you have in memory, if you wish to save it as digital information, you must store it on disk or tape. (Most personal computers today use floppy—thin plastic—disks, although there is a distinct trend to the much-higher-storage-capacity hard disks.) That does not clear memory, for the data is not literally moved when it is saved or stored, but it is copied by the storage device, which is considered to be "peripheral" to the computer, even if it is enclosed in the same housing that surrounds the central computer or computer proper.

The computer operates only on data that is in its memory. So when you use a program, which is usually on disk, you must "load" the program, which means ordering the program loaded, whereupon the computer copies the program into its RAM memory. If the program and/or data on the program disk requires more memory space than the computer affords, it is usually possible to load—copy in memory—only that part of the program and/or data required immediately and to replace it with other parts of the program and/or data, as necessary.

On the other hand, some types of programs can't be used that way because all or nearly all of the program must be in the computer's memory for the program to run properly and to be useful. In such case, it is necessary to have a large enough RAM or forego using the program.

The case of storage is somewhat similar, but far less constraining. It is possible to make-do with less than adequate storage, although it proves to be rather inconvenient, usually, requiring much juggling of data back and forth between memory and storage.

Memory and storage capacity are measured in *bytes*—in *kilobytes*, more accurately. A byte is eight *bits*, and a bit is one electrical pulse, representing a 1 or a 0. A byte is required to represent each alphanumeric character. For example, "abc23" would require five bytes to record it. A kilobyte is nominally 1000 bytes (literally, it is 1024 bytes, but the difference is insignificant and the reason for it is not important here). The typical 64-kilobyte memory of an 8-bit computer therefore represents a memory capacity of approximately 64,000 characters or about 8000 words, equivalent to about 32 pages of double-spaced copy. (The typical memory of a 16-bit computer is twice that, or 128K, but larger memories are common enough today.)

Floppy-disk storage capacities are measured in kilobytes also, and tend to be in hundreds of thousands. My own, for example, are 5¼-inch disks, and the drives operate at double-density (double, as compared with earlier disk storage) and store data on both sides of the disk, so that the drives and the disks are known as double sided, double density. And my system stores 384 kilobytes on each disk, so that the entire system can handle a nominal 832 kilobytes online at one time.

Hard disks are of much greater storage capacity, measured in megabytes (Mb), which means "millions of bytes," and storage capacity of 10 Mb is quite common. Until recently they were too expensive for most owners of personal computers, but the prices have begun to decline as manufacturers have made increasing efforts to develop lower-cost hard disks for personal computers. Probably the trend is tied closely to the increasing trend toward software that requires more and more memory and storage to be run effectively. It may well be that soon it will be difficult to run any but relatively "primitive" programs without the high storage capacity of a hard-disk system.

THE CHICKEN AND THE EGG

As in many things, trying to establish the cause-and-effect relationship between computer hardware and software resembles the chicken-and-egg (which came first?) dilemma. Increasingly sophisticated software requires more and more sophisticated hardware, especially in terms of memory and storage capacity. And computer manufacturers respond with new designs, affecting directly the designs and characteristics of computers being brought to market, as they strive to make their products capable of running the most advanced software. But the reverse appears to be true also, with the development of increasingly more sophisticated software, requiring more and more capacious memory and storage, inspired by and resulting from the introduction of computers with larger memories and storage capacities.

Planning for the future requires that you consider what you are likely to want in the future, as well as what you want and need immediately. If you are going to want only word processing, 64K memory is probably adequate, but it is a bit skimpy for graphics and probably not quite adequate for many of the spreadsheet and integrated software programs. Also, unless 64K systems fall sharply in price in the future, the price differential between 64K and 128K systems—and essentially that is the difference between 8-bit and 16-bit computers—is not very significant, so it appears wise to consider the computer with a 16-bit CPU and 128K memory the absolute minimum acceptable.

CHOOSING THE SOFTWARE

In the first worksheet, in an early chapter, some general areas of general business applications and technical/professional applications of computer usage were listed. You were invited to make some check-offs and/or write-ins, as appropriate, in a first exercise to help you think out your probable needs or at least help determine the areas of your general interest. It is now time to think more seriously about those needs, and it may be helpful to go back to that first worksheet now and review your entries to see if you have changed your mind about any of them before proceeding further, to the third worksheet.

WORKSHEET 3

The suggested review is in preparation for making out another worksheet, Worksheet 3. Because you have now learned a little more about some of the many options open to you as a consultant, while also getting more insight into the kinds of software programs and what you can do with them, this is somewhat more closely related to actual software needs than the earlier worksheet was. It is therefore a closer approach to making some preliminary decisions about the kind of system you will want.

Give serious thought to the choices, and go back to reread some of the earlier material and refresh your memory, if necessary. Try to gain an understanding of what your choices will mean in terms of the software you will need. Part I of the worksheet calls for just that—identifying the kinds of activities you are or will probably be carrying out, in your consulting practice. Spaces are provided to write in other items and/or make notes, since it is virtually impossible to identify all the possible activities and functions. Then, in Part II, convert those activities/functions into the appropriate types of software you will need. (Later, we'll talk about identifying specific progams; for now, let's talk only about *types* of software needed to accomplish everything you want to accomplish.)

PART I: Check off the uses you expect to make of your system.

MARKETING

[ ] Formal proposals [ ] Letter proposals [ ] Brochures
[ ] News releases   [ ] Articles   [ ] Direct mail
[ ] _____
[ ] _____

CONSULTING

[ ] Number   [ ] Presentations   [ ] formal reports
    crunching
[ ] _____
[ ] _____

ANCILLARY INCOME ACTIVITIES

[ ] Seminars   [ ] Newsletters   [ ] Manuals, reports
[ ] _____
[ ] _____

MANAGEMENT AND ADMINISTRATION

[ ] Accounting   [ ] Financial control [ ] Office procedures
[ ] _____
[ ] _____

PART II: Translate those uses into the types of software needed.
[ ] Word processor [ ] File manager   [ ] Database manager
[ ] Spreadsheet   [ ] Integrated   [ ] Communications
[ ] General ledger [ ] Financial manager [ ] Inventory
[ ] _____
[ ] _____

Worksheet 3. Focusing on probable software needs.

SOURCES OF SOFTWARE INFORMATION

Over the past few years the sources of information about available software have grown enormously. Today you can learn about available software from at least these kinds of sources, numbering into many hundreds:

Articles and reviews in general computer periodicals—magazines, mostly, but including tabloids and other newsprint publications—numbering into the hundreds, with at least a couple dozen readily available on well-stocked newsstands. Almost all review software in every issue, often in great depth, and most run frequent articles on generic types of software, such as word processors, spreadsheets, and integrated software packages.

Specialty publications, which specialize in software listings and reviews.

Advertising matter to be found in those publications and catalogs of software products issued by the major software firms. Also advertising matter to be found in retail establishments selling computer hardware, software, and supplies. (Obviously, these kinds of descriptions and coverage are somewhat less objective than those published in general-circulation computer magazines.)

Books published to present compilations of software reviews and descriptions.

Online data from some of the database services.

Conversations with sales personnel. (A risky source, unfortunately, as some salespeople are expert, while others are quite inexpert. Use with caution.)

Fellow members of computer clubs. Some caution is required here, for the same reason that it is required with salespeople: Not all the people you talk to in computer clubs will be truly expert or able to give you reliable information. However, it is also true that many of the computer hobbyists are more expert than the experts—that is, they are more knowledgeable than the professionals. In many respects, computer clubs are the best source of help.

ABOUT "USER FRIENDLINESS"

One major focus of software advertising is on its alleged "user friendliness." This advertising bias is based on the notion that most people are terrified of computers because they are or seem to be so dreadfully technical and nearly impossible for the ordinary mortal to grasp. Therefore, the average prospect needs heavy reassurance that one need not be a Phi Beta Kappa to handle the program. And the notion seems to have taken root in the consciousness of all who write about computer software, even those who do not have a vested interest in selling the software to prospects. In reading articles and reviews about software in the popular literature you often find that same bias toward the friendlier software.

For example, the point has been made in more than one magazine article about database managers that while dBase II is undoubtedly a superior database manager, it offers less help to the user than do many other database managers, and therefore requires a somewhat greater degree of skill—expertise—to use, and this is presented as a negative argument, an argument against this software and for other software that is replete with menus, tutorials, and other evidences of the extended hand and friendly pat on the back.

On the other hand, the president of a computer club, who happens to be a professional computer programmer, recently made the observation that while it might be more difficult to learn dBase II than it is to learn some other programs, the rewards were well worth the extra effort. He remarked, logically enough, that the program is not more difficult to use—might even be easier to use—but was only a little more difficult to learn. And he stated that as a general observation that could be said for many other programs. They are only more difficult to use when the user has not yet learned the program, but that is a condition that will pass, eventually, and even the friendliest program requires some learning.

THE TRADE-OFF

In fact, what we are talking about is really a typical trade-off: To get that extra help known as user-friendliness, you give something up. You give up some of the efficiency and utility the program might otherwise provide. A small excursion into some computer technology basics would be helpful here in understanding this, and it should be most helpful to you later when you are trying to evaluate software.

COMPUTER LANGUAGES

The only language the computer understands is one called *machine language* or *machine code* also sometimes referred to as *object language* or *object code*. This is, in fact, a series of those electrical pulses, representing 1s and 0s, arranged in 8-bit groups (bytes), such as 10011100. In the early days, it was necessary to actually prepare long lists of such groups of 1s and 0s, representing the bits that the machine could understand when they were represented as holes and spaces in a punched card or punched tape, or as magnetic spots on a tape, drum, or other device used as input and output to the computer. (Most often, the codes were punched into those 80-column Hollerith cards that became widely known as "IBM cards," and the cards were then run through a machine that read those codes to the computer.)

Preparing those lists—programs—was a rather tedious job, of course, and it finally occurred to someone that perhaps the computer could itself help in writing those programs. That seemed like a reasonable task for a computer to perform. But someone had to teach the computer how to do the job. So the next step was to develop "high level" languages also called assembly languages. These are codes, using mnemonic—memory assisting—symbols, which are therefore much easier for humans to use, and which the computer is able to translate into the machine codes. This was a major advance in software technology.

Since then, even higher level languages, such as BASIC (Beginner's All-Purpose Symbolic Instruction Code), have been developed and are almost like English, greatly simplifying the task of writing programs, which are then interpreted or translated by the computer into machine language. But the advances have not been accomplished without paying a price for them. They have exacted their own compromises in making the inevitable trade-offs.

One of the sacrifices has been in efficiency. The use of higher level languages requires more memory and it takes longer to run the programs in higher level languages than it does to run them in assembly languages and machine languages. It requires memory and time to install and operate the software that translates the higher level languages into machine languages.

There is also a trade-off to be made between simplicity and versatility. A number of people have complained that the word processor WordStar is complicated and difficult to learn, and sometimes they point to other programs that, they say, are much simpler and much easier to learn. But they overlook the fact that WordStar, as a result of that very complexity which is the bone of contention, is a remarkably versatile and flexible word processor. For one thing, there is virtually no function it does that cannot be done in several different ways, each way more appropriate than the others for some given situation. For example, there are several ways to copy files, part of files, and other material, access swiftly back and forth through a file, use the search and find functions, and do a myriad of other things. (Despite the fact that I have used WordStar for a long time and think I know it thoroughly, I am still discovering useful things I can do with it that I never suspected before were even possible.)

Perhaps it was a bit more difficult to learn WordStar than to learn some other word processors—it was probably a week or more of continuous use before I decided that I did not need the menus any more and preferred to have more free space on the screen—but having once learned it, the chore is done, and I now have the advantage of using the word processor I happen to believe is the greatest of them all, despite some things even I acknowledge are shortcomings.

Give some thought to these things, then, when you consider the benefits of user-friendliness. That quality is probably valuable for software you use only occasionally, for then you probably never really "learn" the program and perhaps you will always need that friendly pat on the shoulder to help you through it. But if you are searching for a program you will use frequently, you will eventually learn it thoroughly, whether you set out to do so deliberately or not, and once you have learned it, its relative difficulty or complexity is more likely to represent benefits than drawbacks. So, under the circumstance of anticipated continuous or frequent use, you may very well be wise to totally disregard the advantages of any alleged user-friendliness and study the true pros and cons of the program. Otherwise you may well pay a greater price than you should for the dubious benefits of that friendly hand.

CHAPTER FIFTEEN

Hardware Is Important Too

The proliferation of hardware is not quite as great as that of software, but it is great enough to be one of the many confusion factors for the nonexpert buying a computer system.

A BRIEF GLANCE AT THE HARDWARE MARKET

Terminology is as confusing on the hardware side of computers as it is on the software side, and ambiguity is one of the complications here. Take, for example, the very word *computer*. Perhaps you think that you know what it means but it does not mean the same thing to everyone or in every use of the word. Generally speaking, most of us use the word "computer" informally to refer to all the items that make up a computer system and which are, in fact, often housed in a single enclosure, as a TV is, except for the printer. (And there are exceptions to that, too, with some systems managing to include even the printer in one monolithic unit.) In fact, being quite technical about it, what most of us call a computer is actually a system of a number of components or subsystems, of which the computer is the central element but which includes all the following as parts of the system, but not part of the computer itself:

Monitor (CRT)
Keyboard
Storage system (disk drives, generally)
Printer
Software (programs)

You must be aware, therefore, that when vendors advertise "computers" at what may appear to be (or are claimed to be) discounted prices, the advertised price is not necessarily referring to a complete computer system, but may be referring to only the computer proper, with most of the system priced separately as add-ons. It is necessary to read carefully when you study the many advertisements offering computers, sometimes at alleged bargain prices, to determine just what is and what is not included. Usually the price will include the keyboard, which may even be enclosed in and part of the same housing that contains the computer (typical of many Apple and Radio Shack models) but it may or may not include all the other items. Many computers are offered with all those other necessities, even the monitor, as options. (This is based on the assumption that you can use an ordinary TV receiver as a monitor, despite the fact that this is not a very satisfactory substitute.) Similarly, in some offers, no storage device is included, on the assumption that you will use an ordinary home audiotape recorder/player as the storage device. This is again not really a very satisfactory substitute for a disk system, if for no other reason than that it is quite a slow method for storing and retrieving digital information.

There is a great tendency today toward the "separates" idea in personal computers as illustrated in Figure 16, in which the highly successful IBM PC is shown. The monitor (unit with the TV-like screen) and the keyboard constitute the "terminal" for the system. The rectangular housing upon which the monitor rests contains the computer per se, but also has two floppy-disk drives. The printer is a completely separate unit.

Figure 16.   The IBM PC in a popular physical arrangement.
(Courtesy IBM Corporation)

This is a fairly popular physical arrangement. (My own Morrow Micro Decisions system is organized the same way.) It enables the operator to move the keyboard around, at the end of its 6-foot cord, a great convenience. (Some users like to type with the keyboard in their laps.)

Of course, the whole system is worthless to you without

software; you have to have programs to get any use out of the computer, and they represent a considerable investment when purchased separately.

Finally, you will not be able to benefit greatly from your system, in all probability, if you do not have a printer. You will therefore almost surely find yourself compelled to buy a printer separately, if one was not included in your original purchase.

On the other hand, there are a great many computers offered as complete systems, including all the components listed here, with some starting software, and often with a rather comprehensive package of software. (The practice of including software with the computer is called "bundling" in the trade and it is becoming a more or less standard practice to include software programs, especially word processors and some version of BASIC, with the system.)

WHAT SHOULD A PERSONAL COMPUTER COST?

It is quite easy to spend $15,000 or more for a desktop computer, if you think your computer needs are that great, but it is unlikely that you need to spend more than $5000, and even that is on the high side for the typical personal computer today, when highly capable personal computers—complete systems, that is—are being offered for well under $3000, many of them even including printers at such prices. However, to get a true appreciation of the market and of the relative values represented, it is necessary to get a more intimate look at the hardware components, with some of the many alternatives offered for each.

PREPARING TO SHOP FOR A COMPUTER

To help you to understand relative values of personal computers offered in the marketplace you need to know what to look for, how to understand what you read and hear, and how to evaluate what is offered. But to do that you need to gain some deeper understanding of computer technology. That compels me to "get technical" to at least some extent but don't get alarmed; it's going to be a brief technical voyage (actually, only a semitechnical voyage) and I will furnish an easy-to-read and easy-to-understand map as we travel. The first steps are to establish some basic definitions, facts, and terminology. Don't try to memorize everything (that is totally unnecessary) but only to get the general essence of it all. Eventually, it will all fall into place and you will remember only that which you need to remember and find useful.

Some Basic Terms and Units of Measure

The central computer is built around the chip called the CPU (central processing unit) or microprocessor. By far the majority of low- and medium-priced personal computers of the microcircuit age used an 8-bit CPU chip until fairly recently. What that means, in practice, is that the CPU handled information in groups of 8 bits. (The term *bit* is derived from the two words *binary digit*, and represents either 1 or 0, since the system is binary, which means that there can only be two values.) Each group of 8 bits is called a *byte*, and one byte is required to represent each alphanumeric character or special symbol. (There are 255 combinations of 8 bits possible, so an ample number of characters and symbols can be represented by assigning each a single byte.)

Most measurements of memory, storage capacity, and other elements of the system are stated in terms of bytes, using either *kilobytes* or *megabytes* as the unit of measure. Kilobytes are generally represented as "K" or "Kb," meaning 1000 bytes (a nominal 1000 since the actual number of bytes in a kilobyte is 1024), and megabytes are generally represented as "Mb" or "M," representing 1 million bytes (actually 1,048,576 bytes).

The Binary System

To understand the significance of these seemingly odd values, you have to understand the binary system. Unlike the decimal system, which has 10 values (1–10), the binary system has only two values,

1 and 0. Both have *positional notation,* which means that the position a digit occupies in a column affects its value. In the decimal system, for example, the figure 1525 actually means this:

$$1000 = 1 \times 10 \times 10 \times 10 \text{ or } 10^3$$
$$500 = 5 \times 10 \times 10 \text{ or } 5 \times 10^2$$
$$20 = 2 \times 10 \text{ or } 2 \times 10^1$$
$$5 = 5 \times 1 \text{ or } 5 \times 10^0$$

1525

Exactly the same philosphy applies in binary notation, although the values are different. That 1024 "K" value thus can be represented by the binary number 10000000000, or 1 followed by 10 0s. To understand that, consider how the binary number 100100 is used to represent the more familiar decimal number 36:

$$100000 = 1 \times 2 \times 2 \times 2 \times 2 \times 2 \text{ or } 1 \times 2^5 \quad (= 32)$$
$$00000 = 0 \times 2 \times 2 \times 2 \times 2 \text{ or } 0 \times 2^4 \quad (= 0)$$
$$0000 = 0 \times 2 \times 2 \times 2 \text{ or } 0 \times 2^3 \quad (= 0)$$
$$100 = 1 \times 2 \times 2 \text{ or } 1 \times 2^2 \quad (= 4)$$
$$00 = 0 \times 2 \text{ or } 0 \times 2^1 \quad (= 0)$$
$$0 = 0 \times 1 \text{ or } 0 \times 2^0 \quad (= 0)$$

Therefore, 2^{10} (1 followed by 10 0s) = 1024, a far easier number to write in binary notation than 1000. (That would be 1111101000. And that also explains why memory and storage capacities of 32 (2^5), 64 (2^6), 128 (2^7), and so on. They are all in the convenient powers of 2, which the binary system can handle with greater ease than it can the decimal quantities (although it necessarily must convert decimal to binary and vice versa, and it uses other number systems, as well, such as octal and hexadecimal). An easy way to remember binary notation is to remember that in each position, from your right to your left as you face the column of numbers, the values double, beginning with 1: 1, 2, 4, 8, 16, 32, 64, 128, 256, 512, 1024, and so on. (The reason it begins with 1 is because the rightmost number is 2^0, and every number to the 0 power is 1, no matter what the number or the base of the system is.)

But don't let all of this trouble you: You do not need to know anything about binary notation or mathematics in general to understand computers. All of this was only to satisfy your curiosity, if you had any, about why we use those odd numbers. Now you can forget it and feel perfectly at ease in doing so.

Bytes, CPUs, and Memory Sizes

Using those chips that handled data in single bytes of 8-bits at a time, the desktop computers tended to have memories of 4, 8, and 16K in the earliest computers, later grew to 32K, and finally became more or less standardized at 64K as the most popular memory size for personal computers. In fact, for a long time it was by the memory size that computers were generally evaluated in a broad sense and became referred to as 32K or 64K machines.

Over recent years, and especially since the IBM PC entered the market, the standard has become more or less one of 16-bit CPUs and 128K or larger memories. There are still many 8-bit, 64K machines being produced and sold, and a great many in everyday use, but with the price differential between the two classes of personal computers being insignificant (if, for that matter, one can even detect a true differential in prices) it seems sensible to consider only the newer computers with their greater capacities. (All of these standards are de facto standards, and the whole industry is plagued by the inherent incompatibility of software and hardware produced for and by the hundreds of hardware manufacturers and software developers.)

Dual Microprocessors

One other factor that has happened along and added further confusion to the picture has been the advent of dual processors in microcomputers. Today a number of computers are offering two CPUs, instead of one, frequently an 8-bit CPU and a 16-bit CPU. This permits the system to handle a wide variety of software and to handle more than one program and more than one task at a time.

(This is referred to in the industry as "multiprogramming" and "multitasking.") It also offers greater flexibility in office automation, lending itself to multiuser applications also.

The Upward Trend in Microprocessors

Computers with 32K CPUs and correspondingly larger memories are also coming along rapidly (the Apple Macintosh is an example of this), and the 32K CPU may be commonplace by the time you read this. (And perhaps the long-heralded 64K microprocessor will begin to become an everyday reality, too, by that time.) Among the things about the computer industry we have learned is that we almost always underestimate what is happening or about to happen in the industry, especially the speed at which it will happen. It's doubtful that anyone would have predicted the marketing of computers with 32K CPUs this early in the game, had you asked them a few years ago. And it was less than 25 years ago that scientists were speculating on and experimenting with the early forerunners of today's microcircuits. (In fact, transistors were a startling new development at the time, but are obsolescent today.)

It's useful to bear this in mind, as you shop for a computer. It would be futile to wait for newer and better models to emerge, because you might wait forever, since newer and better models emerge almost continuously, with frequent major advances in the state of the art. But you might wish to heed the advice of some of the professionals in the field and keep your initial investment as modest as possible, with the aim of amortizing that investment rapidly so that you can write off your computer in a few years and replace it with whatever is the newest and best at the time. (In one conference among a number of experts in the field, Micro Decisions manufacturer George Morrow suggested planning to write off a computer in two years, as a practical response to the rapid obsolescence so common in this industry.) Or, as an alternative to that, you might wish to consider buying only a system that is upgradable or expandable, as many are. For many, the expandability of a system is a significant factor to weigh in making buying decisions.

COMPUTER EXPANDABILITY

All computers are expandable, in theory, but expandability is not always a practical option. In the case of my own system, I can expand the storage capacity by adding disk drives, but I cannot expand the internal memory, except by drastic redesign and changes, an impractical alternative. However, many other machines do permit easy modifications to increase the memory, which usually involve, primarily, replacing a circuit board or adding one to the system.

That is the usual extent of expanding the computer itself. Other changes, such as replacing the CPU with a later chip, are usually not viable options because too much other circuitry would have to be redesigned to make the whole effort worthwhile. However, there are other options when it comes to the peripheral devices— disk drives, keyboards, monitors, printers, and others. These are usually more amenable to being upgraded or replaced with more-capable models.

This is also an argument for buying your system piecemeal, instead of as a single system. But it does carry the hazard that you may wind up with some components that are not compatible with each other. And for that reason the rest of this chapter will be devoted to exploring characteristics of the various peripherals, along with the many options offered you in choosing peripherals. But before going on to that, be aware that there is an additional alternative to gambling that your separates will all work together, and it is, in fact, a hybrid of the two methods (buying the recommended system and designing your own system): Most systems offered include alternatives and can be upgraded, while still giving the assurance that all will work together. In buying my own system, for example, I opted for the maximum memory and storage (I had a choice among four options, for storage) and bought the middle of three levels of printers available. (They varied in size of paper they could handle and in speed, and the tractor feed was also an option.) In most cases, you have such choices offered. And as we proceed through the rest of this chapter, exploring the various peripherals and the many characteristics and features to be found on each, you will come to appreciate just how wide a choice you have and perhaps just how difficult it is to choose from among this panorama of choices.

STORAGE SYSTEMS

By far the most popular storage device used with personal computers today is the floppy disk, also called diskette, in recognition of others of greater physical size and data-storing capacity. The floppy disk, so named because it is made of a thin and flexible plastic, comes in four sizes: 8- , 5¼- , 3½- , and 3-inch size. The latter two are relatively recent developments and are not yet in widespread use (at the time of this writing, at least), although we are promised truly startling breakthroughs in disk-storage capacities with these new ultraminiature disks. (Apple's Macintosh uses a 3½-inch disk, which stores 400K, about equal to that of a double-sided double-density 5¼-inch diskette.) Many systems use the 8-inch floppy, but by far the most popular floppy today is the 5¼-inch size, and all discussions here are with reference to that model, unless specified otherwise.

Despite the fact that this popular floppy represents a quasi-standard of sorts, it has many variations in the formats used with it for filing and storing data and in its total capacity. Essentially, however, this is more the result of variations in the disk drives in which the disk is used than of variations in the disk itself. Drives may be single-sided or double-sided and of single- or double-density. As a result, storage capacity of floppies varies widely, from little more than 100K to approximately 400K per 5¼-inch disk, and even more, in some cases.

Many systems are offered with single drives and with single-sided disk capacity. The cost differentials among the choices are noticeable, although not usually great in terms of overall system cost, but the cost is almost invariably far less than the cost of expanding the storage capacity later. It's always advisable to get the maximum storage capacity you can afford or that is available when you buy the initial system. It is rare that a buyer will not regret failing to do this, for computer storage and memory are very much like money: you never have too much, and usually feel that you could very well do with a bit more.

Virtual Memory

Today's computer software and hardware are both highly sophisticated, so much so that in most modern computers the storage systems may be referred to as "virtual memory." That means that within certain limits the storage systems act as extensions of computer memory and permit the computer to handle many programs and transactions that require more memory than the computer really has by shuttling data back and forth between storage and memory. (The computer does not operate directly on material stored on disk, but it can bring that material into memory to operate on it and then send it back to disk storage, which is what it usually does.)

One example of this is in the handling of operations that require two disk drives when your system actually has only one drive. For example, if you wish to copy material from one disk onto another disk you need two drives, theoretically. But most computers today can transfer some of what you want to copy to memory, instruct you to place the second disk in the drive in place of the first one, and move the information out of memory and onto the second disk. It then repeats the operation, transferring another parcel of data each time, until the entire transfer (copying operation) has been accomplished.

Virtual Disk Drives

This is known as "virtual disk drives," for the same reason that disk storage is often known as virtual memory: Although the system has only one disk drive, Drive A, it can pretend to have another, Drive B, and carry out the work that theoretically requires two disk drives. Of course, the pace is slowed considerably, and it is far better to have two actual disk drives.

In my own case, my system has two drives, A and B. However, the system has two "virtual" drives, C and D, making it possible for me to carry out many operations not otherwise possible. (Drive A is also Drive C and Drive D, if and when I need additional drives.)

Adding Drives

Some systems have the provision to add (actual) drives later. In my own case, although I have two drives, the system will accommodate two more. However, the manufacturer cautions that the power supply will not handle the electrical current requirements of additional drives and that if additional drives are installed, they should have their own power supplies. That is not a burden, however; it's an easy problem to solve.

Floppies Versus Hard-Disk Drives

Until fairly recently, only floppies were being offered as disk drives with personal computers. Hard-disk or Winchester drives (so named for the project code name used during their original development in IBM laboratories) have far greater storage capacity and speed of operation than do floppies, but were formerly impracticably expensive for use with desktop computers.

That has changed, and hard-disk systems are being offered increasingly at fairly high but acceptable costs. More and more, buyers are being offered hard-disk systems as an option. And hard-disk systems offer storage counted in megabytes—5 or 10 megabytes is quite common, for example—and are capable of holding as much as two dozen or more floppies and acting many times faster as well. Still, there are some other factors to consider.

One of these is that even a hard disk must be backed up. In fact, it is even more urgent to back up a hard disk than a floppy because any major mishap striking a hard disk may wipe out far more data than if it struck a floppy: You could conceivably have your entire records for a year or more on a single hard disk.

Few people would find it practicable to back up a hard disk with another hard disk. Instead, some users have a floppy disk to archive (back up) the hard disk, but the more highly recommended and probably more popular hard-disk backup is via a special, high-speed miniature tape cassette. These are used rather commonly for the purpose of preserving older records and freeing the hard disk for more-current data and operations.

The traditional Winchester is a nonremovable disk. The reason for this, and the reason for the great speed of the hard disk, is that it uses something called a "flying head" which does not actually touch the disk surface, as the head in the floppy-disk does, but travels an almost microscopic distance above the surface of the disk. This enables it to travel at far greater speeds than the head in a floppy-disk drive, but the distance is so tiny that even the particles resulting from cigarette smoking can cause a "head crash"—the head striking the surface of the disk—with disastrous results. To prevent this the entire unit is filled with carefully filtered (microscopically clean) air and sealed tightly. (A newer type of hard disk is now available. This one uses a replaceable disk, mounted in a cartridge.)

SUMMARY OF PROS AND CONS OF HARD DISKS VERSUS FLOPPIES

There is no question that hard disks are of far higher capacity than floppies and of almost infinitely greater speed. And perhaps hard-disk drives will eventually compete directly with floppy-disk drives in cost and make floppies far less popular. However, it is problematical if even that would make floppies obsolete for at least the reason that material on hard disks is captive despite the appearance of the hard-disk cartridge, which can be stored and/or transported, but at considerable cost. At present, data can be transported economically only by sending it over a communications link or by transferring it to some inexpensive medium that may be transported, such as a floppy or a tape. (Most software, for example, is delivered to the buyer today on floppies, and many writers are today sending their manuscripts to publishers in the form of floppies.) And since a great deal of data transport is carried out in this manner it seems unlikely that even low-cost hard disks will put the floppy completely out of business. At the moment, the ideal appears to be a hard disk and at least one floppy or high-speed tape serve to back up the hard disk and produce data on some economical storable and transportable medium.

MONITORS

Most computers of that class we refer to as "personal" or "desktop" computers are designed to be used with a TV-type screen as a display. This is known as a "monitor" or "soft display" to distinguish clearly between the volatile or ephemeral screen presentation and the printout, which is referred to as "hard copy." Most computers you buy as complete systems include a monitor, usually a cathode ray tube (CRT) of the same type as that used for TV, although the smaller portables—the "pocket" or "briefcase" portables—generally use an LCD (liquid crystal display), which is a much smaller screen, of course.

The lower-cost systems, such as the game computers and others that are often referred to as "home" computers, are often sold without monitors, and you must either buy a monitor separately or use a TV receiver. Earlier, you may recall, I advised against the use of a TV receiver for this purpose. You will see why shortly.

Resolution Characteristics

The reason for counseling against using a TV set as a monitor is simply that commercial TV receivers do not have good enough "resolution" or sharpness of image to present alphanumeric characters that you can read easily and without fatigue. Despite the fact that the computer monitor is the same kind of device as the TV picture tube, the method of creating the display on the screen is quite different in each case. Computers present their screen data by "painting" the screen with a pattern of dots, very much like the newspapers and magazines print photographs via a "halftone" method. (Examine a newspaper photograph closely and you will see the dots making up the photograph.)

I won't go into technical details, which you do not need to know and which are more likely to confuse than to enlighten. However, to judge the quality of a monitor, should you buy one separately or wish to evaluate the one offered with any system you are considering, you should know just a little about the method. In a nutshell (that is, in a greatly simplified and generalized explanation) it is this: A thin beam of electrons draws lines across the screen, which are slightly diagonal, so that when the beam has drawn 525 horizontal lines (in commercial TV) the beam has reached the bottom of the screen. It then returns to the top to do it all over again. The square of illumination resulting from the stream of electrons exciting the phosphor on the face of the tube is called a *raster*. The beam draws this raster 30 times a second.

The resolution is partly a product of the number of lines in the raster. A 1000-line screen will have higher resolution than a 525-line screen, and most monitors used for computer display have more lines and therefore better resolution than does TV. The number of lines specified for a monitor is one way of explaining the relative resolution quality. [In some cases computers also illuminate the screen, as in TV, and darken it to paint the characters. Most, however, keep the screen dark and lighten it in painting characters, so that the display is a luminous green/amber/blue or other color on black (dark) background, rather than the other way around.]

The "dots" are actually very short segments of the lines (examine a screen display under a powerful magnifying glass and you will perceive this easily) and obviously the more lines there are, the greater the number of dots there will be. And that is the clue to a second way in which monitor-screen resolution is specified. Each dot is regarded as a picture element or "pix" element, and the special term *pixel* was derived from these words. So resolution is also defined as the number of pixels the monitor screen can present. And the measure is given as two numbers: the horizontal and vertical numbers. So if a monitor is rated at 220 × 440 pixels (for a total of 96,800 pixels), it can be compared with others, to determine the relative resolution quality of all. (The ratio of horizontal to vertical pixels varies widely, so that only the total number of pixels offers a measure by which to compare monitors for resolution.)

Color

Of course, there are other characteristics to consider, such as the color of the phosphor. Probably the most popular screen phosphor offers presentations in a luminescent green, but there have been others in blue, amber, and black. And some users have claimed that amber is easier on the eyes than the other shades.

There are also monitors that make presentations in color. These are sometimes referred to as RGB monitors. The letters stand for red, green, and blue, which are the primary colors used to create all the other colors and shades of colors.

Screen Sizes

Monitor sizes vary, just as TV-screen sizes do. Probably 12-inch screens (measured diagonally) are the most widely used size for desktop computers, with 9-inch tubes used for the "transportable" models. (Some earlier transportable computers, such as the Osborne and Kaypro, used 5- and 7-inch tubes, but most such sets today use the 9-inch size so that it has become almost a standard.)

It is possible to get larger monitors, such as 15-inch ones, if you think it is necessary. The display will be the same, probably 24 lines of text, single-spaced and 12 lines if double-spaced, by 80 columns wide, no matter what size monitor you use. (That's 80 characters and spaces; in computers they are called "columns.") Obviously, then, the larger the screen, the larger the characters will be. (That was one of the problems with the 5-inch monitor: it was difficult to read, especially when using it for long periods.)

Screen Orientation

Most computers orient their monitor screens in the same perspective (long dimension horizontal and short dimension vertical) and ratio (3:4) as do TV sets, possibly because all of us now have the TV habit. In one way that is unfortunate because it is the reverse of the paper upon which most of us have worked for many years and continue to work. This is especially unfortunate when using word processors. A few systems have followed earlier tradition and oriented the screen the other way (see Figure 17), so that the display resembles type on paper. That is the exception, rather than the rule, however, and you will probably have trouble finding any recent systems that follow this pattern.

KEYBOARDS

Most keyboards today are of the "qwerty" type, with the keys arranged in what has become the standard typewriter pattern. However, the keyboard also has a few special keys, and many have a special "keypad," a section of the keyboard that resembles an adding-machine or calculator keyboard. This is in addition to the number characters on the regular keyboard, and is provided for your convenience when using your system for "number crunching" kinds of functions. (See right-hand portion of keyboard in Figure 17.)

Fixed Versus Detachable Keyboards

This has been already mentioned, since in some systems the keyboard is built into the computer housing, while it is a detachable unit in others, with the latter the more popular arrangement, apparently. Still, some manufacturers continue to build the keyboard into the computer housing, so evidently at least some users do not insist on a detachable keyboard. (Compare keyboards of Figures 16 and 17.)

"Chiclet" Keys Versus Sculptured Keys

One complaint made about some keyboards—the original model of the IBM PCjr, for example—is that they use what critics call "chiclet" keys, on the premise that the keys resemble that item. Such keys are rectangular and flat, and are rather tiresome to work with for extended periods. Far more popular are sculptured keys, which have slight depressions on their surface, resembling the

Figure 17. Vertical screen orientation.
(Courtesy Eagle Computer Corp.)

keys used in most electric typewriters of recent years and intended to help the fingers get a firm purchase when striking them. (IBM has now replaced the original PCjr keyboard with one that has sculptured keys.)

Key Feedback

It is possible to make the keys of a computer keyboard entirely silent and with virtually no "travel"—exceedingly slight physical motion to make the electrical contact, that is. Many of the earliest keyboards were of that description and were highly unsatisfactory to users. It did not take long for designers to learn that the users wanted some kind of feedback to verify that their fingers had succeeded in what they were supposed to do and the computer had responded properly. They wanted to *feel* and *hear* the keys make the contacts and complete their missions. They also wanted a sense of the familiar: They wanted the keyboard to come closer to providing the kind of sensory feedback the familiar electric typewriter provides. (People do resist change; they hate to give up what they have become comfortable with as a result of its being thoroughly familiar.)

Consequently, most keyboards today are equipped with keys that have typewriterlike "travel" (motion), sound (a click), and feel. And the advice is often given to buyers to try the keyboard out and see if it is comfortable. One reviewer, reviewing the Morrow Micro Decision computers, made a distinction between two keyboards offered, reporting that he found one of them a little too "soft" and too sensitive for his taste, so that it was too easy to accidentally brush a key and generate an unwanted signal; he recommended the other keyboard, accordingly.

Slope of Keyboard

Another factor is the slope of the keyboard. Most users would prefer the same slope as that of the typewriter, but a number of keyboards used with popular computers are rather flattish, so the slope appears to be less critical a factor than some others.

Dvorak Keyboards

The qwerty keyboard is not an efficient one, and deliberately so: It was designed to be inefficient. This is because early typewriters were rather crude, and fast typists had a great deal of trouble with them since their mechanisms could not keep up with the the the typists' speedy fingers. Typewriter designers therefore deliberately designed the inefficient qwerty keyboard layout, which slowed the typists down to the speed the typewriters could handle. It thus became the standard keyboard design, despite the vast improvements ·in typewriter design and mechanisms that followed.

There is a design called the Dvorak keyboard, which is far more efficient and aids users in speeding up their typing. It is possible to get Dvorak keyboards for most popular computers, but there is another solution: There are many computer programs offered that will reprogram a standard qwerty keyboard to convert it to a Dvorak keyboard, with appropriate labels to stick on the keys.

PRINTERS

Having selected your computer, monitor, drives, and keyboard, you have a complete computer system, except for a printer. And here, in selecting a printer, you have as broad a field to choose from as you do when selecting the computer: The diversity of types, makes, and models is that broad and varied.

Basic Types of Printers

One problem in discussing printers is in deciding how to classify them. One way in which some people classify printers is to divide them into two classes: (1) "impact" printers—those that strike paper through a ribbon, and (2) "other" types—those that use a variety of methods, including ink jets, thermal devices, electrostatic methods, and recently, laser printing. By far the majority of printers are of the impact type, however, and we won't go beyond recognizing the existence of these other types.

Impact printers subdivide—if we consider impact versus

nonimpact the first level of classification—into dot-matrix types and formed-character types. Dot-matrix types print in a manner similar to the way characters are painted onto a monitor screen: The characters are formed by a series of dots resulting from pins or needles striking paper through a ribbon. Formed-character printers use a printing element very much like a typewriter does, striking the paper through the ribbon. Most of these printers use a daisy-wheel kind of element, although one uses something called a "thimble," and an occasional one uses the IBM Selectric "golf ball" type of printing element.

Those that use elements with fully formed characters are often referred to as "letter quality" printers on the premise that dot-matrix printing is markedly inferior and not suitable for correspondence. However, makers of dot-matrix printers have been improving their products steadily, and many of their products are now capable of what they call "near letter quality," although they are unmistakably still printing by the dot-matrix method.

Printers Versus Typewriters

The copy that letter-quality or daisy-wheel printers produce is very much like that produced by electric typewriters, and many printers do, indeed, resemble typewriters without keyboards. (See Figure 18.) Others, especially those large enough to handle the 11

Figure 18.   Magna S. L. Printer.
(Courtesy A. B. Dick Co.)

× 14-inch computer printout paper, do not resemble typewriters very much. (See Figure 19.) On the other hand, some typewriters have been converted to serve as computer printers, while still being usable as conventional typewriters. (See Figure 20.)

This latter idea has not caught on very well, possibly because typewriters do not usually make very good printers, unless they are run rather slowly. The typical typewriter simply is not durable enough for the kind of duty required of a computer printer, if the printer is to be used for long periods. Moreover, most people find that once they get a complete system installed and become comfortable with it, they have far less use for a typewriter than they thought they would have. They generally find it most convenient to use the computer and word processor for all or nearly all the things for which they would have formerly used the typewriter.

Printer Trends

There have been several recent trends in printers. One has been to the ink-jet type, in which characters are formed, in a dot-matrix manner, by squirting tiny jets of ink on the paper rather than striking the paper through a ribbon. A great deal of progress has been made in developing practical models of this type of printer, and they are now offered in the marketplace. They have the advantage

Figure 19.   NEC Printer.
(Courtesy NEC Corp.)

Figure 20.   Combination typewriter/printer.
(Courtesy Olympia Corp.)

of being silent or nearly so, and are subject to far less mechanical
wear than are any of the impact printers. They also offer the advantage that the entire print head is a disposable and replaceable
unit.

Laser printing has become increasingly prominent, also, and
several models are offered today. (See Figure 21.) Essentially, the
method is an adaptation of xerographic copying, using a laser imaging technique. The latter is a system of "painting" the copy directly on the selenium copying drum by converting digital data
into laser light pulses. Instead of using a camera to send a photo-
graphic image of original copy to the drum, the laser imaging
subsystem translates the digital data into laser pulses, in a high-
resolution (a great number of dots per square inch) dot-matrix pattern, producing copy of good quality; even with a magnifying glass
it is difficult to perceive that the copy is made up of a series of
dots. A sample of the copy produced by such a printer (the Xerox
8700 system) is shown in Figure 22.

Figure 21. The Xerox 2700 II laser printer.
(Courtesy Xerox Corp.)

Subject, except as otherwise provided herein, to Item X-375 and Supplements 46 and 68.

CHANGE
INCREASE
REDUCTION
REISSUE

SUPPLEMENT 69
TO

CTC-F 2317

ICC CFAE 3700

CANADIAN FREIGHT ASSOCIATION
(For Participating Carriers, see pages 7 and 8 of Tariff)

FREIGHT TARIFF CFAE 3700
COMPUTERIZED TARIFF RETRIEVAL CODE 2HA

Cancels Supplements 62 and 67.
Supplements 59, 69 and the following special supplements contain all changes.
Supplement 13 - Notice of Change of Tariff and ICC Number to New ICC Designation.
Supplement 34 - Non-Application of Special Fuel Cost Adjustment for Account ROCK.
Supplement 46 - Temporary Fuel Shortfall Recovery Surcharge Tariff X-311-S (Ex Parte 311)(Sub. 1-F).
Supplement 56 - Special Supplement, ICC Permission 71-5508.
Supplement 68 - Tariff of increased rates and charges X-386.

COMPETITIVE, JOINT AND PROPORTIONAL FREIGHT TARIFF
— OF RATES ON —
VARIOUS COMMODITIES
CARLOADS

FROM	TO

STATIONS IN THE STATES OF

SHIPPING POINTS
IN
EASTERN CANADA

ALABAMA	LOUISIANA	SOUTH CAROLINA
FLORIDA	MISSISSIPPI	TENNESSEE
GEORGIA	NORTH CAROLINA	VIRGINIA
KENTUCKY		

Governed, except as otherwise provided, by Uniform Classification as more specifically stated herein. (See Item 5).

NOTICE

The provisions published herein will, if effective, not result in an effect on the quality of the human environment.

ISSUED OCTOBER 24, 1980

EFFECTIVE DECEMBER 1, 1980
(Except as otherwise provided herein)

Issued under authority of CTC Special Permission No. 5403 dated July 31, 1978.

Issued by P. J. LAVALLEE, Agent, Canadian Freight Association, 1162 St. Antoine Street, MONTREAL, P.Q. H3C 1B5

(3700)   (LB)

Figure 22. Example of laser printer output.
(Courtesy Xerox Corp.)

Since these printers work directly from transmitted data, as do the other printers discussed and described here, these can be used at the output of individual computers or connected to computer networks. They are still rather costly at present, but future development will probably result in less expensive models.

ONLINE HARDWARE (MODEMS)

To go online and communicate with other computers you need a piece of hardware called a "modem," a word derived from the words *mo*dulator and *dem*odulator. These are technical terms, borrowed from radio terminology because they are appropriate to the technique used here. Without getting into a technical discussion of what these terms mean, here is what a modem does and why it is needed:

Except where they are wired directly together or in other special circumstances, computers communicate with each other over commercial telephone lines, either by dialing up the other computer directly or by using a leased and dedicated telephone line. (The individual entrepreneur will, of course, ordinarily use a dial-up connection.) Telephone lines are used to carry voice signals, but computers produce digital signals, which are silent electronic pulses. Modems convert the digital signals to audible signals, in effect, by the process known as *modulation*, when sending data, and back to digital signals when receiving data from the other computer. (More literally, for those interested in technical accuracy, the modem modulates and demodulates a voice-frequency carrier signal with the train of digital pulses, which is effectively the same as actual conversion of digital data to audio signals.)

Modem Types

As in the case of most computer equipment today, a great variety of modems are available, ranging in prices from well under $100 to those approaching $1000 for modems suitable for typical personal computer use, and even higher for many other uses.

Modems are classified in several ways, as are most kinds of computer hardware. They are rated by their transmission speeds, by whether they are "dumb" or "smart," by whether they are half-duplex or full duplex, by whether they are of the "acoustic" or "direct" types, and by whether they are internal or external types.

Transmission Speeds

Data transmission is rated by a measure known as a *baud,* which is a term derived from the older field of telegraphy. In effect, it equals the number of data bits per second (bps), although this is not its literal translation. The two most common rates are 300 baud and 1200 baud. The latter is generally the upper limit for everyday use, although there are modems designed to operate at higher rates, because most telephone lines were not designed to handle data at a faster rate. So most modems are designed for either or both the rates cited here. (It's wise to get a modem that will transmit and receive at both rates.)

Sometimes these data rates are converted to words per minute, to furnish a better idea of what these data rates mean. The conversion is based on an assumed 8 characters per word (and there are 8 bits or 1 byte per character in the accepted code standard), so 300 baud = 37.5 characters per second = 4.69 words per second = 281 words per minute.

Smart Modems

So-called dumb modems can do little beyond respond to direct commands to transmit and receive at whatever data rates they are designed to handle. But the newer generation of smart modems can do a great many other things because they have their own logic circuits—CPUs and associated electronics—and can do such things as dial-up and answer calls automatically or under commands from the computer, re-ring numbers that are busy (and re-ring continuously or for a specified number of tries only), automatically switch from one transmission speed to another, and do many other things, according to their designs. To a large degree, the "smartness" of a modem consists of or is measured by the degree to which all communications can be managed by the communications software. (This should provide one clear indication of why modem prices vary so widely.)

Half- Versus Full-Duplex Operation

This is a rather simple distinction. A half-duplex modem can both transmit and receive but not at the same time. A full-duplex modem can transmit and receive at the same time, an obvious convenience and time-saver.

Acoustic Versus Direct Modems

The difference between the acoustic and the direct modem is in the way each sends and receives data to and from the telephone line. The acoustic modem has a set of cups into which the telephone receiver is placed, and the modem then sends and receives its signals in the same manner as a human talks and hears, using a telephone. The direct modem bypasses the telephone handset, and is connected to the terminal box that the telephone is connected to, very much in the manner of a telephone-answering machine, so that the handset need not be disturbed when using the modem.

Internal Versus External Modems

Direct types of modems can be either internal or external. As external units they come in some sort of case, usually of modest physical dimensions (my Hayes Smartmodem 1200, a popular model, is in a flattish case about 5.5 inches wide, 9.5 inches long, and 1.5 inches high). But some computers come equipped with internal modems or offer them as options to be added later, if desired, in which case they are usually mounted on a circuit card for installation internally in the computer.

Other than these major characteristics, modems differ in their individual refinements, with each manufacturer offering whatever appear to that manufacturer to be the most desirable and appealing features. There are many such refinements in different makes and models. Some manufacturers even supply their own special software with their modems (and, of course, smart modems have their own firmware built into them). And smart modems generally have an array of indicator lights. The Hayes 1200, for example, has eight such indicators to advise the user of the status or operating condition of the moment. These indicators specify the following conditions or status:

HS	High speed	AA	Auto answer	CD	Carrier detect
OH	Off hook	RD	Receive data	SD	Send data
TR	Terminal ready	MR	Modem ready		

BUFFERS AND SPOOLERS

One problem every computer owner encounters before long is the result of the vast differences in operating speed between the electronic circuits of the computer and the mechanical functioning of the printer. Even the fastest printers cannot approach the speed of the computer. What the computer can pass to the printer in a few seconds takes even a high-speed printer many times that to print, so that even a medium-sized document—say 20 or 30 pages—can easily take from 10 to 30 minutes to print out while you sit impatiently waiting to have your computer back.

The problem is that the computer is tied up during all that time, feeding the data to the printer only as fast as the printer can accept it, so that you cannot use the computer while you are printing out your work. It simply ignores your commands while it is driving the printer, and you have to wait until the printing is done before you can get its attention again. For word processing and many other applications, where you need a hard copy output and especially where you run the printer fairly often, this is an intolerable situation: You are losing much of the benefit the computer was supposed to bring you in the first place.

The solution lies in "buffering" the data on its way to the printer. That term means simply to store temporarily. If the computer can deposit the data somewhere else and turn the job of supplying the printer over to some other device, the computer can go back to doing its other work. That "somewhere else" to deposit the data is, in practice, a print buffer or spooler.

A buffer is another piece of hardware, a piece of "smart" hardware, usually. That means that it has its own logic, including a microprocessor and associated circuits, and will accept the data as fast as the computer can supply it, when the time comes to print hard copy. The buffer will store the data, feeding it to the printer and thus freeing the computer. Most buffers have enough logic to do a number of other things. The Consolink SooperSpooler (see Figure 23) is an example of this. It uses the same Z-80 microprocessor that a great many computers use as a CPU, holds 16K in buffer storage (although this is expandable to 64K), and has a number of features that are typical of printer buffers, including these:

Figure 23.   The Consolink SooperSpooler.
(Courtesy Consolink Corporation)

Formatting.   The buffer permits the user to paginate, set margins, and generate a number of other commands to the printer.

Pause.   The buffer can suspend printing temporarily to permit verification of accuracy or other operator intervention.

Component Interfacing.   Because this buffer can input and output both parallel and serial data, it can be used to interface between two otherwise incompatible systems, matching serial and parallel inputs and outputs to each other.

Single Sheeting.   The buffer can order the printer to pause at the end of each page, to permit the feeding of single sheets to the printer.

Compression.   The density at which data can be stored is increased through use of this feature, which stores consecutive spaces (up to 127 spaces) as a single byte, thereby increasing the overall storage capacity.

Readout.   The digital readout indicator (BUFFER STATUS) reports the amount of material stored in the buffer at the moment.

Some manufacturers use the term "spooler" to identify their print buffers, as Consolink has done, although the term "buffer" is more commonly associated with a piece of hardware designed to buffer data destined for the printer. The term "spooler," on the other hand, is more commonly used to designate a kind of software that accomplishes the same function. And although spooler software does not offer all the features and conveniences of buffer hardware, spooler software does offer a few advantages of its own. For one thing it is a far less expensive way to buffer the printer data, as you will see in a moment. Also, it generally offers far greater storage capacity than do most buffers commonly available.

The typical hardware buffer offers 16, 32, or 64K storage, and usually costs about $500–600 for the maximum capacity. A spooler program costs a fraction of that and can provide several times greater storage. Here is my own case, as a fairly typical example:

I installed a spooler program called SPL, supplied by Blat Research + Development Corp. of Edmonds, Washington. The program cost me $139, and in my case can provide up to 164K storage for printer data. I say "in my case" because the amount of buffer storage the program provides depends on the computer system with which it is used and how the operator chooses to use it.

In this case, the spooler sets aside a portion of memory or disk, at the option of the user, for buffer storage. If you use memory, you can set aside only up to 15K. If you use disk, you can set aside as much disk capacity as you have available or wish to provide. In my case I have set aside 100K of the same disk on which the program is installed, but I have another 164K available, if I want to use it, and could even stretch that by another 84K, for a total of 348K. (I have so far never had need for even 100K, much less for additional storage.)

The advantage of using memory, instead of disk storage, is speed: The system works fast enough with disk storage, but is even faster when using memory. (That is because access to memory is entirely electronic, and electrons speed around the circuits so fast that they appear instantaneous to our human senses, but access to disk requires the use of the read-write head, a mechanical device, which slows things down.)

It is possible to queue items in a spooler, loading in as much material as you wish. The spooler will print them out in the same order in which they were loaded in. (In fact, the buffer store on disk is called a "queue file," reasonably enough.) So if you want more than one copy printed, you have to either order each copy individually or use another method, one I use myself, of copying the document in the file, so that the file itself consists of more than one copy. (You can do this in a matter of seconds.) On the other hand, some buffers include among their features capabilities for ordering the printer to make more than one copy, even to make many copies of whatever they have stored away in their memories. So there are pros and cons to each alternative method for solving the problem. But there is a third possible approach, also:

Some computers come equipped with built-in spooler software, and you may wish to inquire into the possibility of this when you go shopping, since you will probably decide you need some kind of buffer or spooler after you have experienced some of the frustration of waiting for the printer to finish its work so you can get back to your computer chores.

SURGE SUPPRESSORS

One problem you may one day face is that of surges on the power line. The ordinary house current on which personal computers operate is a nominal 115 volts or thereabouts. (It is rated between 105 and 125 volts because it can easily vary between those limits.) The computer's microcircuits operate at very small voltages, which are supplied through the computer's own power supply, a subsystem that converts the 115 volts input to whatever output voltages are required by the various elements of the computer. One problem, however, is that of voltage surges or spikes occurring in the supply. They cause the voltage to increase greatly for fleeting moments, but even a fleeting moment of overvoltage can damage the microcircuits, leading to costly repair jobs. Such transient surges can be caused by any of a great variety of things, even by other appliances or the air-conditioning system cycling on or off.

To counter this and minimize the possibility of damage to your computer, many vendors offer devices that act as surge suppressors, opposing any increase in voltage. They are relatively inexpensive, ranging generally from as little as $25 to about $90, and are probably good insurance.

RFI SUPPRESSION

Radio frequency interference (RFI) is another possible hazard. This is a different type of aberration that may appear in your computer. It is of extremely small voltage and so is not a hazard to the equipment itself, but is is a possible hazard to the data—it can scramble the data and produce errors. Many surge suppressors include devices to combat RFI, too, and it is probably a good idea to buy a surge suppressor that includes RFI suppression.

UNINTERRUPTED VOLTAGE SUPPLIES

Computer memory is volatile: When the current is turned off the memory is erased. That is one reason why it is wise to do frequent "saves" (store what is in memory by writing it on one of your disks) during the day. Then, if a power failure occurs, you will not lose everything you have done. Even a momentary power failure, one that lasts for a fraction of a second and causes only a flicker of the lights, can erase the memory completely.

To prevent that disaster, many computer owners buy special devices called uninterrupted or uninterruptible power supplies. These are devices that have standby battery power, and the computer is switched over to battery power instantaneously in the event of a power failure. The battery power may be sufficient only for a few minutes' operation, but that is long enough to do a save and transfer memory data to a disk, so that there is no loss of data. There are, however, some systems that can operate the computer on battery power for longer periods. And there are some computers that come with an integral uninterruptible power supply of this type.

CHAPTER SIXTEEN

Doing the Research

> Buying a computer is not a casual purchase, but is serious
> enough to justify—even require—a substantial amount of pre-
> liminary research.

WHY RESEARCH?

Buying a computer is not the same as buying an automobile or TV
receiver. Buying a computer is a commitment, and the initial purchase is only the beginning, somewhat like "seeing" the first raise
in a poker game: You may be sure that it will require additional
investments to cover the first one, with some uncertainty as to just
how many such additional investments you will need or how large
your total investment is likely to become. (You may be sure that if
you buy a computer suitable for serious business/professional
purposes, you will invest at least several thousand dollars immediately and more in the future.) Even though you buy a computer
system completely bundled and complete with a printer, it is extremely likely that you will sooner or later make additional investments for your system. In my own case, and despite the fact that I
researched, studied, and pondered the market for many months

before deciding what I would buy, I did not escape without at least some additional investment soon after my initial purchase. I calculated my needs meticulously and was careful to buy the maximum configuration in the system I did finally choose: the largest memory and storage available, and the larger of the printers available. (But there was a third printer, of the same size as the one I bought but nearly twice as fast, and I now regret not being wise enough to buy that one.) I bought a system that was heavily bundled with what appeared to me to be a complete complement of hardware and software: word-processing, spreadsheet, database management, programming languages, and several other programs. I was sure that it would be a long, long time, if ever, before I would need anything else. Still, before many months had elapsed I bought three additional pieces of hardware and three additional software programs and I already plan to buy more of both hardware and software. But I am thankful that I did do as much research as I did and so managed to avoid making any serious errors in my selections, other than my lack of foresight regarding which printer to buy. I shrink from speculation on what other, perhaps far more serious, blunders I would have made had I not "done my homework" before choosing a system. I certainly have no doubt that I would have made them.

These pages of information can get you started on the road to acquiring and enjoying the benefits of a personal computer in your practice. They can provide you with a few ideas and a basic orientation in what I hope you will find as exciting an adventure as I have found it. (I confess that this was a surprise to me; I did not expect to have more than passing enthusiasm for computers, and I saw my acquisition of a computer as only the act of gaining a more efficient way of turning out my books. My growing enthusiasm for and dedication to learning more and more about computers has enriched me in ways I did not foresee.) But that is all the information on these pages can do—give you a beginning and embark you on a course of further research and investigation. Here, we will scratch the surface for you, but there is much more you will want to research and investigate, more that you *should* research and investigate so that you will make the right decisions when you enter this information age as an active participant.

THE SOURCES OF INFORMATION

In some field, research is difficult because there is a scarcity of information or the information is not easily accessible. Perhaps it is fitting, even poetic justice, that this field of information offers too much information that is too easily accessible. There is so much information about computers accessories, software, and supplies that it is an almost unmanageable abundance. Merely to understand and catalog the sources of information and the kinds of information available itself requires some considerable effort, and that is where we will start here: surveying the field overall.

In general, the sources readily available fall into several broad classes, and reading alone can help you become most knowledgeable about computers, especially since so much computer literature is written for the lay person especially. One word of caution: In the beginning, you will find much of the information utterly confusing. Even in my own case, armed with some prior experience in computers (but, unfortunately, experience confined to larger machines—mainframes—of an earlier time and confined, also, primarily to the hardware/engineering considerations), I found much of the information and the jargon utterly confusing. However, just plod on patiently and absorb whatever you can understand. This will furnish you with bridges to the other, more cryptic information, and as time goes on you will read with ever-greater understanding.

Here are some of those many information sources, arranged by the general classes they fall into:

Periodical publications: magazines, newsletters, occasional publications

Books

Computer clubs

Manufacturers' literature

Retail outlets

Electronic bulletin boards

Public databases and information services

Let us discuss these one at a time, to place them all into proper perspective.

PERIODICALS

To survey the field represented by periodicals we have to classify and subclassify this segment of the information spectrum. There are, first of all, a great many periodicals, most of them relatively new, that are intended for the lay owners of computers, owners who are not terribly knowledgeable about computers in a technical sense. There are literally dozens of these periodicals, thick and thin, slick-paper monthly journals, heavy with advertising and full of articles about generic hardware and software and reviews of specific hardware and software items. Many of these can be found on the well-stocked newsstands, although some are available by subscription only or only on the especially well-stocked newsstands.

If there is any universal or common cement among all these periodicals it is that they are written with reference almost exclusively to personal or desktop computers, rather than to the larger mainframes and or minicomputers, and they are addressed to computer owners and users who are not computer professionals. (There are other computer periodicals that are addressed to the computer professionals, but these are not likely to be very helpful in your case.) Aside from this one factor, the magazines fall generally into several classes. Many of these magazines are directed to the general interests of the individual interested in buying a personal computer for any reason, personal or business, as well as to those readers who are already owners of personal computers. But others are addressed to narrower interests and narrower definitions of intended readership. Some address only business owners, some address only those interested in intercomputer communications, some address hobbyists ("hackers"), some address owners of some specific machine (such as the IBM PC or an Atari), some address those interested primarily in what is happening in the computer industry, some address those interested primarily in programming, and some address various other esoteric and specialized interests with regard to personal computers. Here are the titles of just a few of those most popular magazines (a more complete list is furnished later):

Popular Computing	*Personal Computing*
Creative Computing	*Byte*
Link Up	*InfoWorld*
Compute!	*PC World*
Office Administration and Automation	*Computer Decisions*

These and others to be listed later (some of which will be aimed at computer professionals and "hackers," those computer enthusiasts who are more expert than the professionals) are computer magazines. But there are other magazines, magazines on other subjects, that carry at least occasional computer articles, some of which are quite helpful. First of all, all those popular electronic magazines—*Radio Electronics* and what was formerly *Popular Electronics* and now has become *Computers & Electronics*, to name just two—run frequent articles about computers. The popular other semitechnical magazines, *Popular Mechanics* and *Popular Science*, for example, likewise cover the subject of computers frequently. But even that is not all. Articles about computers have appeared in all kinds of magazines. *Money* magazine ran extensive articles, including a rather detailed survey and review of most of the popular computers, not too long ago. James Fallows has written on the subject in the *Atlantic Monthly*. Business magazines such as *Inc.* have not neglected the subject, either, nor have the professional journals in many fields. The subject is so popular today, as personal computers have become so completely pervasive in our society, that the subject is now fair game for coverage in almost any kind of periodical, no matter what main field of interest it is addressed to.

Finally, there are a great many newsletters also, some of which are quite helpful, although not as useful to the beginner in the field as are the magazine articles.

BOOKS

The outpouring of books about computers has been truly aston-
ishing, and these have fallen into several general categories, just as
the computer periodicals do. But the books tend to fall into an
even greater number and diversity of categories, making it rather
difficult to classify them. Here are some of the apparent types and
classes:

Introductory and "made simple" books
   Introduction to computers
   How to buy a computer
   Introduction to computer programming
   Programming made simple
   Understanding CP/M (PC-DOS, MS-DOS, UNIX, etc.)
   Understanding BASIC (assembly language, C language, etc.)
Programming books
   More advanced books on programming in BASIC (C language,
assembly language, etc.)
Machine-specific books
   Programming the Atari (Apple, Macintosh, PC, etc.)
Computer dictionaries
Miscellaneous
   Where to get free software
   Directories (to public databases, bulletin boards, etc.)

So far there has been no noticeable slackening in this deluge,
despite the apparent oversupply of books about computers. At
least one computer book has been on national best-seller lists, a
rather surprising event, since no one would ordinarily expect the
appeal of a computer book to be wide enough to qualify for that
degree of success. But, as with the periodicals, the supply of information is obviously far too great to digest all of it, so the problem
becomes one of selecting that which is most appropriate and
useful.

There are at least two mistakes that writers of introduction-to
and made-simple books have made rather commonly. The first
mistake has been to assume that readers are all interested in learn-

ing how to write programs for computers. The second is to assume that readers are all interested in becoming technical experts in computer technology.

The fact is that readers can be classified in three ways, as regards programming computers: Those who have programming as an original and abiding interest; those who develop an interest in programming only later, after becoming familiar and comfortable with their computers; and those who never develop an interest in programming, but who want only to become expert in using their computers.

Of course, very much the same thing can be said for readers regarding technological detail: By far the majority of readers are not interested in learning that functional/technical detail, at least not in the beginning.

Armed with an awareness of this, you can review computer books for their relevance to your true interests.

COMPUTER CLUBS

Joining a computer club is one of the best things for the beginner in computers to do. And it is not a case of the blind leading the blind, as you might be tempted to suspect, for in the typical computer club you will find others as green and eager for help as you, but you will also find others who have owned their computers for a long time and have become quite expert with them (often even more expert than many professionals) and you are likely to find a few computer professionals—programmers and engineers, for example—as well.

One of the advantages of belonging to a computer club is the mutuality of interest vis-à-vis the systems. Some clubs are based on all the members having machines that have the same operating system—CP/M, MS-DOS, or other—and some are even based on all members owning the same make of computer—Apple, Atari, IBM, or other. (I belong to an MUG—Morrow Users Group.) This enables members to be of great help to each other. Here, for example, are some typical events and activities at club meetings:

Announcements and club business.

Buy and sell public domain software (usually downloaded from a bulletin board by one of the club's officers or a volunteer and sold to members at the cost of the disks only, usually under $5).

Demonstration (often a guest, such as a salesperson, local dealer, or factory rep, demonstrating some hardware or software product).

"How-to" presentation (miniseminar in some pertinent subject) by a member.

Question and answer session (members ask questions and whoever has answers or ideas offers them).

Breakout meetings of SIGs (special-interest groups).

Buy and sell between members (usually selling surplus or items no longer needed).

Some computer clubs even operate their own electronic bulletin board, for those who are interested in that activity. And some put on occasional special events, such as "swap meets" or the computer equivalent of a yard sale.

Frequently fellow members can direct you to the best magazines and books for your needs and some even run internal lending libraries or members arrange to lend each other books. Certainly, it is an excellent source of directly useful information and often virtually a free consulting service. However, it is also a route to a consulting service, for some members of such clubs are computer consultants and will provide their regular professional services to fellow club members at discounted rates. (And possibly fellow members of a consultant or other professional society you belong to are also members of a computer club.)

It is not difficult to discover what computer clubs exist in your area. There are several ways to do so. Some of the computer periodicals list computer clubs, for one. Computer retailers usually know what computer clubs exist in the area. (That's how my own computer club and I learned about each other's existence.) The computer manufacturers' public relations departments (which are often part of their marketing divisions) usually are aware of all computer clubs. And the local daily newspaper may carry announcements about computer-club meetings.

MANUFACTURERS' LITERATURE

Some manufacturers' literature consists of slender little pamphlets that are only extravagant blurbs. But some manufacturers offer most useful and helpful booklets, some of which are quite substantial and expensively produced, the equal of books you might buy for many dollars. Ordinarily these will cost you nothing more than a postage stamp. Lists of major computer manufacturers and software developers with their names and addresses will be furnished later. A simple request for information about their products will bring you substantial rewards, many of them quite worth the effort.

RETAIL OUTLETS

Computer retailers have sprung up throughout the country. Some of them are chains: Sears, for example, has a chain of computer showrooms and sales outlets; the Radio Shack stores market their own computers; and there are newly formed chains and franchises selling computers and related supplies and accessories. But there are also many local independents selling computers today in virtually every city and town in the United States; you will certainly have no difficulty in finding a few such retailers.

It is the usual practice of anyone buying a computer to "shop" in these stores for some time, trying to educate themselves about both computers and the market for computers—the relative price structures, that is—for there is heavy competition in this field, with consequent price wars and discounting by both the manufacturers and the retailers.

Unfortunately, a great many such shoppers have reported that far too many salespeople in these outlets are not very knowledgeable about the products they sell and can do little more than quote from manufacturers' literature. Still, there are exceptions, and if you persevere you stand a chance of finding a knowledgeable and helpful salesperson eventually.

Do try to get demonstrations whenever you can. Many retailers keep demonstration models available and will offer such help. These are most helpful in contributing to your general knowledge.

Some retailers offer free seminars, usually lasting an hour or two, as sales promotions. Try to find and attend these for the information you will glean from them.

Aside from that, the retail establishments are a source of manufacturers' literature, some of which may be helpful (although you usually must write the manufacturer to get the more substantial and more helpful literature).

ELECTRONIC BULLETIN BOARDS AND PUBLIC DATABASES

You have to have a system and a modem to communicate with the electronic bulletin boards and public databases, of course, but once you are equipped to "go on the air" in this manner, you can begin adding to your knowledge rapidly through the contacts available via these networks. You can have "real time" or "live" conversations and dicussions, and you can have "offline" conversations, in which you read what others have said, add your own comments, and return a day or two later, engaged in an extended conversation, which is something like playing chess by mail.

WORKSHEET 4

Earlier in this book you were invited to make out the first worksheet, which represented your early, even preliminary, estimate of your probable uses for a computer. It was divided into those general business applications, such as accounting and marketing, and those technical/professional applications, such as analysis and project management. Later, at the appropriate point, you were invited to do something similar (Worksheet 3) for your probable software needs. Now, armed with the knowledge you have accumulated in this reading and study, it is time to sharpen those estimates and start identifying your needs more precisely so

---

TYPES OF PROGRAMS MOST LIKELY TO
GET EXTENSIVE APPLICATION

INSTRUCTIONS: Enter numbers, starting with 1, to indicate probable priority; write in others in blanks provided, as necessary.

[ ] Word processors	[ ] File/list managers
[ ] Database managers	[ ] Inventory programs
[ ] Accounting programs	[ ] Spreadsheets
[ ] Communications	[ ] Integrated software
[ ] Financial management	[ ] Decision support systems
[ ] Project management	[ ] PERT/CPM software
[ ] Market research	[ ] Graphics
[ ] Office administration	[ ] Analysis, qualitative
[ ] Statistical analysis	[ ] Educational software
[ ] Maintenance	[ ] Hospitality
[ ] Personnel	[ ] Membership organization
[ ] Health care	[ ] Import/export
[ ] Transportation & travel	[ ] Publishing
[ ] Training & human resources	[ ] Insurance
[ ] Music	[ ] Research & development
[ ] Social sciences	[ ] Statistics
[ ] _____	[ ] _____
[ ] _____	[ ] _____
[ ] _____	[ ] _____

NOTES_____

Worksheet 4. Probable software priorities.

that you can choose and buy wisely. There will be several more worksheets offered to help you do this. The next of the worksheet series, Worksheet 4, is intended to help guide you in determining the right questions to ask salespeople or otherwise seek answers to, based on doing some introspective analysis regarding the kinds of challenges you face and functions you are required to perform in the course of providing your consulting services to clients. As a first step you are invited to study the kinds of software listed in Worksheet 4 (some are generic, some are more specific) and select those you believe correlate most closely with the chief functions your consulting work requires you to perform, and check those off. But rather than simply placing check marks in the boxes, write numbers in them, in the order of probable priority of use (1 for the highest priority, that is, software you will probably use most often and most extensively). If you cannot find the types of software listed that you believe to be most important in your own practice, use the blanks provided for write-in names.

HOW THIS RELATES TO COMPUTER SELECTION

If you were going out to buy a system today, as I write this, you would probably be unwise on general principles to buy one that does not have at least a 16-bit CPU, 128K memory, and 700K storage because such a system will not cost you appreciably more than one of lesser qualifications. Such is the state of the art at this moment. However, when you read this and go in quest of your system, the state of the art may have risen considerably (there is an excellent probability that it will have), and those measures may be obsolete as reflections of the current state of the art. You should therefore be sure that you do whatever is necessary to make yourself aware of the *minimum* characteristics and features you should settle for at that time.

However, that aside, you need to determine what your individual and possibly special needs are. Perhaps the minimum system you should buy (that which I just referred to here) will satisfy your need, but that is by no means certain, nor can you take that for granted. The data you entered in Worksheet 4 is a first step in identifying your own individual need by pinning down the kinds of functions and software you will use most extensively. You therefore need to translate this into computer characteristics and features by determining what these various kinds of software require in the way of memory, storage, and other facilities and characteristics. That is, what are the minimum memory, storage, and other characteristics you require, to handle the functions/software you have decided are among your most important requirements?

If you have any doubts regarding how to answer that question, it is one you need to seek answers to, and the entries you have made on Worksheet 4 should be a great help to you as a definition of what your system has to measure up to. By making it clear what you wish to use your computer extensively for, you have, in effect, specified your need. A competent salesperson should be able to help you match that need to the right system. At least you know what you need answered, with regard to the needs that you have decided are your chief ones.

One way to begin developing answers to your questions is to begin studying the software programs to determine the typical needs of the programs. If you research database management systems today you find enough of them specifying that they are designed to work with CP/M-86 to perhaps influence you in favor of a computer using the CP/M-86 operating system. And if you continue your research you soon discover how much memory you are likely to require as a minimum requirement for any kind of software you choose and as an absolute requirement for some specific program.

On the other hand if you anticipate a great need for a system that will generate graphics—various charts and graphs, for example—you will want a dot-matrix printer or perhaps even a plotter. And if you also expect to use a word processor very often and generate a great deal of material for publication, you may decide that you need both a letter-quality printer and dot-matrix printer or plotter.

WORKSHEET 5

Worksheet 5 offers you a means for making some firm commitments about the specific kinds of components your system is to have and the minimum characteristics in terms of storage and memory. This should then become a reference to guide you in your quest for a system.

Even if you are not certain at this point exactly what your final requirements will be, enter your best estimates. You can revise them later, as you undertake some independent research, but

---

ENTER HERE YOUR BEST ESTIMATES OF
YOUR PROBABLE NEEDS OR DESIRES

INSTRUCTIONS: Check all appropriate boxes and/or write in entries as necessary.

Memory Requirement

[ ] 128 K   [ ] 256K   [ ] 512 K   [ ]_____K

Minimum Storage Requirement

[ ] 400 K   [ ] 700K   [ ] 1M   [ ]_____

Storage Device(s)

[ ] Floppy disk   [ ] Hard disk   [ ] Tape   [ ]_____

Hard Copy Output Requirement

[ ] 8½ × 11-inch copy   [ ] 11 × 14-inch printout
[ ] Letter-quality printer   [ ] Dot-matrix printer [ ] Plotter
[ ] Tractor feed   [ ] Cut-sheet feeder

Soft Display, Color

[ ] Green screen [ ] Amber screen [ ] RGB   [ ]_____

Soft Display, Size

[ ] 9-inch   [ ] 12-inch   [ ] _____-inch

Modem

[ ] Acoustic   [ ] Direct, external   [ ] Direct, internal

Miscellaneous

[ ] Surge protector   [ ] Uninterruptible-power system
[ ]_____[ ]_____
[ ]_____[ ]_____
NOTES_____

Worksheet 5. System component requirements.

your investigations and studies will be far more productive as guided research by having some specific premises established in advance to act as an anchor. Otherwise you find yourself in the position of the child in the candy store, bewildered by the vast array and unable to choose from among so many beckoning goodies.

HOW TO READ MANUFACTURERS' LITERATURE

You are going to read a great deal of manufacturers' literature, both in their own publications and in the advertising you find in the various periodicals. To get any useful information from this material you must understand a few facts about such literature and advertising copy.

First of all, there are two basic kinds of product information published: general descriptive text and specifications. They are quite different from each other, and the easiest way to distinguish one from the other is by the very nature of the copy: General descriptions are loaded with adjectives and adverbs—hyperbole frequently—reflecting generalized opinions or claims more than objective fact. General copy says such things as "easy to use" and "something extra," while a list of specifications says such things as "12-inch screen" and "128K memory."

There are actually two kinds of specifications, performance specifications, or what the system will *do*, and equipment specifications, or what the equipment *is*. Figure 24 is one example of specifications for two printers marketed by the A. B. Dick Company. Note that the lists provide *quantified* information, which is a distinguishing feature of specifications. (Be wary of "specifications" that are not specific in the sense of providing quantified data.)

Figure 25 is a specification for software, the CP/M Release 2.2 operating system. Note that although this is software, not hardware, the specification offers quantified data primarily, as in the case of the printers.

The important thing to remember is that in general descriptions the manufacturer feels a great deal of freedom to make claims, but specifications are a different matter. Here it is necessary to state absolute facts because specifications, by their nature, must be factual, usually quantified. Therefore, to get the true picture, learn to regard the general descriptions with a large grain of tolerance and seek the specifications to get a truer picture.

The A.B.Dick Magna-Writer Printers are designed for use with the Magna-Writer Information Processing System. The Magna-Writer Printers are capable of printing high-quality, fully formed characters using daisy-type printwheels. These versatile printers provide application flexibility and superior print quality at a low-cost.

Magna-Writer 20 CPS Printer (Product Number – 2715)

This printer is capable of printing fully formed characters at a speed of 20 Characters Per Second minimum using a new 98 character plastic printwheel. This new printwheel, available in most of the popular typestyles in 10, 12 and 15 pitch, is part of a unique "drop-in" system which allows the printwheel to be "dropped-in" without removing the ribbon cartridge. The Magna-Writer Printer Electronics interprets coding on the print-wheel to set Pitch and Font automatically.

Specifications

Print Speed: Up to 25 characters per second.

Printwheel: 98-character plastic "drop-in" wheel

Type Styles Available:

Courier 10	Pica 10
Courier 12	Pica 10 WP
Courier Italic 12	Elite 12 WP
Prestige Elite 12	Pica 10 Multilingual
Prestige Pica 10	Bookface Academic 10
Letter Gothic 12	Orator 10
Letter Gothic 15	Script 12

Ribbon: Single-Strike or Multi-Strike. Up to 440,000 characters per cartridge

Forms Width: 15.2 inches maximum

Interface: Serial. RS-232-C/V24; 300-1200 baud; Bell type 103A, 113A and 212A modem compatible.

Multi-copy Controls: 1 to 5 part forms, no adjustments

Power Requirements:
120V AC, 60 Hz, 2 Amp
220V AC, 50 Hz, 1 Amp
100 watts typical

Dimensions: Height: 9.25", Width: 24.5", Depth: 17.4"

Weight: Less than 50 lbs. including shipping container

Safety Certifications: Meets UL and CSA requirements and FCC Class B requirements.

Magna-Writer 40 CPS Printer (Product Number - 2690)

The Magna-Writer 40 CPS printer produces excellent print quality at a speed of up to 40 Characters Per Second and includes many standard features such as Ribbon Out, Paper Out and Cover Open sensors. This printer features a 96 character plastic printwheel available in a wide variety of typestyles in 10, 12 and 15 pitch.

Specifications

Print Speed: Up to 40 characters per second.

Printwheel: 98-character plastic wheel

Type Styles Available:

Letter Gothic 12	Elite 12
Letter Gothic 15	Prestige Elite 12
Pica 10	Artisan Legal 12
Courier 10	Dual Gothic Legal 12
Emphasis 10	Forms Gothic S10
General Scientific 10	

Ribbon: Multi-Strike. Up to 360,000 characters per cartridge

Forms Width: 16.0 inches maximum with paper out; 16.53 inches without paper out

Interface: Serial. RS-232-C/V24; 110, 150, 300, 600, 1200, 1800, 2000, 2400, 4800, 7200 and 9600; Bell 103A, 113A, 212A modem compatible.

Multi-copy Controls: 1 to 6 part forms (typical) accommodated by a 2-position carriage lever

Sensors: End of ribbon, top paper out, cover open, copy control

Power Requirements:
120V AC, 60 Hz, 2 Amp
220V AC, 50 Hz, 1 Amp
100 watts typical

Dimensions: (RO configuation) Height: Less than 8.25" w/o forms tractor; Width: 22.4" Depth: 18.25"

Weight: Less than 60 lbs.

Safety Certifications: Meets UL, CSA and VDE 0804 and 0871 requirements

A.B.Dick Company
5700 West Touhy Avenue
Chicago. Illinois 60648
87-0190

Figure 24. Specifications for two printers.

The CP/M® Operating System, one of the most widely used today, allows your Magna III or Magna-Writer™ to perform personal computation applications in addition to their extensive word processing capabilities. Now data processing and word processing can be performed at the same workstation and the results printed on high-quality printers. CP/M Release 2.2 requires only software, no hardware modifications are necessary. Various utilities have been provided to increase ease of use when performing housekeeping tasks such as copying or deleting files.

Specifications

Operating System: CP/M Release 2.2, Digital Research, Inc.

Diskette: 5¼ Inch, Dual Sided, Double Density

User Available Diskette Capacity: 248,000 Characters Per Diskette

Number of Diskette Drives Supported: 2

Memory Size: 64K System with 56K available User Memory

Screen Size: 24 lines by 80 characters

Maximum Number of Directory Entries: 256

Clock Speed: 3 Mhz.

Printers Supported: Magna-Writer Printers

Interface: RS-232C Serial Port

Standard Communication Buffer: 255 Characters

User Definable Communications Buffer: Up to available Memory Size less 16K reserved

SOFTWARE SET-UP PROVIDED:

Baud Rates: 300 - 19,200

Protocol: XON/XOFF, Toggle RTS

Word Length: 5, 6, 7, 8 Bits

Parity: Even, Odd, None

Stop Bits: 1, 1.5, 2

Character Attributes: Bold, Blink, Highlight, Underscore

Key Click: Low, High, Off

SCREEN FUNCTIONS SUPPORTED:

Direct Cursor Positioning Non-Destructive Cursor Movement: Up, Down, Right, Left

Character Attributing: Off, Bold, Blink, Highlight, Intensify

String Attributing: Off, Bold, Blink, Highlight, Intensify

Erase to End of Line

Erase to End of Screen

Home Cursor

Clear Screen

Documentation Provided: User Manuals from Digital Research, Inc.
Skil/Pak for A.B.Dick Utilities

Utilities

Standard utilities from Digital Research, Inc. are provided. A.B.Dick utilities include various tools to aid in file maintenance and system set-ups.

And a world of CP/M based software. . .from A.B.Dick

For Programming	For Financial Planning	For Terminal Emulation
Microsoft® BASIC	SuperCalc™	DEC® VT52
		3270
		2780/3780
		HASP

. . .And over 100 software packages are available for purchase from Lifeboat Associates

For further information about CP/M and applications software call your local A.B.Dick Representative.

CP/M is a registered trademark of Digital Research, Inc.
DEC is a registered trademark of Digital Equipment Corporation
SuperCalc is a trademark of Sorcim Corporation
Microsoft is a registered trademark of Microsoft, Inc.

ABDICK ®
Information Systems Group
We're putting frustration
out of business.

A.B.Dick Company
5700 West Touhy Avenue
Chicago, Illinois 60648
87-0195

Figure 25. Specifications for software.

287

CHAPTER SEVENTEEN

Accessories and Supplies

The personal-computer industry has spawned the creation of an ample number of satellite industries that provide the many accessories and supplies necessary to support the computers.

ACCESSORIES AND SUPPLIES ARE DURABLES AND CONSUMABLES

Computers, like any other major item, require support of a variety of accessories. Some of the accessory items are durables, of which you buy only one or two and which you rarely, if ever, need to replace. Surge suppressors and modems are examples of such items. But there are also many accessories which are consumables and which you must buy on a continuing basis and even maintain in stock in your own inventory. These include disks, tape, paper, and ribbons, among other items. They represent an important enough element of your computer commitment and its cost to merit their own chapter. The time you spend reading these pages will probably reward you substantially, for like the computer industry itself the accessories business is highly competitive, and a bit of advance guidance can save you a great deal of money over the course of a year.

DISKS

Disks are a significant item of cost because they are not inexpensive and you tend to use them up rather rapidly, no matter what your disk configuration happens to be. Even the popular 5¼-inch disk, the one you will probably use (because it is by far the most widely used one today), can run as high as $65–70 per package of 10 disks. As an example of how many disks you are likely to need I can cite my own case. In the past year I have purchased approximately 70 disks, which does not represent a particularly high incidence of use. Some users consume a far greater number of disks per year than that, and computer owners employ several different approaches to minimize the cost of the disks. To appreciate these methods, however, a few words of explanation about disks are necessary:

The disk is coated with an iron oxide, a material that can be magnetized and is thus suitable for magnetic storage devices. Moreover, the disks are coated on both sides with the iron oxide, so that either one or two sides of the disk may be used. Also, data may be packed on a disk at the regular (original) density, at the more-advanced double density, and more recently even at double-double or quadruple density. (Techniques have improved steadily, resulting in the steadily increasing efficiency of storing data on disks.) Disks are therefore rated as single- or double-sided and as single, double, or quadruple density, and disk ratings include designators of whether they are for one- or two-sided use and at what density of data storage they are rated; disk ratings include all combinations of these two rating factors.

The designations you will find therefore include these:

SS   =   single sided
DS   =   double sided
SD   =   single density

DD   =   double density

Quad =   quadruple density

Ironically, the disks are not different from each other, for it is not any characteristic or feature of the disk per se that determines whether it is double- or single-sided or at what density data may be packed on its surfaces; it is the disk drive mechanism and circuitry that determines this. A disk that is rated as SS/SD (single sided/single density) can be used as a double-sided/double-density disk. The difference lies in the disk manufacturer's guarantees. The manufacturer tests the disks and guarantees them as SS/SD, SS/DD, and so on, and sets prices accordingly: The SS/SD is the lowest priced and the DS/quad-density is the highest priced.

The disk has a notch cut into one side of the sleeve (see Figure 26) and the disk must be inserted into the drive so that the notch appears in the right orientation. The disk will not work when inserted so that the notch is not where it must be for the drive to read and write to the disk. The notch is, in fact, known as a "write-

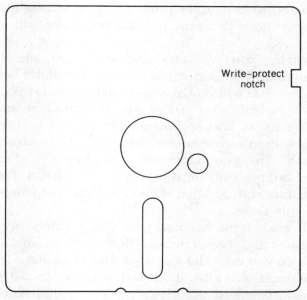

Write–protect
notch

Figure 26.   A 5¼-inch disk in sleeve.

protect notch," and when it is covered with a bit of tape the computer cannot write to it—record on it, that is. So if the disk is turned around, the computer sees the disk as being write-protected—that is, as having the notch covered.

To overcome this, some owners of computers with single-sided disk drives cut a notch on the other side of the sleeve, and in fact the support industry sells special devices to cut the notch with exact precision so that it matches the factory-cut notch. The disk may then be turned around and the other side can be used to record and store data.

Manufacturers caution against this practice and against using disks for drives other than those designated—that is, against using single-density disks in double-density drives, single-sided disks in double-sided drives, and so on. They stipulate that it is at the user's risk, for the disk has been tested and guaranteed only for the use its code indicates. However, I long ago began buying SS/SD disks for my DS/DD disk drives and have had no difficulties whatsoever, so far, and have cut my disk costs about 60 percent in so doing. (I admit that I did so with great trepidation, at first, despite my awareness that the disks should perform satisfactorily, but I was prepared to encounter problems. Happily, there have been none, at least none that I did not encounter also with disks rated for my drives.)

Incidentally, you will find that disks are offered in both preformatted and nonformatted versions, but don't become confused by this. You will probably use soft-sectored disks, which are the more popular ones. These are formatted by magnetically designating tracks and sectors on the surface so that the disk operating system can record where files are stored and can find them again. In some cases you can buy the disks already formatted, but probably most users prefer to format them via their own computer software that is provided with the machines, since it is a simple task.

Entirely aside from this, disk prices vary widely, depending on manufacturer (the "brand name"), dealer's discounts, and quantities in which you buy. The standard pack is 10 disks, but they are offered in packs of 50 also, at somewhat lower per-disk prices, and some dealers offer sliding scales of prices on still-larger quantities.

If you take the time to read the advertisements in the popular periodicals you will see this for yourself very quickly. With many dealers asking for about $3–7 per disk for disks in 10-packs and somewhat less in 50-packs, you can find others offering the same brand names at far less. I have, for example found a source that sells Wabash disks (a brand name) for as low as $1.35 per disk for single-side/single-density disks in 10-packs, with even lower prices in larger quantities. (I have also used "generic" brands and had no problems with them.)

PAPER

Paper is another item you are likely to use in quantity, since you will almost surely need hard copy—paper printout. And here you will find an even greater diversity of products offered, although the diversity in pricing is not as great.

If you refer to Worksheet 5 you will recall being asked to decide whether you will want to print out 8½ × 11-inch or 11 × 14-inch hard copy, and whether you will want to use a cut-sheet paper-feeder or a tractor-feed mechanism with your printer. This will affect your costs somewhat, but your personal convenience and what you order in paper supplies will be affected by these decisions. The difference between the two choices is not insignificant.

The cut-sheet feeder fits on your printer and supplies individual sheets of paper, using the friction- or pressure-feed mechanism, in the same manner that a similar mechanism feeds paper through a conventional typewriter. Such sheet feeders are relatively expensive–on the order of $500–600—and are reported to be somewhat troublesome mechanically or at least less reliable than tractor-feed mechanisms.

The latter use paper in a continuous train, fan-folded, and with sprocket holes along the vertical margins. The paper is perforated so that the edges of the paper can be detached and the sheets separated from each other after printing. The system provides excellent control of the paper and is simple and trouble-free. Some of the paper sold for this use is perforated in such a way that there is a clearly discernible sawtooth edge all around each sheet after detaching the sides and separating the sheets. However, it is possible to buy "microperforated" paper that leaves a clean edge after separation, as though cut sheets had been used.

The paper is available in conventional after-separation sizes of 8½ × 11 inches (conventional business size), 8½ × 13 (legal size), and 11 x 14 inches (that familiar size used for printout by large, mainframe computers). It can be bought in a variety of packages, from 250 sheets to boxes containing well over 3000 sheets. The cost is slightly higher than that of cut sheets, but not excessively so—if you shop carefully.

Paper is available also in various forms, including one with blue borders which is referred to as a "proposal paper," carbon sets, which produce carbon copies, a variety of forms, labels, and other such items. You can also have your own stationery made up— letterheads and envelopes—to be fed through your printer with your tractor-feed mechanism.

PRINTER RIBBONS

If you use any kind of impact printer (and by far the majority of printers in use and being offered today are impact types) you will need to use ribbons of the same type as those used in conventional typewriters, but usually in a cassette or cartridge package for instantaneous insertion and removal. This makes the ribbons easy to use but also relatively expensive.

The ribbons come in various types, as they do for typewriters. In my own case I am offered fabric, polyester film single-strike, and polyester film multistrike. I use the latter, at $7.35 per cartridge, but since it delivers approximately 300,000 impressions it is still less costly than the single-strike film, which costs about $3.50 but delivers only 85,000 impressions. (I tried the fabric ribbon but was dissatisfied with it.)

The Silver Reed is an excellent printer, but it is not nearly as widely used as are some others, such as the Diablo. It uses an Olivetti ribbon, which is also not as widely sold as are some other printers. Therefore the competition to make and sell ribbons for it is less sharp than in the case of some other printers. This is very much a factor in availability and prices of supplies. [There are manufacturers of ribbons and various other supplies, and they make supplies of just about every description for the most popular machines, usually at lower prices than such supplies are sold by the OEMs (original equipment manufacturers)]. In fact, in some cases those who manufacture the supplies for the OEMs (and, of course, also label them for the OEMs) also package the identical items with "private-brand" labels and sell them at far lower prices than do the OEMs. This is quite a common business practice in just about every industry, so that the label is often not a reliable indicator of who the actual manufacturer or original source is.)

PRINT WHEELS

If you use a letter-quality printer you will probably have a daisy-wheel type of printing element. (A few printers use the IBM ball type of element, and the NEC printer has its own patent "thimble" type of element, but almost all others use the daisy wheel.) Again, the availability of supplies and suppliers is directly related to the popularity of the machine.

Most daisy wheels come in both plastic and metal versions. The metal versions are more expensive and expected to be longer-lived, although the plastic wheels appear to be quite durable. Prices vary from as little as $4–6 to as much as $18–25, and brand names again play an important part in pricing.

PART FIVE

Useful Information and Guides to More of the Same

Both Albert Einstein and Henry Ford are on record as rejecting the idea of trying to memorize information that can be looked up readily. And others have expressed similar ideas, some pointing out that education is not memorizing a great many facts, but instead knowing how and where to find them when needed.

The wisdom of that philosophy is more apparent than ever today as we find ourselves threatened with a tidal wave of information, much of it highly specialized but yet useful and even necessary. In the pages that have preceded this one I have been able only to peel off the top veneer of information about computers and how they affect or should affect you as an independent consultant. In Part Five you will get two other kinds of assistance:

1. An introduction and general guide to the online services, commercial and public, which, if you use these services well, are likely to become one of your most valuable resources in the near future.

2. An assortment of reference data—glossary, recommended reading, and vendor lists, among other items—to help you in various ways to choose your system, accessories, and supplies, and to serve you subsequently as a first reference resource.

CHAPTER EIGHTEEN

The Many Sources of Useful Information

The store of valuable information has been growing exponentially—at an ever-increasing rate—throughout the history of humankind, and it is only the computer that has enabled society to cope with it at all. But now the next evolutionary step has arrived, that of making the information readily available to everyone who has use for it.

THE ROLE OF INFORMATION TODAY

It has been long recognized that information is an important key to success in all undertakings, and one of the advantages the large corporation has long had over the small business has been the larger organization's vastly greater stores of and access to useful information. (Large organizations, for example, can establish and maintain their own research departments or, alternatively, contract such work out to other organizations who specialize in gathering data.) That is changing rapidly now, since the personal computer has become readily available to everyone and, through it, so has access to the growing online services, namely, the myriad of public databases and the information services that make these public databases available to subscribers.

What this means is that in our now-acknowledged information society, information itself has become a commodity to be bought and sold, and it is no longer the private preserve of the supercorporations. Today you can utilize your personal computer and modem to gain access to virtually all of the world's information that is not specifically guarded as proprietary, personal, or vital to a government's security. Moreover, today you do not have to put a researcher to work to spend many hours poring over stacks of printed material to search out what you need to know: The host computers will do the searching for you in a matter of minutes— even seconds, sometimes. It's all yours, at acceptable costs in most cases, and even without cost in many cases.

TELECOMMUNICATIONS SYSTEMS

Earlier in this book you were made aware of the existence of online systems, both those that are commercial ventures and require the payment of subscription and use fees and those that are free or require only nominal fees. In fact, these are elements of what might be referred to overall as "telecommunications systems," which, for better understanding, can be divided into three basic types (although these have variants):

Bulletin Board Systems (BBSs), which are those systems that usually are operated on personal computers by hobbyists, computer clubs, and local businesses. They usually have only a single telephone line, and you often have trouble getting through for that reason, if the service is a popular one. However, their "amateur" status and limited access does not necessarily diminish their potential usefulness to you. They can be useful in several ways. For one, you can gain a great deal of valuable experience with your computer system and enrich your computer knowledge generally at no cost except for telephone charges. But you can also make valuable "contacts" by spending a little time with these systems, and thereby carry out some of your PR work from the comfort of your own office.

Local-Area Services, which are something like local newspapers and local directories, albeit electronic ones, and which charge a small fixed fee, usually, and often no fee at all. These range widely in what they have to offer, and they include such things as an electronic "yellow pages" directory, local bulletin board, and electronic library, as well as a news source.

National Networks, which are analogous to a radio or TV network in that they are national in scope and tied to some communications web into which you can connect your own computer by dialing a telephone number, usually a local one. Most of the major public databases and information systems who provide access to these databases are connected to one or more of these national networks and are so usually available through a local telephone connection. (The subscriber is charged for the network connection, but this is less costly than the regular long-distance dial-up telephone line would be.)

These are known as *value-added networks* and also as *packet-switched networks*, which is a technical designation that refers to the transmission methods used. (Data is sent in packets, that is.) The company that operates the network, which is not necessarily the same organization as the one operating the *information utility* or host computers sending the information, is thus logically referred to as the *value-added carrier*. As an example, here are some of those value-added carriers and the value-added networks they operate:

GTE Telenet Communications Corporation:	Telenet
Tymnet, Inc.:	Tymnet
Transcanada Telephone System:	DataPac
British Telecom International:	PSS

In this chapter you are going to learn more about the full extent of these services, what they offer, what they require, and how to gain access to and use the commodities they offer users. But first some preliminary explanations are offered to assist you generally in gaining a fuller understanding of computer-to-computer communications.

COSTS

Most of the major commercially based public-database/ information systems charge for their services on the basis of time charges for "connect time," either by the hour or by the minute. However, actual billings are by the minute and/or fractions, in both cases, and there are generally several different base rates. Service is divided into prime time and nonprime time: prime time consists of the normal business hours, and nonprime time consists of after-hours and weekends. But in many cases these are subdivided according to speed cf transmission, usually on the basis of one rate for a 300-baud transmission and a higher rate for the faster 1200-baud transmission.

In many cases, where the service provides access to many different databases (many of which they do not own but must pay fees to use), there are extra charges and even extra subscription fees for access to and use of various such databases.

If you call the service directly you will pay long-distance toll charges, but since most of the services belong to one or more networks or have gateways (connections) to several networks, you can usually dial a local number and be connected to a network at a lower rate than the AT&T long-distance line would cost you.

Many of the services also impose a minimum monthly fee, which can be quite small or quite large, and more than a few prefer or even require that you provide a credit-card number for billing purposes, since they prefer to automatically bill your credit card for all charges and send you simply a copy of their billing document.

DIAL-UP CONNECTIONS

When you use your modem to call another computer—and all these public-database/information services are brought to you via computer-to-computer conversation—you either dial the telephone number of the other computer or, if you are using a smart modem and appropriate communications software (as you should be), you type the number on your keyboard and the system dials it up. (You can also have the numbers recorded and dial up a number by simply pressing one code letter, if you have a smart modem and proper software.)

Unless the line is busy or you have made some mistake in dialing, you will get a response by the word "CONNECTED" or "ONLINE" and/or by the line identifying itself and welcoming you, which advises you that you are now connected to the other system. If it is a subscription-type system (and in some cases, even if it is free of charge) you will be asked to type in your name, identification code, and password. (The latter would have been issued to you when you subscribed or when you registered to use the system for the first time.) When your credentials have been examined and approved by the other computer (or by its software program, more literally), you will be asked a few questions, unless you have made the connection before and the other service has already recorded the answers for future reference when you call again. These depend on the kind of terminal you are using [you may be using a teletype (printer) kind of terminal, instead of a CRT and screen], how many columns you can display or print, whether you need line feeds or can advance each line yourself, your baud rate (most systems can transmit at either 300 or 1200 baud, and the commercial systems usually charge more for 1200-baud transmission, although that saves you money because it is four times faster than 300-baud transmission), and other such criteria. Then you will get an opening menu, from which you can pick your choices. A typical opening menu might look something like the following:

1	LATE NEWS SUMMARIES
2	STOCK MARKET REPORTS
3	SEARCH SERVICE
4	SHOPPERS' MALL
5	AIRLINE SCHEDULES
6	TV SCHEDULES

7   CHANGE ID OR PASSWORD

8   MENU OF OTHER SERVICES AVAILABLE

TYPE NUMBER OF SERVICE OR OTHER MENU DESIRED AND PRESS ENTER

That action then either brings the item on-screen or brings you another menu to choose from, as the instructions stipulate.

When you use a full-duplex modem, one that transmits and receives at the same time, whatever you send is echoed by the other computer, thereby appearing on your own screen so you can verify that what you sent was received correctly. (The exceptions to this are identification codes and passwords, which are not echoed so that others cannot pick up your identification code or password by seeing them on their screens.)

Some systems use *keywords* instead of menus. These keywords are listed and explained in the user's manual you get when you subscribe and the system often also presents the keywords on-screen. And some also permit or even encourage the use of *direct commands*, which are like keywords in that they ask the system to do something specific. The user's manual also explains the direct commands you can issue from the command line.

IT'S NOT ALL DATABASES

Not all the services these systems offer is purely the provision of or access to databases, although this is the most prominent and most commonly cited benefit. In fact, among the various services made available through these various systems are these:

Communications in both real time (spontaneously) and in sending messages in a kind of electronic mail or cable system.

Timesharing and data processing support, in permitting subscribers to utilize larger software packages and mainframe computers on a rental or fee basis.

Access to special online classified help-wanted advertising as aid in seeking high-technology jobs.

Sending your own résumé via online connections to prospective employers.

Online conferencing.

Gateways to other networks.

Online advertising.

Online newsletters, magazines, and directories on a variety of subjects.

Online games.

Electronic shopping, ordering items to be shipped out to you by some means or buying materials that can be sent to you immediately over the link you have by "downloading" the items and charging them to credit cards.

DOWNLOADING

There are three ways to receive and handle the information that is provided by the online services. The immediate delivery is in the form of on-screen presentation, and you can settle for that only. However, you can usually also print out anything you are receiving, if you want a hard copy to read at your leisure or for any other use. But that takes time, since printing is relatively slow, and it is costly because you are paying for connect time in most cases. However, you can usually write the input data to go to disk far more rapidly than your printer can print it out (especially when you are using a 1200-baud transmission) and store the data on disk to be printed out later, when you are offline and are no longer piling up charges for connect time.

This latter practice of recording and printing out the data transmitted is known as "downloading" in the jargon, although the term is usually used to refer to a slightly different practice, wherein you specifically order a file downloaded to your own system and do not see it displayed on-screen. (What you get on-screen is information advising you that the downloading transmission is in progress and keeping you informed of the status of the transmission as it proceeds.) "Uploading" is, naturally, the opposite process: sending a file to another computer.

The exact procedure for downloading and uploading will vary somewhat in its details from one case to another, depending on how your own system and communications software are designed and on how the system you are communicating with is designed. You will get an instruction manual of some sort with your software (although if you get free public-domain software, you may find the manual is on the disk and has to be printed out or displayed on-screen). You'll also get online instructions from the various systems, explaining their own procedural requirements, and if you subscribe to one of the major networks you will get some kind of instruction manual as well.

WHAT IS TO COME

The rest of this chapter will be devoted to presenting directories of the three kinds of systems described, starting with the major national systems. The descriptions will necessarily be somewhat brief, and the listings are not represented as complete, since new facilities are almost constantly being established. But the listings and the descriptions, brief as they are, are representative and furnish a general idea of the kinds of information and services typically available on these systems. To get more complete information you can write to some of them (the major networks, for example) for more information, since the addresses and telephone numbers are provided here. Moreover, other directory listings in this final part of the book will give other sources, especially bibliographic references to other sources, which will provide such details as hours of operation, rates, and other information.

NATIONAL NETWORKS AND SERVICES

ADP Network Services, Inc.
175 Jackson Plaza
Ann Arbor, MI 48106
(313) 769-6800

Business databases, forecasts and projections, timesharing, and data-processing services.

Boeing Computer Services, Inc.
7990 Gallows Court
Vienna, VA 22180
(703) 827-4603

Economic and financial databases, securities/stock-market information.

Bolt Beranek and Newman, Inc.
50 Moulton Street
Cambridge, MA 02238
(617) 497-3505

Timesharing, electronic mail, mathematical and statistical library, text processing.

Brodart Co.
500 Arch Street
Williamsport, PA 17705
(800) 233-8467
(800) 692-6211 (in PA)

Database, supports libraries. References over 1 million monographs. Book orders can be placed online.

Broker Services, Inc.
8745 E. Orchard Rd., #518
Englewood, CO 80111
(303) 779-8930

Access to 100+ stock-analysis/investment programs.

BRS/Bibliographic Retrieval
Services
& BRS After Dark
1200 Route 7
Latham, NY 12110
(518) 783-1161
(800) 833-4707

Access to 80+ databases in medicine, education, engineering, science, business, financial, other areas.

BRS/Executive Information Service
John Wiley & Sons, Inc.
One Wiley Drive
Somerset, NJ 08873
(201) 469-4400

Databases summarizing recent major business articles from 600 periodicals, abstracts of other business articles/information.

CBD Online
United Communications Group
8701 Georgia Avenue, Suite 800
Silver Spring, MD 20910
(301) 589-9975

Commerce Business Daily online, search capabilities, other services.

Chase Econometrics/Interactive
Data
486 Totten Pond Road
Waltham, MA 02154
(617) 890-1234

Historical and forecast databases from all countries, all U.S. counties, on labor, energy, savings, insurance, government, other related topics.

Chemical Abstracts Service
2540 Olentangy River Road
POB 3012
Columbus, OH 43210
(614) 421-3600

Online search service, access to Registry File of structural information of 6.4 million substances, related data.

Citishare Corporation
850 Third Avenue
New York, NY 10043
(212) 572-9600

Computer support, economic–financial-securities databases, stock quotations, related data, services.

Commodity Information Services
327 S. LaSalle, Suite 800
Chicago, IL 60604
(312) 922-3661

Databases on financial, agricultural, other futures, updated daily, accompanied by extensive library of programs for analysis, trading models.

CompuServe
5000 Arlington Centre Blvd
Columbus, OH 43220
(614) 457-8600
(800) 848-8990

Variety of databases and services for general consumer—news, stock market reports, schedules, banking and travel services, electronic mail, games, business news, other databases and services for professionals.

The Computer Company
POB 6987
1905 Westmoreland Street
Richmond, VA 23230
(804) 358-2171

Timesharing, access to various business databases in banking, energy, and transportation industries.

Computer Directions Advisors, Inc.
11501 Georgia Avenue
Silver Spring, MD 20902
(301) 942-1700

Profiles of 6000+ public companies, updated daily as filed with SEC; covers institutions, other organizations.

Comshare, Inc.
3001 S. State Street
Ann Arbor, MI 48104
(313) 994-4800

Decision support systems for financial planning, marketing, personnel applications. Also demographic data.

Connexions
55 Wheeler Street
Cambridge, MA 02138
(617) 938-9307

Employment positions online; online résumé services; electronic mail.

Control Data Corp.
Business Information Services
500 West Putnam Avenue
POP 7100
Greenwich, CT 06836
(203) 622-2000

Marketing, financial, other business databases on a variety of business topics; profiles of companies, industries, consumers, markets.

Cornell Computer Services
G-02 Uris Hall
Ithaca, NY 14853
(607) 256-4981

Database featuring 1000 time series on various economic factors, including car sales, consumer buying and forecasts, financial indicators, and help-wanted advertising.

Customer Service Bureau
Box 36
Riverton, WY 82501
(800) 446-6255
(800) 442-0982 (in WY)

A network that offers subscribers gateways (access) to a variety of other networks and databases.

Data Resources, Inc.
1750 K Street, 9th floor
Washington, DC 20006
(202) 862-3700

Business and investment data, data on various companies, business patterns, and financial information.

Delphi
3 Blackstone Street
Cambridge, MA 02139
(800) 544-4005
(617) 491-3393

Databases on travel, finances, stock quotes, investments, commodities, and securities. Also, online brokerage, games, and conferencing services that permit buying and selling via online connection.

Dialog Information Services, Inc.
3460 Hillview Avenue
Palo Alto, CA 94304
(800) 277-1927
(415) 858-3785

Contains hundreds of databases, including CBD Online, business, advertising, economics, politics, government, medicine, other topics.

Dow Jones News/Retrieval Service
POB 300
Princeton, NJ 08540
(800) 257-5114

27 databases business/economic and financial/investment services.

Dun & Bradstreet Corporation
299 Park Avenue
New York, NY 10171
(212) 593-6800

Timesharing and such business services/information for which D&B is already well known.

General Electric Information
Services Co.
401 N. Washington Street
Rockville, MD 20850
(301) 340-4000

Teleprocessing and data processing services, access in 700 cities and 20 countries, hundreds of software programs available.

GTE Telenet
8229 Boone Blvd
Vienna, VA 22180
(800) TELENET

Electronic mail, intercomputer communications/network service, medical, pharmaceutical, clinical practice information; stock quotes.

GML Information Services
594 Marrett Road
Lexington, MA 02173
(617) 861-0515

Technical databases on computers and related technologies.

InnerLine
95 W. Algonquin Road
Arlington Heights, IL 60005
(800) 323-1321

News and other information for bankers: banking news, money market funds, related databases.

Interactive Market Systems, Inc.
19 West 44th Street
New York, NY 10036
(212) 869-8810
(800) 223-7942

Access to media- and marketing-related services, timesharing services, legal-research services.

ITT Dialcom, Inc.
1109 Spring Street
Silver Spring, MD 20910
(301) 588-1572

Databases for Fortune 100 companies, government agencies, other large organizations; electronic mail, airlines schedules, other services.

Mead Data central
POB 933
Dayton, OH 45401
(513) 865-6800

LEXIS for legal research; LEXPAT
for patent information; NEXIS for
general news service.

NewsNet
945 Haverford Road
Bryn Mawr, PA 19010
(215) 527-8030 (in PA)
(800) 345-1301

Business information utility
distributing a variety of online
business newsletters and wire
services and providing search
services.

The Source
1616 Anderson Road
McLean, VA 22102
(800) 336-3366

One of the oldest, if not the
oldest, online database services
for general consumers: news
schedules, TV listings, stock
quotes, and so on.

TRW Information Services Div.
Business Credit Services and
Credit Data Service
500 City Parkway West, Suite 200
Orange, CA 92668
(714) 937-2000

Provides both business and individual consumer credit as the
names reveal, plus related business information.

Westlaw
West Publishing Co.
50 West Kellog Blvd
POB 43526
St. Paul, MN 55164
(800) 328-9352

Legal research and related information, plus news and index coverage of several financial and general newspapers.

THE DATABASES

What has been presented here as a listing of networks and information services represents only a fraction of all the online services
available and makes only general references to the various
databases made available through the services. Space limitations
made it impossible to provide complete descriptions of the services and information available from each of the listed services. In

fact, there are thousands of databases accessible today, and together they cover virtually every sphere of human activity—sciences, business, industries, social life, education, and others. Some of these databases are available uniquely through only one network or service, while others are available through several networks and services. Complete listings and descriptions would constitute a book in itself. However, a sampling of the several general types of databases, selected from a relatively small portion of the databases offered (approximately 300) is given here to furnish an idea of the storehouse of data available and of the sheer diversity of the data. The information in these databases is derived from various kinds of sources, which include abstracts from, reports on, and/or complete transcripts of news accounts in popular media, articles in trade journals and professional publications, books, the proceedings of professional societies and their conferences, and sundry other such sources:

- Business, management, industry information abstracted from several hundred periodicals.
- Online encyclopedia (full text).
- Accounting, auditing, tax, investments, financial information, and financial management, with quarterly updates.
- Marketing data (consumer behavior) based on series of regional types.
- Weekly summaries of civil suits and court decisions.
- Index to advertisements in a number of consumer periodicals, cross-referenced by various keywords/search terms.
- Abstracts, reports on print coverage of agricultural subjects.
- Reportage, bibliographic listings on history and area studies of America.
- Air pollution coverage.
- Information about marine life, aquatic sciences, fisheries data.
- Water and waste water.
- Radio and TV ratings, measurement reports.
- Petroleum prices.

- Sales information on art sales.
- Asbestos information, reports.
- Statistics index.
- Data on arctic areas.
- Index of audiovisual material for teaching health sciences.
- Banking information, reports from official reports, other information of interest to bankers.
- Biological/biotechnological information, citations, abstracts, reports, news.
- Chemical sciences, engineering, industries, economics.
- Bibliographic data on books catalogued at/by various organizations.
- Child abuse and neglect.
- Patent information, claims, cases, abstracts.
- Commodities, futures, prices.
- Conferences and papers.
- Construction industry, costs.
- Economic indicators, factors, forecasts.
- Medical data, diagnostic assistance.
- Food, food technology, food industries.
- Forest products.
- Textiles, related science, news, bibliographic citations.
- Zinc, lead, and cadmium abstracts on production, properties, and uses.
- Adoption, information about children waiting for adoption and families wishing to adopt children.
- Transcripts from the *Wall Street Journal*.
- Full text of *Washington Post* articles.
- Toxic substances information.
- Ownership information on American corporations.
- Sports information.
- Health care socioeconomic information.

- Roper reports on public attitudes in range of subjects.
- Technical papers and reports from Society of Automotive Engineers.
- Business data on Canadian industries, economics, financial matters.
- Text of stories, features appearing in *Philadelphia Inquirer*.
- Press releases issued by U.S. corporations, full texts.
- Official Airline Guide on domestic flight schedules.
- Management literature, conference proceedings and bibliographic citations.
- Mathematical research literature, worldwide.
- Literature on metals, alloys, related processes, properties.
- Mineral processing abstracts, index of related literature.
- Technical database on securities.
- Index of approximately 400 popular general-interest magazines.
- Abstracts of journal articles on language and language behavior.
- Pharmaceutical abstracts, all phases of drug development and uses.
- Index of mechanical engineering, engineering producting, and engineering management, articles from 200+ professional journals.
- Labor/industrial relations; economic and social development, related laws; demography; education: journal articles and monographs.
- World literature on physics, electrical engineering, computers.
- Monthly catalog of publications issued by Government Printing Office.
- Grant programs of federal, state, and local governments and of other organizations.
- Directory of foundations having assets of $1 million or more or awarding grants of $100,000 or more annually.

- Index of foreign traders—manufacurers, wholesalers, services, agents, retailers, distributors, and cooperatives in 130 foreign countries.

APPLICATION PROGRAMS

Among the network services listed (and especially many others not listed because of space limitations) were those that offer services, as well as access to databases. The services listed represent only a relative few of all the services available. A great many of those listed and a great many that were not listed here offer timesharing on computers larger than your own personal computer, access to other software, and assistance of various kinds in data processing, including having the service actually run your programs (using their own software) and acting as a computer service bureau. The following is a listing of the kinds of applications and application programs you can gain access to and/or get help with through many of these services:

General Applications

Accounting

Cash management

Database management

Electronic mail

Energy auditing

Financial analysis

Flow charting

Forecasting

Income tax computation

Inventory control

Job costing

Mailing list maintenance

Management information systems

Mechanical

Numerical control

Order entry

Payroll

Personnel management

Pension management

Photocomposition

Plotting/graphics

Simulation

Statistical analysis

Miscellaneous

Advertising

Computer-aided instruction

Foreign exchange analysis

Investment analysis

Market research

Medical diagnostics

Real estate appraisals

Industry Specific

Agribusiness

Professional time and cost records

Project planning and control
Report writing

Text Processing

Engineering/Technical

Architectural

Aviation

Banking

Broadcasting

Brokerage

Commodities/futures

Communications

Chemical/petrochemical

Civil/structural

Communications network design

Construction

Econometric modeling

Economics

Education

Electrical

Electrical construction

Employee benefits

Government

Graphics/mapping

Insurance/pension

Investments

Land development

Law

Libraries

Manufacturing

Market research

Media research

Medical

Oil/gas/mining

Pharmaceuticals

Printing

Publishing

Retail trade

Restaurant/theatre/sports

Science R&D

Energy

Environmental health and safety

Geophysical/geological

Transportation/shipping

Waste disposal

LOCAL AREA SERVICES

A-T Videotext
320 Nelson Street
Tiffin, OH 44883
(419) 447-4493

Local news, UPI news, farm news, business and financial news, other general information.

Buy-Phone
POB 29307
Los Angeles, CA 90029
(213) 474-2220

Electronic "yellow pages," listing 10,000+ businesses, services, products.

CLEO (Computer Listings of Employment Opportunities)
2164 West 190th Street
Torrance, CA 90504
(213) 618-0200
Other telephones
Los Angeles: (213) 618-8800
Orange County: (714) 476-8800
San Diego County: (619) 224-8800
San Jose/Santa Clara: (408) 294-2000
San Francisco/Oakland: (415) 482-1550

High-tech help-wanted (job openings) in California area.

Data Trac Information Service
2848 Westerville Road
Columbus, OH 43224
(614) 476-5895

Bulletin-board/electronic message service.

Fantasy Plaza
POB 6055
Burbank, CA 91510
(213) 840-8211

Online shopping service for software, peripheral equipment, supplies and accessories, other merchandise.

Harris Electronic News
300 W. 2nd
POB 356
Hutchinson, KS 67501
(316) 662-8667
(800) 362-0283

News, local and national; weather reports, farm news, commodity prices.

Microshare
POB 11N
Milwaukee, WI 53201
(414) 241-4321

CP/M public domain software.

BULLETIN BOARD SYSTEMS AND FREE SOFTWARE

The bulletin board systems in the United States are far too numerous to list here (there are well in excess of 500, at the lowest estimate) but they are listed in such periodicals as *Link-Up*, *Microsystems*, and others. However, they are organized usually on the basis of makes of computers and/or operating systems, and they offer generally the same basic features. Here are some of the bases on which these systems are organized:

CP/M	Radio Shack/TRS-DOS computers
PC-DOS/IBM-PC/PCjr computers	Atari computers
MS-DOS/IBM-compatible computers	Commodore computers
Apple computers	Morrow computers
Heath–Zenith computers	Osborne computers
Kaypro computers	Sanyo computers

By and large the BBSs have similar offerings and features. Here are the features found commonly on these systems:

- Chat with system operator and/or other callers.
- Conferencing, discussion groups.

- Games.
- Downloading free (public domain) software.
- Electronic mail.
- Shopping.
- Text files, various subjects, usually related to computers.
- Computer club information.
- List of other BBSs.

Some of the systems have rather special or unusual features, such as the following:

- Matchmaking ("lonely-hearts" club).
- Pen-pals.
- Educational programs.
- SIGs—special interest groups—service, including technical news/information about computers, games, video, ham radio, audio, other special interests.
- Sale of software programs, games, other computer-related items.
- X-rated messages, materials.
- Swap/sell notices between subscribers.
- Text files about UFOs, parapsychology researchers, and related topics.

A few of these are operated by for-profit companies and various other organizations or for/by special-interest groups, such as the following, for example:

Atlanta Computer Society CBBS,   300 baud
Atlanta, GA
(404) 636-6130
Sponsored by the Society, a
general-interest system.

Apple Medical BBS, Iowa City, IA   300 baud
(319) 353-6528
Concerned with computers in
medicine.

Dickenson's Movie Guide, Mis-   300 baud
sion, KS
(913) 432-5544
Operated by a local movie chain
to provide a directory of movies,
primarily, with other services similar to those of most BBSs.

Online Beta Sigma Phi, Overland   300 baud
Park, KS
(913) 384-2196
Operated by Beta Sigma Phi gift
shop, offers online shopping.

PMS—The Floppy House, San   300 baud
Diego, CA
(619) 280-1958
Rents time on micros, explains
their service via online text file.

PMS—McGraw-Hill Book Com-   300 baud
pany, New York, NY
(212) 512-2488
Offers BBS list, catalog, message
center; lists McGraw-Hill books
about computers, which can be
ordered by credit card.

A large number of these BBSs offer free software, which are
public-domain programs that can be downloaded for your own
use. These are programs in just about every category—games,
word processors, file managers, database managers, spreadsheets,
communications programs, and others. There are literally thousands of such programs offered, many of them of quite excellent
quality, although many also have bugs in them or are not efficient
programs. (An inefficient program is one that requires far more
time and memory than absolutely necessary, and it is far easier,

usually, to write an inefficient one than to write an efficient one.) There are also many free files containing useful information. All of this is readily available, much of which is useful for your amusement only, much is for your general education and familiarization with computers, and much has direct and indirect application to and value for your independent consulting practice.

CHAPTER NINETEEN

The Original Equipment Manufacturers

Here are mailing lists if you want useful literature.

GO TO THE SOURCE FOR THE BEST INFORMATION

Among the best sources of information about computers are the OEMs—the original equipment manufacturers. The lists offered here do not contain all the manufacturers supplying the computer industry, but instead contain some of the most prominent ones. Most will gladly send you brochures, press releases, and other information about their products, and you will find much of that information well worth the trouble of sending for it and the time waiting for it. Especially ask Data General Corp. for their free booklet *The Insider's Guide to Small Business Computers* and Honeywell for their publication *About Computers*. These two publications alone are an education in the subject.

COMPUTER MANUFACTURERS

A. B. Dick Co.
5700 West Touhy Avenue
Niles, IL 60648

Altos Computer Systems
2360 Bering Drive
San Jose, CA 95131

Apple Computer Co., Inc.
20525 Mariani Avenue
Cupertino, CA 95014

Atari, Inc.
1196 Borregas Avenue
Sunnyvale, CA 94086

BMC Computer Corp.
860 Walnut Street
Carson, CA 90746

Burroughs Corp.
Burroughs Place
Detroit, MI 48232

Canon USA
One Canon Plaza
Lake Success, NY 11042

Casio, Inc.
15 Gardner Road
Fairfield, NJ 07006

Columbia Data
8290 Route 108
Columbia, MD 21045

Commodore Business Machines
Computer Systems Division
487 Devon Park Drive
Wayne, PA 19087

Convergent Technologies
2500 Augustine Drive
Santa Clara, CA 95051

Corvus Systems, Inc.
2029 O'Toole Avenue
San Jose, CA 95131

Cromemco, Inc.
280 Bernardo Avenue
Mountain View, CA 94040

Data General Corp.
4400 Computer Drive
Westboro, MA 01580

Datapoint Corp.
9725 Datapoint Drive
San Antonio, TX 78284

Digital Equipment Corp.
Maynard, MA 01754

Dynabyte
521 Cottonwood Drive
Milpitas, CA 95035

Eagle Computer
983 University Avenue
Building C
Los Gatos, CA 95030

Epson America, Inc.
3415 Kashiwa Street
Torrance, CA 90505

Franklin Computer Corp.
7030 Colonial Highway
Pennsauken, NJ 08109

Heath Company (Zenith)
Benton Harbor, MI 49022

Hewlett-Packard
1820 Embarcadero Road
Palo Alto, CA 80535

Honeywell Information Systems
200 Smith Street
Waltham, MA 02154

IBM Systems Products Division
POB 1328
Boca Raton, FL 33432

Imsai Corp.
Division Fischer-Freitas Corp.
910 81st Avenue
Oakland, CA 94521

Lanier Business Products
1700 Chantilly Drive, NE
Atlanta, GA 30324

Morrow Designs, Inc.
600 McCormick St.
San Leandro, CA 94577

NCR Corp.
Stuart Street and Patterson Blvd
Dayton, OH 45479

NEC Home Electronics
1401 Estes Avenue
Elk Grove, IL 60007

NEC Information Systems, Inc.
5 Militia Drive
Lexington, MA 02173

Olivetti Corp.
155 White Plains Road
Tarrytown, NY 10591

Olympia USA, Inc.
Box 22
Somerville, NJ 08876

Otrona Corp.
4755 Walnut Street
Boulder, CO 80301

Panasonic
One Panasonic Way
Secaucus, NJ 07094

Perkin-Elmer Computer Systems
2 Crescent Place
Oceanport, NJ 07757

Pertec
12910 Culver Blvd
Los Angeles, CA 90009

Radio Shack/Tandy Corp.
One Tandy Center
Fort Worth, TX 76102

Sanyo Business Systems
51 Joseph Street
Moonachie, NJ 07074

Scientific Data Systems
344 Main Street
Venice, CA 90291

Seattle Computer
1114 Industry Drive
Seattle, WA 98188

Sharp Electronics Corp.
10 Sharp Plaza
Paramus, NJ 07652

Sony Corp. of America
Micro Products Division
7 Mercedes Drive
Montvale, NJ 07645

Texas Instruments, Inc.
POB 73
Lubbock, TX 79408

Wang Laboratories, Inc.
One Industrial Avenue
Lowell, MA 01851

Xerox Corp.
6416 Wrenchwood
Dallas, TX 75252

Zenith
1000 Milwaukee Avenue
Glenview, IL 60025

PRINTER MANUFACTURERS

Apple Computer Co., Inc.
20525 Marani Avenue
Cupertino, CA 95014

Bytewriter
125 Northview Road
Ithaca, NY 14850

C. Itoh Electronics, Inc.
5301 Beethoven Street
Los Angeles, CA 90066

Data General Corp.
Route 9, 15 Turnpike Road
Westboro, MA 01581

Diablo Systems, Inc.
26460 Corporate Avenue
Hayward, CA 94545

Digital Equipment Corp.
One Iron Way
Marlborough, MA 01752

Epson America, Inc.
3415 Kashiwa
Torrance, CA 90505

Fujitsu America, Inc.
2945 Oakmead Village Court
Santa Clara, CA 90505

NEC Information Industries
5 Militia Drive
Lexington, MA 02173

Okidata Corp.
111 Gaither Drive
Mount Laurel, NJ 08054

Olivetti Peripheral Equipment
505 White Plains Road
Tarrytown, NY 10591

Qume Corp.
2350 Qume Drive
San Jose, CA 95131

Radio Shack/Tandy Corp.
One Tandy Center
Fort Worth, TX 76102

Smith-Corona
65 Locust Avenue
New Canaan, CT 06840

Teletype Corp.
5555 Touhy Avenue
Skokie, IL 60077

Wang Laboratories
One Industrial Avenue
Lowell, MA 01851

Xerox Corp.
Xerox Square
Rochester, NY 14644

MODEM MANUFACTURERS

Anchor Automation
6624 Valjean Avenue
Van Nuys, CA 91406

Bizcomp Corporation
Box 7498
Menlo Park, CA 94025

Datec Modem
200 Eastowne Drive
Chapel Hill, NC 27514

General DataComm
One Kennedy Avenue
Danbury, CT 06810

Hayes Microcomputer Products,
Inc.
5835 Peachtree Industrial Blvd
Norcross, GA 30092

Lexicon Corp.
1541 NW 65th Avenue
Fort Lauderdale, FL 33313

MFJ Enterprises, Inc.
921 Louisville Road
Starksville, MS 39759

The Microperipheral Corp.
2643 151st Place, NE
Redmond, WA 98052

Novation, Inc.
18664 Oxnard Street
Tarzana, CA 91356

Omnitec Data
405 S. 20th Street
Phoenix, AZ 85034

Racal-Vidic, Inc.
222 Caspian Drive
Sunnyvale, CA 94086

Rixon, Inc.
2120 Industrial Parkway
Silver Spring, MD 20904

CHAPTER TWENTY

The Software Producers

There are even more software producers than there are hardware producers.

There are probably at least 2000 developers of proprietary software in the United States today, ranging from the tiny kitchen-table entrepreneurs to the large and successful software corporations. [This is aside from and in addition to the vast numbers of firms who do custom programming for organizations operating large mainframe computer systems, few of whom develop and "publish" (market) proprietary software for personal computers.] There is little point in trying to list all of them here. The following list was chosen at random, as a representative sampling of these software developers, and there is no significance in the fact that some companies are included here while others are not.

Addison-Wesley Publishing Co.
Applications Software Division
One Jacob Way
Reading, MA 01867

Ashton-Tate
9929 W. Jefferson Blvd
Culver City, CA 92030

Convergent Technologies
2441 Mission College Blvd
Santa Clara, CA 95050

Dakin 5 Corp.
7000 North Broadway
Denver, CO 80221

Digital Equipment Corp.
4 Mount Royal Avenue
Marlboro, MA 01752

Digital Research
POB 579
Pacific Grove, CA 93950

dilithium Press
8285 SW Nimbus, Suite 151
Beaverton, OR 97005

Disco-Tech
600 B Street
POB 1659
Santa Rosa, CA 95402

Dorsett Educational Systems, Inc.
POB 1226
Norman, OK 73070

Dow Jones & Co., Inc.
POB 300
Princeton, NJ 08540

Eagle Computer, Inc.
983 University Avenue
Los Gatos, CA 95030

Hayden Software Co.
POB 8428
600 Suffolk Street
Lowell, MA 01853

Hayes Microcomputer Products,
Inc.
5923 Peachtree Industrial Blvd
Norcross, GA 30092

Howard W. Sams & Co., Inc.
4300 West 62nd Street
Indianapolis, IN 46268

Informatics General Corp.
401 Park Avenue South
New York, NY 10016

Informatics General Corp.
9441 L.B.J. Freeway
Dallas, TX 75243

International Business Machines
(IBM)
POB 1328
Boca Raton, FL 33432

John Wiley & Sons, Inc.
605 Third Avenue
New York, NY 10158

KAYPRO
533 Stevens Avenue
Solana Beach, CA 92075

Krell Software
1320 StonyBrook Road
Stony Brook, NY 11790

Lotus Development Corporation
161 First Street
Cambridge, MA 02141

Micro Mike's, Inc.
POB 1440
Amarillo, TX 79105

MicroPro International Corp.
33 San Pablo Avenue
San Rafael, CA 94903

Microsoft Consumer Products,
Inc.
400 108th Avenue, NE, Suite 200
Bellevue, WA 98004

Microsoft, Inc.
10700 Northrup Way
Bellevue, WA 98004

NewsNet, Inc.
945 Haverford Road
Bryn Mawr, PA 19010

Peachtree Software, Inc.
3445 Peachtree Road, NE
Atlanta, GA 30326

Pearlsoft
POB 13850
Salem, OR 97309

Pickles & Trout
POB 1206
Goleta, CA 93116

Prentice-Hall, Inc.
Englewood Cliffs, NJ 07632

PrimeSoft Corp.
POB 40
Cabin John, MD 20818

PromptDoc, Inc.
833 W. Colorado Avenue, Suite 113
Colorado Springs, CO 80905

Quadram Corp.
4357 Park Drive
Norcross, GA 30093

Random House, School Division
400 Hahn Road
Westminster, MD 21157

Rapidata Division, National Data Corp.
One National Data Plaza
Corporate Square
Atlanta, GA 30329

Reader's Digest Services, Inc.
Microcomputer Software Division
Pleasantville, NY 10570

STSC, Inc.
2115 East Jefferson Street
Rockville, MD 20852

Smoke Signal
31336 Via Colinas
Westlake Village, CA 91362

SofTech Microsystems
16885 West Berardo Drive
San Diego, CA 92127

Software Products International
10343 Roselle Street
San Diego, CA 92121

Sorcim Corp.
2310 Lundy Avenue
San Jose, CA 95131

Vector Graphic, Inc.
500 North Ventu Park Road
Thousand Oaks, CA 91320

Versa Computing, Inc.
3541 Old Conejo Road
Newbury Park, CA 91320

Wang Laboratories, Inc.
One Industrial Avenue
Lowell, MA 01851

CHAPTER TWENTY-ONE

Other Information Sources

Probably no subject in history has ever been as thoroughly publicized, documented, and written about on a daily basis as the
computer and the information industries.

WHAT WAS A FREE-FLOWING STREAM HAS BECOME A BOILING RIVER

Even before the personal computer appeared on the scene a few
years ago there was an abundance of freely available published information about computers and the information industry. By far
the bulk of it was directed then to the professionals in the
industry—the engineers, programmers, analysts, and others
whose career interests were tied directly to computers and data
processing. But there were quite a large number of people in those
categories, so there were at least a dozen computer journals, ranging from the relatively "popular" ones written for the workaday
programmer and computer user to the professional journals written for information scientists. And there was also at least an equal

number of computer newsletters written for those same people. A number of books, especially those of the highly scientific, even abstruse, category was also available. Anyone who wanted to "read up" on computers could find literature with which to do so without great difficulty.

Microelectronics and the personal computer changed that radically. They created a mass market for computers, inspired the almost overnight creation of at least 200 computer manufacturers and hordes of satellite industries, spawned millions of computer aficionados and hobbyists—some call the latter "hackers"—and spun off an unprecedented avalanche of books, magazines, and other literature dealing with microcomputers and what one can do with and through them. There have been at least 200 periodicals—magazines, newsletters, and tabloids—and many hundreds of books, mostly paperbacks, created in the first few years of this decade alone. It is almost impossible to avoid becoming "computer literate" today, to at least some degree, and our children are now being taught the subject as part of their regular required education.

You can hardly help becoming aware of some of this torrent of literature today, even if you are not interested in computers. But if you are you should become aware of all or at least most of it so that you can select for your reading that which is most appropriate to your own needs and interests. This chapter contains lists of various kinds of literature, with remarks if and as it appears appropriate to make comments. Many of the peiodicals can be found on well-stocked newsstands, but others are available only by subscription because it is a rare newsstand that has room for all the periodicals being published today. It is obviously a problem to decide which to read, because it is impossible to read them all.

Books offer the same kind of problem. For example, if you want to learn the popular computer language, BASIC, you have a choice of several dozen paperback books, each of which assures you absolutely that it is the easiest method for learning the language and implies that no one else really knows how to teach it. The same problem occurs when you want to buy a book to learn the CP/M or PC-DOS operating system, or any other popular OS, for that matter. (At the moment, attention is beginning to focus on the C language and the UNIX operating system, and we are beginning to see extensive coverage of those on the bookshelves, as more and more computers adopt that operating system and programming language.)

Some books are about special kinds of software, such as graphics, spreadsheets, word processors, or integrated software, and they tend to run in cycles, as a particular kind of software catches the fancy of a great many computer owners and becomes currently the most popular kind of software.

Many of the books deal with hardware—specific computers, that is—and the popularity of the computer is a key to how many books will be written about it. Of course, there is a superabundance of books about the IBM PC computer, and there are many about Apple, Commodore, Atari, and Radio Shack computers, for the same reason.

Of course, while this book deals with computer applications, it also deals with the related subjects of the kinds of things you can do with a computer, and this invokes some other kinds of books, so not all the books that should interest you and be useful are computer books. Some of the books listed here are therefore on such other subjects as proposal writing, applications of word processing, marketing, and administration.

BOOKS

There is no intention on my part to compile anything resembling a complete selection of books on computers or on any other relevant subject, and certainly the following lists are not represented as even approaching complete coverage. Even if I could do so it would serve no good purpose. The books listed here will be those I have read, have in my personal library, or simply know of and think useful to mention. Instead of the typical bibliographic listing these will be arranged by their titles and grouped in terms of their general subjects or subject areas because I believe that to be the most helpful presentation. In most cases I want to bring them to your attention for reasons that should be readily apparent in each case.

Where it appears necessary (where it appears that you would require the information if you wished to order the book) the publisher's address is furnished, along with the title, my own remarks, and any other information I can furnish and which I believe to be useful.

Online Databases and Bulletin Board Systems

Going On-Line with Your Micro, Lou Haas, Tab Books 1984. Excellent how-to.

The Computer Phone Book, Mike Cane, New American Library 1983. A directory of online networks, services, databases, and BBSs, complete and well done, with helpful reports on most of these by an author who obviously has personally tried out a great many of them.

Directory of Computer-Based Services, GTE Telenet, Corporate Headquarters, 8229 Boone Blvd, Vienna, VA 22180. This is a complimentary publication from this large corporation. They sent me the 1984 edition at my request, and they will probably send you whatever is the then-current edition in response to your own request. It offers many helpful lists of online information and services accessed via Telenet.

How To Win with Information or Lose Without It, Andrew P. Garvin and Hubert Bermont, The Consultant's Library, POB 309, Glenelg, MD 21737. Garvin is in the information business and knows the subject well. Bermont is a consultant and publisher of information for consultants.

How To Get Free Software, Alfred Glossbrenner, St. Martin's Press 1984. Over 400 pages of information and clear instructions on how, when, and where to get an abundance of public-domain software via online connections.

The Free Software Catalog and Directory, Robert A. Froehlich, Crown Publishers, Inc., 1984. This is a large paperback, full of useful information.

Money-Making Computer Applications

How To Make Money with Your Personal Computer, Paul and Sarah Edwards, Alfred Publishing Co. 1984. A small book packed with good information from a well-known husband and wife team.

Home Computers Can Make You Rich, Joe Weisbecker, Hayden Book Company 1980. A pioneering book still in the book stores, which says something for it.

How To Make Money with Your Micro, Herman Holtz, John Wiley & Sons 1984. My own contribution to this field.

Programming

The Art of Computer Programming, Donald William Drury, Tab Books 1983.

25 Graphics Programs in Microsoft BASIC, Timothy J. O'Malley, Tab Books 1983.

The BASIC Cookbook, Ken Tracton, Tab Books 1978.

Computer Programming for the Complete Idiot, Donald McCunn, Design Enterprises of San Francisco 1979.

A Bit of BASIC, Thomas A. Dwyer and Margot Critchfield, Addison-Wesley 1980.

30 Computer Programs for the Homeowner in BASIC, David Chance, Tab Books 1982.

General Books About Computers

Computers for Everybody, Jerry Willis & Merl Miller, dilithium Press 1981.

Without Me You're Nothing: The Essential Guide to Home Computers, Frank Herbert with Max Barnard, Pocket Books 1980. This is the Frank Herbert of the Dune best-sellers in science fiction.

Understanding Computer Science, Roger S. Walker, Ph.D., P.E., developed and published by Texas Instruments Learning Center, distributed by Radio Shack. A "serious" work written with obvious engineering approaches to the subject and a scientist's attention to detail and precision.

1001 Things To Do with Your Personal Computer, Mark Sawusch, Tab Books 1980. Covers the waterfront of hobbyist applications, but with some applications to business and professional pursuits.

Troubleshooting & Repairing Personal Computers, Art Margolis, Tab Books 1983. Margolis is an old hand at electronics maintenance and writing about it, with many books and articles to his credit. Even if you never want to pick up a screwdriver or soldering iron this book is an education in how computers work and why they sometimes do not.

How To Buy the Right Personal Computer, Herman Holtz, Facts on File 1984. A work book, with many worksheets to help you develop your own specifications and go shopping properly armed.

Word Processing for Business Publications, Herman Holtz, McGraw-Hill 1984. Details of how to produce proposals, manuals, catalogs, newsletters, and other office "paper," using word processing efficiently.

Getting the Most Out of Your Word Processor, Arnold Rosen, Prentice-Hall 1983.

Word Processing Primer, Mitchell Waite and Julie Arca, McGraw-Hill 1982. Excellent explanations.

General Books About Related Subjects

The Newsletter Editor's Desk Book, Marvin Arth and Helen Ashmore, Parkway Press, Box 8158, Shawnee Mission, KS 66208. Authoritative information by two true professionals in the newsletter game.

The Newsletter Yearbook Directory, Howard Penn Hudson, Editor, The Newsletter Clearinghouse, 4 West Market Street, Rhinebeck, NY 1252. Published every year or two by the editor/

publisher of the "Newsletter on Newsletters," who is also active in other affairs concerning newsletter publishing.

The Writer's Market, Writer's Digest Books, 9933 Alliance Road, an annual publication listing thousands of publishers and related information. Virtually a bible for professional writers, growing substantially in size each year. (The latest edition at the time of this writing is over 1000 pages.)

The Winning Proposal: How To Write it, Herman Holtz and Terry Schmidt, McGraw-Hill 1983. Detailed how-to on writing formal proposals with many examples and illustrations.

Writing with a Word Processor, William Zinsser, Harper & Row 1983. By a well-known writer, an author of a successful earlier book. This is not a technical book and really adds nothing to anyone's knowledge of word processing, but instead is a disappointing account of the author's "triumph" over the frightening boxes of hardware that arrived at his office when he succumbed to the blandishments of word processing.

PERIODICALS

The situation with periodicals is very much the same as it is with books. There are a great many magazines, newsletters, tabloids, and occasional periodicals dealing with computers and related subjects of interest to the independent consultant. Many are of general interest, while many others are centered on special interests. Many, for example, are aimed directly at owners of specific kinds of computers, while many address various other interests, as many of the titles suggest. Publisher's addresses are given for periodicals known or suspected to be not easily found on newsstands.

Computer Periodicals

A.N.A.L.O.G. Computing, POB 23, Worcester, MA 01603, for Atari owners.

Ahoy, Ion International, Inc., 45 West 34th Street, Suite 407, New

York, NY 10001, for owners of Commodore 64 and VIC 20 computers.

A+, the Independent Guide to Apple Computing, Ziff-Davis, 1 Davis Drive, Belmont, CA 94002, for Apple owners, of course.

Antic Magazine, the Atari Resource, Antic Publishing Co., 524 2nd Street, San Francisco, CA 94107.

Business Computer Systems, the Magazine for Business Computer Users, Cahners Publishing Co., 221 Columbus Avenue, Boston, MA 02116.

Business Computing, the PC Magazine for Business, Penn Well Publishing Co., 119 Russell Street, Littleton, MA 01460.

Business Software Magazine, 2464 Embarcadero Way, Palo Alto, CA 94303.

Byte, monthly, slick paper, quite thick and heavy with advertising, articles, somewhat more technical than many others.

Canadian Datasystems, 481 University Avenue, Toronto, Ontario M5W 1A7, Canada. Technical, semitechnical, and popular coverage, but aimed primarily at professionals and managers in computers and data processing fields.

Christian Computing, 72 Valley Hill Road, Stockridge, GA 30281.

Closing the Gap, Random Graphics, Box 68, Henderson, MN 56044. Bimonthly tabloid on computers for handicapped people.

The Color Computer Magazine for TRS-80 Color Computer Users, Ziff-Davis, Highland Mill, Camden, ME 08483.

Commodore Microcomputers, Commodore Business Machines, 1200 Wilson Drive, West Chester, PA 19380.

Compute! The Leading Magazine of Home, Educational, and Recreational Computing.

Computer Dealer, Gordon Publications, Inc., POB 1952, Dover, NJ 07801.

Computer Decisions, the Management Magazine of Computing, Hayden Publishing Co., Inc., 10 Mulholland Drive, Hasbrouck Heights, NJ 07604.

Computer Design, 119 Russell Street, Littleton, MA 01460.

Computer Graphics World, 1714 Stockton Street, San Francisco, CA 94133.

Computer Merchandising, the Magazine for High Technology Retailers, Eastman Publications, 15720 Ventura Blvd, Suite 222, Encino, CA 91436.

Computer Retailing, 1760 Peachtree Road, Atlanta, GA 30357.

Computer Trader Magazine, Lambert Publishing House, 1704 Sam Drive, Birmingham, AL 35235. A fast-growing publication for computer enthusiasts and ham radio hobbyists. Many "wanted to buy/sell/swap" classified advertisements, from whence comes the name.

Computer Update, Boston Computer Society, Inc., One Center Plaza, Boston, MA 02108.

Computer User, for the Tandy/Radio Shack System, McPheters, Wolfe & Jones, 16704 Marquardt Avenue, Cerritos, CA 90701.

Computerworld, 375 Cochituate Road, POB 880, Framingham, MA 01701.

Computers & Electronics, formerly *Popular Electronics,* has succumbed to the trend and become a computer magazine; aimed at enthusiasts and hobbyists.

Compute!'s Gazette, for VIC 20 and Commodore 64 owners.

Computing Canada, Canada's Bi-Weekly Data Processing Newspaper, Plesman Publications, Ltd., 2 Lansing Square, Willowdale, Ontario M2J 4P8 Canada.

Creative Computing, general coverage.

Data Management Magazine, the Magazine for Information Processing Professionals, Data Processing Management Association, 505 Busse Highway, Park Ridge, IL 60068.

Datamation, 666 Fifth Avenue, New York, NY 10103. Aimed at professionals in the field.

The DEC Professional, Professional Press, Inc., POB 362, Ambler, PA 19002.

Desktop Computing, 80 Pine Street, Peterborough, NH 03458.

Digital Review, the Magazine for DEC Microcomputing.

80 Micro, for owners of Tandy/Radio Shack TRS-80 computers.

Hardcopy, the Magazine of Digital Equipment, Seldin Publishing Co., 1061 S. Melrose, Suite D, Placentia, CA 92670.

Home Computer Magazine, Emerald Valley Publishing, 1500 Valley River Drive, Suite 250, Eugene, OR 97401.

Home Electronics & Entertainment, Harris Publications, 79 Madison Avenue, New York, NY 10016.

Hot Coco, the Magazine for TRS-80 Color Computer and MC-10 Users, Wayne Green, Inc., 80 Pine Street, Peterborough, NH 03458.

ICP Series & Business Review, formerly *ICP Interface Series*, 9000 Keystone Crossing, Indianapolis, IN 46240.

inCider, 80 Pine Street, Peterborough, NH 03458. About Apple computers.

Information Systems News for Information Systems Management. Biweekly tabloid for staffs of major computer installations.

InfoWorld, the Newsweekly for Microcomputer Users. Focuses largely on industry news, "inside stories," and reviews of software and hardware.

Interactive Computing: The Journal of the Association of Computer Users, ACU Research & Education Division, Inc., POB 9003, Boulder, CO 80301.

Interface Age: Computing for Business and Home, 16704 Marquardt Avenue, Cerritos, CA 90701.

Journal of Systems Management, 24587 Bagley Road, Cleveland, OH 44138.

jr Magazine, for IBM's Home Computer, Wayne Green Publications, 80 Pine Street, Peterborough, NH 03458.

Link-Up, Communications and the Small Computer, On-Line Communications, Inc., 6351 Cambridge Street, Minneapolis, MN 55426.

LIST, Redgate Publishing Co., 3381 Ocean Drive, Vero Beach, FL 32963. Premier semiannual for software listings.

Macworld, the Macintosh Magazine, PC World Communications, Inc., 555 DeHaro Street, San Francisco, CA 94107.

Micro Communications, Miller Freeman Publications, 500 Howard Street, San Francisco, CA 94105.

Micro: The 6502/6809 Journal, 34 Chelmsford Street, Chelmsford, MA 01824.

Microcomputing, formerly *Kilobaud Microcomputing*, Wayne Green, Inc., 80 Pine Street, Peterborough, NH 03458.

Micro Moonlighter Newsletter, 4121 Buckthorn Court, Lewisville, TX 75028. For computer owners trying to earn a few dollars by moonlighting.

Microsystems, the Journal for Advanced Microcomputing, Ziff-Davis Publishing Co., 1 Park Avenue, New York, NY 10016.

Mini-Micro Systems, 221 Columbus Avenue, Boston, MA 02116.

News/34-38, for Users of IBM Systems 34/36/38, Duke Corporation, 295 East 29th Street, Suite 210, Loveland, CO 80537.

Nibble, the Reference for Apple Computing.

Office Administration and Automation, Geyer-McAllister Publications, Inc., 51 Madison Avenue, NY 10010.

Online Today, the Computer Communications Magazine, CompuServe, Inc., 5000 Arlington Centre Blvd, Columbus, OH 43220.

PC: The Independent Guide to IBM Personal Computers.

PC World, the Comprehensive Guide to IBM Personal Computers and Compatibles.

PCM, the Magazine for Professional Computer Management, Falsoft, Inc., 9529 U.S. Highway 42, POB 209, Prospect, KY 40059.

Personal Computer Age, the Definitive Journal for the IBM Personal Computer User, 8138 Foothill Blvd, Sunland, CA 91040.

Personal Computing.

Popular Computing Magazine.

Portable 100, the Magazine for TRS-80 Model 100 Users, Computer Communications, Inc., 15 Elm Street, Camden, ME 04843.

Programmers Software Exchange, 2110 N. 2nd Street, Cabot, AR 72-73.

Rainbow Magazine, Falsoft, Inc., 9529 U.S. Highway 42, Prospect, KY 40059. For users of TRS-80 Color Computers and Dragon 32 computers.

Selling Micros, Wayne Green, Inc., 80 Pine Street, Peterborough, NH 03458.

Small Systems World, 950 Lee Street, Des Plaines, IL 60016.

Softalk for the Personal Computer, Softalk Publishing Inc., 11160 McCormick Street, North Hollywood, CA 91601.

Softside Magazine, Softside Publications, Inc., 10 Northern Blvd, Amherst, NH 03031.

Syntax, Syntax ZX80, Inc., POB 457, Bolton Road, Harvard, MA 01451.

Systems User, 119 N. Belmont, Suite 103, Los Angeles, CA 90026.

Telesystems Journal, OSI Publications, Ltd., Fort Lee Executive Park, Two Executive Drive, Fort Lee, NJ 07024.

UNIX/World, Your Complete Guide to the Frontiers of the Unix System, Tech Valley Publishing, Inc., 289 S. San Antonio Road, Los Altos, CA 94022.

CHAPTER TWENTY-TWO

Glossary of Terms

Computer "language" refers not only to programming languages, such as BASIC and COBOL, but also to the ever-changing and ever-growing jargon of personal computers, which is so mystifying even to those experienced in computers.

WHY A GLOSSARY IS NECESSARY

Computers have been through several "generations" already, from the primitive models with thousands of vacuum tubes, through the order-of-magnitude improvements via transistors and printed-circuit boards, to today's revolutionary microchip sophistication. The jargon peculiar to computers has kept pace, growing and changing at least as rapidly and as drastically. For the newcomer to the field, the jargon is itself a Great Wall of China obstructing understanding.

The terms listed in the following glossary are by no means all the special terms you will meet in reading the popular and not-so-popular literature about personal computers; I have made a deliberate effort to keep the list as small as possible to make it less awesome. I have, in fact, tried to limit the list of terms to those encountered most frequently and most commonly, and I hope the

345

list represents at least a beginning in learning the strange language of microcomputers.

Access method. Technique or means for finding and moving data between storage and input/output or channel.

ACK (acknowledge character). Signal sent by receiver in data transmission to verify character or accuracy.

Acoustic coupler. Modem (also acoustic modem), a device for converting data signals into audible signals and vice versa for transmission via telephone lines; equipped with receptacles for ordinary telephone handset, so it requires no wired connection.

Address. Code for location of data in computer memory.

Alphanumeric. Adjective generally, referring to both letters and numerals, as in alphanumeric character set, alphanumeric codes, and so on.

ANSI. American National Standards Institute, an organization for setting voluntary standards in the United States.

Applications programs. Software designed to solve specific problems or carry out specific end-functions, such as accounting, word processing, and so on.

Archive. Storage or backup copy of data.

ASCII. American Standard Code for Information Interchange, standard for representing characters and symbols with bytes (8 bits); widely accepted in computer industry.

Assembler. Program that assembles instructions written in high-level language and translates them into machine codes.

Assembly language. High-level programming language, using mnemonic (memory-jogging) terms.

Auto-answer. Modem feature that automatically detects and answers incoming telephone calls.

Auto-dial. Modem feature that initiates calls.

Backup. Duplicate copy of data or program, usually stored on another disk, held for safekeeping against accidental loss of original data or program.

BASIC (variations: MBASIC, BAZIC, CBASIC, other). Beginner's All-Purpose Symbolic Instruction Code, a popular high-level programming language.

Baud, baud rate. Technically a modulation/signaling rate, but practically a unit in which rate of transmission in bits per second, especially over telephone lines, is expressed.

BCD. Binary coded decimal, a system of using binary data (groups of bits) to represent decimal quantities.

Bidirectional (printing). Ability/action of printers printing in both directions, printing right to left on "carriage return" cycle.

Binary. System used by digital computers, in which there are only two (mutually exclusive) values—1,0; up,down; true,false; and so on.

Binary digit (bit). One of the two values (e.g., 1/0); acronym *bit* is derived from these two words.

Boot. Program/routine/action that initiates computer operation, usually clearing memory and loading or auto-loading a program.

Boot, cold. Booting from cold start, usually from already cleared memory or having just turned system on.

Boot, warm. Boot initiated during operations by clearing files or portion of memory, often by entering a control-C on the keyboard.

bps. Bits per second, measure of transmitting rate.

Break. Interruption in communications originated at transmitting end, usually hardware function.

Buffer. Device used for temporary storage of data to adjust for differences between elements in their rates of transmission and reception (sometimes used to refer to software, but more often refers to hardware device).

Bug. Error or problem in software that must be corrected to get proper operation.

Bus. A common electrical or electronic main pathway to which many components and subsystems are or may be connected.

Byte. Group of digital bits processed as a group, currently defined as 8 bits, representing one alphanumeric character.

Cathode ray tube (CRT). Tube with screen for displaying data of all types with phosphorescent illumination; same type of tube, generally, as that used for TV.

Central processor, central processing unit (CPU) microprocessor. See CPU.

Character. Individual letter, numeral, symbol, or diacritical mark, normally defined and/or represented by one byte.

Chip. Functional electronic element consisting of an entire circuit or set of circuits etched into a tiny wafer of silicon, such as RAM, ROM, and microprocessor (CPU) chips.

Clock. Circuit emitting precisely timed pulse to synchronize events in a system; also the pulse itself (each pulse is sometimes referred to colloquially as a "clock," meaning clock pulse).

COBOL. Common Business-Oriented Language, a popular language used in business and science applications.

Command. Order/instruction to the computer.

Communications software. Programs of instructions for computers to exchange information over telephone lines via modems or by other links.

Compiler. A program that translates high-level input language into machine language.

Connect time. Measure of time in which station (computer or terminal) is connected to database or terminal is connected to computer; generally used as a basis for charges in systems on subscription to database services.

Control characters. Codes to control flow, display, and/or printing of data.

cps. Characters per second, usually used to specify rate of printing.

CP/M. Control Program for Microcomputers, a popular operating system, especially in microcomputers.

CPU. Central Processing Unit, the essence of the computer, a single microchip.

CR. Carriage return; same as RETURN or ENTER.

Crash. Refers to loss of data, collapse of program, power failure, or other such disaster.

CRC. Error detection for verifying transmission accuracy using Cyclic Redundancy Check characters.

CRT. See Cathode ray tube.

Cursor. Symbol on screen, under operator control usually, showing where next action will take place or directing computer program to site of next action.

Daisy wheel. Flat print wheel used in most letter-quality printers.

Database. A store of related or coherent data readily accessible from various programs and/or sources.

DBMS. Database management system.

Debug. Correct errors in program.

Dedicated (system, computer, etc.). Item designed and/or designated for single function, kind of work, or user.

Default. Options chosen by the program or operating system as standard procedures if the user does not opt for an alternative ("defaults").

Digitize. Convert analog data to digital form.

Disk. Metal or plastic disk coated with magnetic oxide and serving as storage medium. See also Floppy.

Disk drive. The hardware device that reads/writes to disk.

Display, soft display. Presentation of data on screen (CRT or other, such as LCD—liquid crystal display).

Documentation. Written copy, such as manuals and specifications.

DOS. Disk operating system, also operating system.

Dot matrix. Screen displays and printing by dot patterns in matrix (e.g., 7 × 9); usually refers to printers.

Double density. Technique that doubles the amount of data that can be stored on magnetic disk or tape.

Double pass. Ability/action of printers, usually dot-matrix type, to print each character twice, the second time on a return—right to left—print cycle. See also Bidirectional (printing).

Download.   Receiving information from a mainframe or other computer (e.g., a remote database) and storing it or printing it out on another system.

Dual intensity.   Characteristic/capability of terminal to present data at both full and reduced brightness.

Dumb terminal.   Terminal, usually keyboard and monitor, without processing capability.

Dump.   To lose all data in system, as a result of power failure or other problem; also used to denote deliberate transfer of information in bulk to another medium or storage location. See also Crash.

EAROM.   Electrically Alterable Read-Only Memory, which is normally alterable only with ultraviolet signals; often used as storage for alphabet fonts, for various languages, in dot-matrix printers.

EBDIC.   Extended Binary Coded Decimal Interchange Code; code for representing characters, used primarily by IBM.

Echo.   Repeating information received (causing it to appear on sender's CRT screen) to confirm reception and accuracy to sender.

Echo check.   Using echo to compare with original transmission as check on accuracy.

Editor, text editor.   Portion of word processor program responsible for entering, correcting, and manipulating text.

Electronic mail.   Sending and receiving messages, on-screen or via hard copy, through computer communications.

ENTER/RETURN.   Both are used to enter commands and, usually, to start a new paragraph; see also CR.

EPROM.   Erasable   ROM   (via   ultraviolet   light),   hence programmable.

File.   Set of related records in storage or in work, identified by unique name; may be of any size, depending on computer.

File insertion.   Adding to or altering contents of file, especially computer's capabilities for so doing.

Firmware.   Program material/instructions permanently inscribed in computer logic, as in ROM.

Floppy.   Colloquial for floppy disk or diskette, a flexible plastic disk, encased in a paper sleeve, 3, 3½, 5¼, or 8 inches in diameter, used to store data on its magnetic coating.

Flowchart.   Chart used to organize and analyze information, used widely by computer specialists to develop programming strategy and to explain software logic to others.

Formatter.   Portion of word processor that permits operator to organize/reorganize copy for printer or other output peripheral device and/or issue instruction to the output device; may be separate program.

Full duplex.   Mode in which transmission and reception can be carried out concurrently.

Function key.   Terminal key that transmits command or code with single press.

Glitch.   Electrical spike, other signal aberration.

Global search (and replace).   Refers to ability of word processors to find any/all references/uses of a word or term and, if ordered, to replace that word/term with another.

Graphics.   Drawings, other illustrations; in software applications this usually refers to ability of computer systems and programs to generate drawings of charts, graphs, plots, and other such representations of data.

Handshaking.   Exchange of signals by two data devices establishing communication.

Hard copy.   Printed output.

Hard disk.   Rigid disk with high storage capacity and high speed of access; also called Winchester.

Hertz.   Unit of frequency, equal to one cycle per second.

Hexadecimal.   Base-16 number system used in computers, counting 1 to F (0–9, A–F; A–F represents 11–16).

High-level language.   English-like language used for programming.

Host computer.   Primary or controlling computer in network such as public database.

IC.   Integrated circuit, technical name for chips, microcircuits.

Impact printer.   Printer that strikes ribbon against the paper.

Input, input data.   Information entered into system.

Input/output, I/O.   Refers to computer data being entered into the system and/or output from the system; also an adjective for various computer hardware and software elements.

Insert.   Copy marked to be inserted as addition to existing copy, especially convenient to accomplish electronically in word processors; also used, in direct mail circles, to refer to materials used as part of package in envelopes.

Insert mode.   An optional mode of word processor operation.

Instruction.   Command to computer.

Intelligent terminal.   See Smart terminal.

Interface.   Connection or juncture between two devices connected for information exchange, processing, or other functions.

Interleaving.   Splitting memory into two sections, each with path to CPU, to speed processing.

Interrupt.   Signal that permits suspension of current process in favor of higher priority request.

Justification.   Aligning lines of copy so that each line begins and/or ends at exactly the same place, resulting in absolutely even margins; generally accomplished by adjusting spacing between words, letters, or both. Most word processors can justify automatically. Also called *right justification* and *justified right* because left justification is taken for granted as the result of beginning each line of copy at the same place.

K,Kb.   Abbreviations for kilobyte; K also abbreviation for prefix *kilo*, used commonly to mean thousand.

Kerning.   Refers to word processor capability of tightening spaces between characters to justify, condense type, or of other purposes.

Keypad.   A separate set of numeric keys, arranged in calculator style on keyboard.

Kilobyte, Kb.   Nominally 1000 bytes (actually 1024 bytes).

Kludge.   Improvise, use makeshift method.

Letter quality.   Applied to printers producing fully formed characters, such as those from daisy wheel.

Line oriented.   Characteristic of word processor in which copy is stored by lines, rather than by individual characters, and entire line must be addressed for changes or corrections.

Line printer.   High-speed printer usually used with mainframe computers.

Live screen.   Characteristic of word-processing program which enables changes at any time, without changing mode—that is, editing and formatting can be done without changing mode; see also Screen oriented.

Load.   Verb describing entering of program or files into memory; also electrical drain on circuit.

Logic.   Name applied to digital circuits, microchips, especially microprocessors; also general rationale of cicuit design.

Machine language.   Digital codes actually used within computer circuits, which machine "understands."

Magnetic tape.   Tape coated with iron oxide, used to store data as "bits."

Mail merge.   File-merging capability that enables operator to combine contents of files in printout, such as automatically printing form letter from one file, with names and addresses (mailing list) from another file.

Mainframe.   Colloquialism for big computer.

Megabyte, Mb.   One million bytes.

Memory.   Internal circuits of computer that store information, generally on a temporary basis, usually known as RAM (random access memory) in small computers.

Menu.   Index or table of contents on computer screen to guide user through program options and define commands for each option.

Microprocessor.   Central processing unit (CPU); main logic unit, a chip.

Microsecond.   One millionth of a second.

Millisecond.   One thousandth of a second.

Modem.   Term derived from *mo*dulator–*dem*odulator, a device that enables computers to communicate (transfer data) over telephone lines.

Modulation.   An encoding process to enable a carrier signal to carry the signals representing the message.

Monitor.   Usually refers to "soft copy" or "soft display," represented by CRT (cathode ray tube) screen, liquid crystal display, or other such presentation, as distinct from "hard copy" (printed output).

MP/M.   Multiprogramming control program for microprocessors: a multiuser version of CP/M.

Multiplexing.   Techniques for permitting near-simultaneous transmissions over single channel.

Multiprocessing.   Having more than one microprocessor, hence able to process more than one command at a time.

Multitasking.   Sharing routines, data space, files; able to execute several jobs at same time.

Multiuser.   System that permits more than one user/work station to address CPU and other devices.

Nanosecond.   One billionth of a second.

Network.   Interconnected group of computers/digital devices that share resources and communicate with each other.

Nodding.   Characteristic of printer to incline print head slightly for second and succeeding passes to darken copy for boldface characters or to increase dot density and so increase quality of dot-matrix output.

Number crunching.   Refers to computers and/or functions concerned mainly with arithmetic operations, especially complex mathematics.

Object code/language.   Machine language, especially that produced by assembler, compiler, or interpreter translating high-level language into machine language.

OEM.   Original equipment manufacturer; assembles end-item, may or may not manufacture components making up end-item.

Offline. Equipment in inactive state; processing or other operations conducted after actual event.

Online. Connected and processed during main running cycle, as compared with being processed later; opposite of offline.

Operating System (OS). Program (software and firmware) used to administer and manage internal computer operations and direct peripheral devices.

Output. Data delivered by device.

Output device. Any device that delivers information—CRT, printer, or other device.

Page display. Word-processing term for displaying entire page on-screen or for showing where page begins and ends to help operator fit copy.

Parallel interface, parallel transmission. Port/information exchange by sending out (usually) entire byte or word (8 or 16 bits) at a time, rather than serially (bit by bit).

Pascal. High-level programming language named for Blaise Pascal; suitable for relatively sophisticated programming uses.

Password. Character string used as identification code for security purposes.

pc board. Printed circuit board.

PC DOS. IBM's copyrighted disk operating system for the PC computers.

Peripheral (equipment). Equipment used in connection with but not part of central computer—keyboard, CRT monitor, printer, modem, buffers, or other equipment.

Personal computer. Any microcomputer, desktop computer, home computer.

Pixel. Term derived from words *picture element*, referring to dots on-screen used to construct text and illustrations on-screen; expressed as ratio—for example, 270 × 640 pixels—indicating number of pixels (dots) per horizontal and vertical inch (per pixel block) so that figure serves as measure/indicator of resolution or ability to present fine detail.

Plotter.   Device that draws on paper with pens, under computer direction (via graphics program).

Port.   Input and/or output connection to computer or other equipment.

Printer.   Typewriter-like machine used to create hard-copy output.

Program.   Software set of instructions for computer; "word processor" refers to program, as well as to machine.

PROM.   Programmable read-only memory; a ROM that can be programmed or reprogrammed, usually via ultraviolet signals.

Prompt.   Signal from computer announcing completion of instruction and signaling readiness for next one.

Queue.   Refers to lining up of messages, print orders, files, or other items/operations to be handled in sequence, as in queue file.

Ragged right.   Opposite of right-justified.

RAM.   Random access memory; device that constitutes memory for most small computers; this is generally referred to by such designations as "64K computer" or "16K" memory, which denote capacity of RAM.

Random access.   Access to any location at any time, as contrasted with access at only beginning or end, or only under certain conditions.

Random access device.   Memory or storage device that allows random access, such as disk and RAM, and distinct from tape, which does not permit random access.

Random access memory.   See RAM.

Read-only memory.   Designated as ROM, refers to internal device (microchip) with fixed program which cannot be changed, containing instruction set for computer.

Read–write.   Indicates ability to read what is stored and/or write—add to or change what is written there—as in the case of RAM; used as adjective to designate "read–write head" and other components that permit read–write functions.

Real time. Happening during actual event, as "real time processing." See Online and Offline.

Refresh. Renewing signals to screen to keep presentation from decaying; also, refreshing signals in other circuits subject to signal decaying or fading.

Refresh rate. Frequency of refreshing signals.

Resolution. Ability of monitor screen and/or printer to present detail clearly, usually as a consequence of number of pixels or dots per screen; dependent partly on hardware quality and partly on software.

RETURN. See ENTER and RUN.

RGB. Red, green, blue, identifying CRT as color tube.

ROM. See Read-only memory.

RS-232. Recommended Standard (RS) 232, commonly used serial connection; standard connection with computers, terminals, printers, and so on.

RUN. Command for some computers, similar to ENTER and RETURN.

Screen. Face of CRT, in word-processing hardware references; to display, in software references; also, data/material displayed may be present screen, last screen, next screen, and so on.

Screen oriented. Characteristic of program in addressing individual characters and doing both editing and formatting in same program, on-screen, achieving "what you see is what you get" effect—presenting copy exactly as printer will print it (except for nonprinting control or "embedded" commands).

Scrolling. Moving copy up, down, or side to side on-screen, so as to view pages other than one currently on-screen; can be used to view any portion of file, usually.

Search and replace. See Global search (and replace).

Sector. Area of disk used for storage.

Serial interface, serial transmission. Port through which data is transferred bit by bit; contrast with parallel.

Simplex. Characteristic of being able to transmit in only one direction.

Smart Terminal.   Remote terminal or work station that can input to, as well as draw information from, system (host or main computer). Also known as intelligent terminal.

Software.   Programs and other computer instructions that may be changed readily.

Spelling checker.   Program that includes dictionary and reviews words for spelling; many are designed to permit additions by user.

Spooler.   Buffer device, used to store information temporarily to permit computer to do other work while printer is operating; see also Buffer.

Spooling.   Storing data temporarily for later use or printing.

Subprogram.   A routine within a program, usually a branch, not able to operate independently.

Sysop.   Jargon for *system operator*, used usually in connection with electronic bulletin boards and similar systems.

Terminal.   Remote unit, usually including CRT and keyboard, connected to main system; see also Smart terminal.

Throughput.   Amount of work accomplished by computer in a given period.

Upload.   Transfer information to another computer or terminal.

UNIX.   A multiprogramming, multiuser operating system, based on the C language and regarded as a powerful manager of computer operations; favored for many network and multistation systems.

VDT.   Video display terminal; usually CRT, usually with keyboard.

Virtual.   Apparently, although not actually, in virtual memory.

Virtual memory.   Storage capacity arranged for such immediate and ready accessibility as to appear to the computer to be part of internal memory, thereby achieving "virtual" increase in size of memory.

Volatile.   Usually refers to internal memory's transient nature— that is, dumping of data when power is interrupted.

Wild card.   Special functions/symbols used in computer systems to implement special commands.

Winchester.   Name of metal disk and drive used for storage.

Window.   Portion of screen on which displayed data is shown, generally used when program permits several "windows" to display portions of more than one file.

Work station.   Remote unit, usually terminal of some sort; may be microcomputer.

Write protection.   Ensuring that disk cannot be accidentally erased.

Index